INSURGENTS, RAIDERS, AND BANDITS

INSURGENTS, RAIDERS, AND BANDITS

How Masters of Irregular Warfare Have Shaped Our World

JOHN ARQUILLA

Ivan R. Dee
Chicago

Ivan R. Dee
An imprint of The Rowman & Littlefield Publishing Group, Inc.
4501 Forbes Boulevard, Suite 200, Lanham, Maryland 20706
www.ivanrdee.com

Estover Road, Plymouth PL6 7PY, United Kingdom

Distributed by National Book Network

British Library Cataloguing in Publication Information Available

Library of Congress Cataloging-in-Publication Data:

Arquilla, John.
  Insurgents, raiders, and bandits : how masters of irregular warfare have shaped our world / John Arquilla.
    p. cm.
  Includes bibliographical references and index.
  ISBN 978-1-56663-832-6 (cloth : alk. paper)—ISBN 978-1-56663-908-8 (electronic)
  1. Irregular warfare—History. 2. Asymmetric warfare—History. 3. Guerrilla warfare—History. 4. Military history, Modern. I. Title.
  U167.5.I8A77 2011
  355.02'18—dc22

                                                          2010054367

∞™ The paper used in this publication meets the minimum requirements of American National Standard for Information Sciences—Permanence of Paper for Printed Library Materials, ANSI/NISO Z39.48-1992.

Printed in the United States of America

For Hy Rothstein
(Colonel, U.S. Army Special Forces, ret.)
One of the modern masters

CONTENTS

MAPS

PREFACE

For all the hope of peaceful progress that accompanied the turn of the new millennium, its first decade ended with more than thirty armed conflicts still in progress. Most were civil wars, but some involved the presence of foreign troops, like the lingering American intervention in Afghanistan. Yet the salient fact about the ongoing conflicts of our time is that *all* are irregular in nature. That is, they are primarily conducted through acts of terrorism or more classic guerrilla hit-and-run tactics. Those who face insurgents and terrorists have learned—as the Americans did in Iraq—that conventional responses will not suffice. Thus the forces of order and stability have been ineluctably drawn to mount irregular small-unit raids of their own, and have often found themselves teaming up with local tribesmen and a range of other groups in all manner of unusual field operations.

In the conventional realm of warfare the best strategies are generally gleaned from the careers of the so-called great captains, such as Julius Caesar, Frederick of Prussia, and Napoleon Bonaparte. Choosing the most effective of the moderns usually sparks a lively discourse, one that often ends with heads nodding in George Patton's direction. But even insights that might be drawn from the near great who ended in defeat, like the Confederacy's noble Robert E. Lee or Germany's Erwin Rommel, the "Desert Fox," are closely studied. The literature is large indeed.

Yet when it comes to the great captains of irregular warfare, the same can hardly be said. While there are many accounts of daring commando raids, and more thoughtful works that explore the complex relationships between elite military advisors and friendly indigenous fighters, there is precious little study of the principles that might be distilled from the stories of those whose campaigns have proved exemplary. To be sure, the memoirs of Mao Zedong, Vo Nguyen Giap, and Che Guevara provide important general insights. But they only begin to poke holes in the darkness. In order to understand the strategic implications of this new age of insurgency, terrorism, and other forms of irregular warfare, we must look closely at the earlier "masters."

I have sought to fill this gap by telling the stories of some of the greatest guerrillas, raiders, and counterinsurgent experts of the past 250 years. This period coincides roughly with the span of the Industrial Age and also covers the heydays of both modern imperialism and nationalism. The era of post–World War II rebellion against colonial rule and the conflicts that raged around the edges of the Cold War also come under close scrutiny. The survey ends in the near present, a time when rising networks of non-state actors have come into bitter conflict with leading nations, with no apparent end in sight.

The action itself ranges across the world, beginning in the eighteenth-century North American wilderness. There the opening markers are the deaths of British general Edward Braddock and more than a thousand of his troops in 1755, ambushed by a very small Franco-Indian force, and the formation of a colonial ranger unit better able to wage such wilderness warfare. The narrative crosses to Europe during the Napoleonic era, and from there branches out to Africa, South America, Arabia, Asia, and eventually encompasses the wide reaches of the Pacific during World War II. The masters whose stories drive the principal action come from many cultures: American, Spanish, Russian, Arab, Italian, Boer, British, German, Croat, Vietnamese, and Chechen.

The death in 2005 of the Chechen leader Aslan Maskhadov—who a decade earlier had beaten the Russians using an irregular swarming concept of operations—frames the near end of this survey. But between Braddock's death and Maskhadov's are the stories of many remarkable individuals. Their fighting skills aside, they are often obsessed with the importance of "branding," especially in their manner of dress.

Despite their origins in so many different cultures, and style issues aside, the masters of the irregular have a great deal in common, most conspicuously their sheer indomitability. Robert Rogers led his rangers through unimaginable hardships in the wilderness war in North America. A generation later during the Revolution, Nathanael Greene lost virtually every pitched battle he fought, yet he kept coming at Lord Cornwallis and his Redcoats to distract them and create new and better opportunities for his dispersed guerrilla forces.

Rogers and Greene were hardly alone in overcoming adversity. The leader of irregular resistance to Napoleon's occupation of Spain, Francisco

Espoz y Mina, had his main force wiped out on no less than three occasions by his tough, smart French opponents. Yet he was able to reconstitute his insurgent forces again and again, finally prevailing.

Another kind of indomitability was reflected in a key campaign of the famous American Indian fighter George Crook. Instead of taking thousands of troopers into the Sonoran desert to chase after Geronimo, Crook ventured forth with just a few hundred, most of them "friendly" Apaches. He tracked Geronimo relentlessly, then walked into the enemy camp alone one day and talked the great warrior into giving himself up.

Similar panache was shown by the German commander in East Africa during World War I, General Paul von Lettow-Vorbeck. Beset on all sides by vastly superior enemy forces, he nonetheless launched a multipronged irregular offensive and continued raiding right up to the armistice. The list of such achievements goes on and on, as the masters of the irregular all seem to have been imbued with this sort of daring.

Beyond the great captains of irregular warfare, a few key supporting characters make recurring guest appearances in the pages that follow. The most frequent is Winston Churchill, who appears on the scene at the outset of the Boer War in 1899, returns to support T. E. Lawrence's pan-Arab policy goals after World War I, develops a friendship with Tito, the Yugoslav partisan leader during World War II, and exits only after lobbying President Dwight Eisenhower not to come to the aid of the French as they were losing to Vietnam's gifted insurgent leader Vo Nguyen Giap at Dienbienphu in 1954.

Another supporting character who comes close to Churchill's half-century-plus of involvement in irregular matters is Jan Smuts, who started out as a Boer insurgent but later ran the British East African campaign against von Lettow-Vorbeck during World War I. He reappears again during World War II as a bureaucratic thorn in the side of Britain's master of "deep penetration" tactics, the military mystic Orde Wingate, who is rescued from oblivion by—no surprise—Churchill.

Churchill, Smuts, and other characters like Louis Napoleon of mid-nineteenth-century France—a captor of the great Arab insurgent Abd el-Kader and a principal opponent of the Italian nation builder Giuseppe Garibaldi—help connect the individual stories to larger themes and tides of global events that influenced, and were in turn influenced by, the various masters. In this respect a sort of alternate history of the past two-and-a-half centuries is told, as seen both through the eyes of these larger players and through the lens of the irregular.

Yet another kind of service is performed by some of the great adversaries who opposed the masters. For example, Nathanael Greene's contribution to the winning of American independence, and the skill he showed in doing so, cannot be fully appreciated without knowing that his main opponent, Lord Cornwallis, was exceedingly able, probably the best general the British had in the field. Thirty years later the Spanish guerrilla leader Mina had to face off against Marshal Louis-Gabriel Suchet, considered by Napoleon Bonaparte to be the most skillful of all his commanders. George Crook, America's premier Indian fighter, had his mettle tested by Sitting Bull as well as Geronimo.

And so on. This is a book filled with hard-fought and fascinating duels, played out over raids, ambushes, and cordon-and-sweep counters to them. The stories are replete with evidence that irregular warfare operations often proved crucial to the outcomes of the larger wars of which they formed component parts—far more so than general military histories tend to suggest.

If a few individuals with a turn of mind toward the irregular have had profound effects on world events, the same is also true of the less epochal undertakings. Garibaldi, using his "Thousand" in swarming style, led Italy to unity over and against the desires and forces of France, Austria, and the Pope. And even those who strove in similar fashion in the cause of nationhood and failed, from Abd el-Kader of Algeria to the great Boer leader of insurgents, Christiaan de Wet, demonstrated the profound power of "the few" when skillfully employed against regular forces. Where most nineteenth-century anticolonial rebellions failed, the great lessons provided by leaders like Abd el-Kader and de Wet lived on, helping guide independence-minded fighters to victory again and again in a powerful wave of twentieth-century insurgencies.

Another important theme highlighted by the lives and campaigns of the masters of irregular warfare is their ever-deepening encounter with advanced technology. Conventional armies have always prized the possession of the latest weapons and the swiftest transports and means of communication. But irregulars have realized that the greater reliance of conventional troops on these advanced systems makes them highly vulnerable to disruption; and some masters have aimed at achieving just such an effect.

Nathan Bedford Forrest of the Confederacy was perhaps the first to realize just how significant a strategic impact could be achieved by disrupting railroad links and telegraph lines during the American Civil War. T. E. Lawrence, as much as he is associated with the importance of having deep cultural expertise, was most successful in leading the Arab revolt during

World War I because he blew up so many Turkish troop trains. Indeed, the tribesmen he led into battle came to call him "Emir Dynamite." And the great Vietnamese leader Vo Nguyen Giap created a whole new concept of irregular operations based on exploiting the limitations imposed on the American military doctrine of heliborne "air assault" by the rough terrain of Southeast Asia. In short, conventional warriors are greatly nourished by technical advances; irregulars often concentrate their efforts on exploiting mass armies' deep dependencies on such sustenance.

This aspect of the story is not confined to land warfare. As trading states from the mid-eighteenth century on came to depend on the freedom and security of the seas, repeated efforts were made to prey upon the sea lines of communication in wartime. A great deal of damage was done, in many wars, by sea raiders, most notably by Confederate captains during the Civil War and German U-boat skippers in both world wars. But none of these came close to the achievements of the relative handful of American submariners during the Pacific War who, under the inspired leadership of Admiral Charles Lockwood, brought the Empire of Japan to its knees.

Aside from the challenge posed by Lockwood and his "undersea wolves," Japanese military leaders also had to cope with the first serious use of air power to enable and sustain Allied deep-penetration field operations in the Burma theater. It was here that Orde Wingate pioneered what may come to be a future model of deploying one's forces with little reference to such constraints as front lines, rivers, or mountain ranges. With a few brigades he caused mass disruption in an entire theater of war. Nearly seventy years later, his feat has yet to be duplicated in scale or effect.

Wingate and the others I have mentioned here, along with the rest of the masters of irregular warfare whose stories form this book, are important precisely because of their continuing ability to shape the future of conflict—and thus the future of the world system. I have attempted to highlight the particular lessons to be drawn from each of the masters, keying on such themes as the possibility of transforming an entire military; integrating irregular and conventional operations; pursuing nation building from the grassroots up; infiltrating insurgent and terrorist groups; and building networks and crafting a capacity for employing swarm tactics.

All these issues lie at the heart of military affairs in our time, an era of perpetual irregular warfare. The great captains of traditional forms of conflict have little to tell us about this. Nor can the classical principles of war provide much help, in particular the notion of the sheer power of mass, which has lived on until now in the form of Colin Powell's doctrine of "overwhelming force" and other concepts like "shock and awe." Such ideas were already faltering by the time of the Vietnam War; today it is clear that attempts to retool them against insurgent and terrorist networks will prove just as problematic.

For those who nod sadly at this point, resigned to the notion that irregulars will always remain a step ahead because traditional militaries must continually ready themselves to fight conventional foes, I have good news. "Master lessons" in irregular warfare will not only help us defeat the al Qaedas of the world; they can provide a new way to fight against big, old-style opponents too—with smaller but more effective forces. So this looming age of irregular warfare is not only one characterized by grave new threats but also by amazing opportunity.

J.A.
Monterey, California
December 2010

ACKNOWLEDGMENTS

For the past two decades I have been teaching irregular warfare in a graduate-level course of study for elite American and international military officers. This program exists today largely because my colleague Gordon McCormick has nurtured and protected it. I am deeply grateful to him for offering me the opportunity to contribute to its success. My gratitude also extends to the officers who have studied with me over the years and taught me so much along the way. Another colleague at the Naval Postgraduate School, the soldier-scholar Hy Rothstein, to whom this book is dedicated, has given me the benefit of his "master lessons" for many years. He continues to do so.

Major Matt Zahn, U.S. Army, played a crucial role in helping me decide to focus this book's penultimate chapter on the great Chechen insurgent leader Aslan Maskhadov. Professor Misha Tsypkin then guided me through the subtleties of conflict in the Transcaucasus, pointing the right way ahead at each twist and turn. The indefatigable staff of the Dudley Knox Library once again found every last obscure source I needed, sometimes putting into my hands centuries-old books whose pages I almost feared to turn. Almost.

Ryan Stuart created beautiful, clear maps that will allow the reader to follow the story in each chapter more easily. Sherry Pennell searched tirelessly for just the right picture to capture the spirit of each character profiled in this study. Mary Marvel helped keep materials readily available and well organized.

Ivan Dee once again provided exceptional editorial guidance, right from the start and on through to completion of the manuscript. It has been the great privilege of my professional life to work with him. At Rowman and Littlefield, Jon Sisk, Darcy Evans, and Julia Loy have devoted considerable energy to making sure that this book will "be all that it can be." I am much obliged to all of them for their efforts.

Finally, as this book touches on historical themes that still resonate in our time, especially the early manifestations of network warfare and swarm tactics, I am grateful to David Ronfeldt for having explored these areas with me over many years. It is growing ever clearer that we were cutting a valuable trail, one that others will no doubt join in enlarging and taking out to ever farther reaches, to the undiscovered places where the future of military affairs is to be found—and perhaps will be reshaped in ways that make our world more peaceful and secure.

INSURGENTS, RAIDERS, AND BANDITS

Watch, then, the band of rivals as they climb up and down
Their steep stone gennels in twos and threes, at times
Arm in arm, but never, thank God, in step.

—W. H. Auden

If a man does not keep pace with his companions, perhaps it
is because he hears a different drummer. Let him step to the
music which he hears, however measured or far away.

—Henry David Thoreau

Two things have altered not
Since first the world began:
The beauty of the wild green earth
And the bravery of Man.

—T. P. Cameron Wilson

1

WAR "OUT OF THE DARK"

War is among the most complex and perilous of human undertakings. Its complexities include those introduced by nature itself, as conflicts are conducted on virtually every type of terrain, on and beneath the surface of the sea, in the skies, and, perhaps one day soon, in outer space. Then there are the challenges posed by weapons systems of all sorts and of ever-increasing ingenuity, and the creative concepts of operations to guide their use. Such complexities are further compounded by the fact that all these elements—terrain, technology, and techniques—are wielded by thinking adversaries against each other, both striving for even the slightest edge that so often divides victory from defeat in wars between near equals.

And what of conflicts in which one side is markedly superior, as in the countless nineteenth-century struggles between advanced, imperial powers and indigenous peoples? The long history of warfare is replete with such unevenness. Parity, as existed between the leading states at the outset of World War I in 1914, is rare. In a world of unfair fights, only human creativity allows the chance to take on one's betters with some hope of prevailing. So it is that an innovative turn of mind toward unusual tactics and strategies, arising largely in response to material inferiority, lies at the heart of conflict's area of greatest complexity: irregular warfare.

Where conventional conflicts—on land, at sea, or in the air, and with whatever weapons—all tend to conform to the consistent, straightforward pattern of employing large masses of forces, fleets, and air wings, irregular warfare is primarily distinguished by the small size of its fighting units and their penchant for stealth and hit-and-run surprise attacks. Instead of a division of infantry charging forward against fixed defenses, an irregular approach would feature, say, a dozen commandos slinking across the lines to blow up the enemy's key defenses. Or perhaps an entire corps (several

3

divisions) would be broken into small "packets" of infiltrators capable of raiding and exploiting gaps, as Japanese general Yamashita chose to do with his forces in the amazing conquest of Malaya early in 1942. At sea, instead of the head-on clash of large battle fleets, one or a relative handful of stealthy submarines might be lurking, swarming, preying—like German admiral Karl Doenitz's U-boats in the Battle of the Atlantic.

Tactics aside, the fundamental and defining characteristic across the range of forms of irregular warfare is the small unit. These examples from World War II suggest that the small can be useful even in the biggest of wars. Thus a central aspect of irregular warfare is the employment of small military units in innovative ways, primarily against larger, more traditional formations.

A second form of irregular warfare is that conducted by guerrillas, their name derived from the small bands of Spaniards who effectively resisted occupation of their country by Napoleonic forces between 1808 and 1814.[1] While introduced in its current incarnation more than two centuries ago, guerrilla warfare did not come into its own as a dominant concept of operations until the eruption of a series of anticolonial wars of liberation waged from the late 1940s to the mid 1970s. In the heyday of these struggles, ranging from Mao Zedong's victory in China in 1949 to Vo Nguyen Giap's successful campaign against U.S. forces some two decades later, irregulars and their "pop-up" mode of attack proved exceptionally effective. Small bands of fighters put large professional militaries on the run again and again during this period, in a string of startling victories that brought colonialism to an almost complete end. Even in those instances where insurgents were defeated militarily—in places like Algeria, Kenya, and Malaya—colonial overlords departed anyway. The cost of continuing to try to control various rebellious peoples who had become habituated to the ways of irregular warfare was seen as too great.

How different this result was from most colonial wars of the nineteenth century, when indigenous peoples all too often tried to fight the armies of the great powers head-on and were slaughtered in the process. The Battle of Omdurman in the Sudan in 1898 was emblematic. In this clash a vastly outnumbered Anglo-Egyptian force—eight thousand British and about double that number of native levies—used a mix of machine guns, light artillery, and gunboats operating on the River Nile to decimate a force of more than sixty thousand Muslim zealots in just a few hours. And this was the general pattern during the "scramble for Africa," as well as in colonial ventures in other venues, such as the bloody repression of Chinese religio-nationalists at mid-century, which saw at least twenty million killed in the Taiping Rebellion. Firepower regularly overcame native valor, and by century's end much of the surface of Asia and Africa had fallen under colonial control.

There were a few exceptions. The plains Indians of North America fought guerrilla style, staving off inevitable defeat at the hands of a much more numerous and technologically advanced foe: Americans in pursuit of their "manifest destiny." The Russians, following their own expansionist dreams, ran into difficulties against the Chechens of the Caucasus mountains, who used similar hit-and-run tactics to hold out for many years—a form and spirit of resistance that would awaken once again late in the twentieth century. Even the British, riding high in the wake of victory over the Dervishes at Omdurman, soon found themselves deeply embroiled with the South African Boer *kommandos*, a few thousand fighters whom it took an expeditionary force of more than five hundred thousand troops to contain.[2] On the whole, however, the first wave of resistance to expanding industrial powers collapsed quickly, in large part because of the indigenous peoples' choice to employ conventional tactics when they enjoyed an initial edge in numbers over colonial expeditionary forces.

The third leg of an irregular warfare triad is terrorism. This is yet another mode of conflict based chiefly on the notion of employing small units in innovative ways—the aim in this case being to kill the innocent in hope of coercing or blackmailing others into compliance with one's wishes. To be sure, large conventional forces have occasionally been used for terroristic purposes—the deliberate firebombing of cities during World War II being an example of such a misuse of airpower. But in the main, terror tends to be practiced by the few as a means of challenging those more powerful. As opposed to irregular military operations, which seem to find a useful niche in most major conflicts—and in less conventional settings too—and guerrilla warfare, which has blossomed over the past half century and currently accounts for most of what can be called "irregular," the record of terrorism has been problematic. While it has been hard to extirpate terrorist organizations, it has proved just as difficult to point to many cases in which they have achieved their aims. In the judgment of the military historian Caleb Carr, terrorism "has been one of the most self-defeating tactics in all military history."[3] A quick glance at more than forty years of fruitless Palestinian terrorism in pursuit of statehood suggests just how hard it can be to make this form of warfare support the achievement of one's aims.

If the three faces of irregular warfare—small units, guerrilla tactics, and terrorism—suggest far more complexity than exists in traditional conflict, still greater depths remain to be plumbed. There are no neat dividing lines between the three forms. For example, standing militaries that establish elites in order to have a capability for the *coup de main* commando strike sometimes find themselves forced to employ these units to conduct guerrilla style insurgencies.[4] During World War II, for example, the Russians found themselves detaching some of their best soldiers to fight, far behind the lines, with partisan forces whose job was to attack the Nazi invaders' supply lines. Similarly, the U.S. Army Special Forces—the Green Berets—were formed in 1952 with the idea that they would lead insurgent resistance to Soviet occupation forces in any new European war that might break out. This tradition lives on today in what the Special Operations Command calls "unconventional warfare," an activity that features small numbers of American soldiers fighting "by, with, and through" indigenous bands of friendly forces in remote theaters of operations in the ongoing struggle against terror networks.

Beyond simply adopting partisan tactics to confront traditional aggressors and terrorists, military elites may also employ other irregular warfare techniques—including commando-style raiding—to defeat guerrilla movements. This is the basis of a major strand of thinking in the field of counterinsurgency, though it should be noted that military experts have often tried to defeat insurgents by using big units, traditional tactics, and overwhelming firepower against them—the approach that the U.S. military eventually settled upon and lost with in Vietnam. Thus military special operations forces' irregular warfare missions often overlap substantially with guerrilla techniques and may be employed to fight other militaries or terrorist organizations as well.

Similarly, guerrillas often go beyond using straight insurgent tactics against standing militaries and incorporate significant elements of terrorism. Certainly Mao and Giap, in their respective campaigns, were not at all averse to liquidating the innocent in order to make a point. This was a dark pattern seen in many guerrilla wars of liberation in their heyday over half a century ago, from the Mau Mau in Kenya to Chinese Communist operations in Malaya, to many other salient examples from the 1950s. Much more recently, the late insurgent/terrorist Abu Musab al Zarqawi virtually fused insurgency and terrorism, blending resistance to the American occupation of Iraq with calculated violence aimed at so-called Muslim apostates.[5]

Lest we assume that this linkage is something only benighted peoples fall prey to, consider the period of the American Revolution, when guerrilla tactics against British redcoats went hand-in-hand with systematic terrorism conducted against the Tories, those colonists whose loyalties remained with King George III. The Tories themselves showed considerable skill at mixing insurgency and terror. The conflict was so unremitting that, in the wake of defeat, the vast majority of surviving Tories chose to leave the country, settling in Canada. In this respect—that is, in the remorseless brutality of the connection between insurgency and terror—the conflicts in colonial-era America and modern Iraq have something very much in common.

*   *   *

Given the several facets of irregular warfare, and the large areas of overlap between them, it should not be surprising that attempts to grasp these complexities have often foundered. The best, and certainly most troubling, example of conceptual confusion can be found in the most recent attempt by Pentagon experts to define irregular warfare: "A violent struggle among state and non-state actors for legitimacy and influence over the relevant population."[6] While this view captures some sense of irregular warfare arising in unequal fights between nations and, say, networks, it misses the notion that either the weak *or* the strong may resort to special operations, insurgency, and terrorism, using small units. Further, this official document—issued on the sixth anniversary of 9/11—reflects a curious lack of attention to the idea that irregular warfare may be employed by a standing military in a general conflict.

Academic attempts to understand irregular warfare have been either too inclusive or restrictive. For example, one of the latest texts covers insurgency and terrorism, but excludes military special operations—and then adds such events as civil war, revolution, and coup d'état.[7] The range of battlefield special operations, to which most militaries show at least some attention, is missed. Further, one need only look to the American Revolution and the Civil War to see that these types of conflicts may be conducted in a mix of conventional and irregular ways. The same is true of overthrowing a sitting government from within. The fascist generals who sought control of Spain in 1936 did so primarily by means of a conventionally waged civil war that saw nearly a million Spaniards killed.

Efforts to simplify the concept of irregular warfare have tended to slight the complex elements that are so necessary to a proper understanding of the phenomenon. More than twenty years ago the notion of "fourth-generation warfare" was introduced—the four generations represented by line-and-column musketry some centuries ago, fire and movement tactics, mobile maneuvering, and, most recently, insurgency.[8] The problem with this formulation—which is wildly popular within the U.S. military—is that the generational phenomenon simply doesn't exist historically. The Mongols, a completely mounted force, were masters of mobile maneuver nearly four centuries *before* massed volley fire. Insurgents predated the Mongols by more than a millennium, if one goes back to the Sicarii Zealots who opposed the Roman occupation of Judea. And so on. The generational concept is simply inaccurate. Better to think in terms of conventional and irregular warfare always coexisting, sometimes quite uneasily, with one or the other ascendant in different eras.

The second major attempt to organize our thinking about irregular warfare came in the early 1990s with the introduction of the notion of "asymmetric conflict." Initially the idea was limited to explaining why weak nations sometimes attack their betters and how the use of innovative military means helps make this possible.[9] After 9/11 this concept was embellished to include any acts an aggressor might undertake that a more "civilized" defender would refrain from imitating: attacks with chemical weapons, actions directly against the environment, hostage taking, and a host of other forms of violence, most associated with terrorism.[10] But this concept too has a limitation: it falls afoul of the problem that virtually all warfare consists of actions intended to be asymmetric. The checkerboard deployment scheme of ancient Rome's many legionary maniples was an asymmetric response to the massed Hellenistic phalanx—but it was regular, not irregular, warfare. Lord Nelson's notion of "breaking the line" of opposing ships was an asymmetric response to classic line-ahead naval formations. The tank was an asymmetric technological response to trench warfare. Military affairs have long been the realm of the asymmetric, whether having to do with the irregular or not.

This brief survey of definitions brings us back to the need to focus on the heart of the matter: small units, used creatively across the three fundamental forms of irregular warfare: insurgency, terror, and special operations. At least one definition has been advanced that reflects this formulation and provides a common root for thinking about all of irregular warfare. It comes from the German nobleman, legal scholar, and World War II paratroop commander Baron Friedrich August von der Heydte. Writing in 1972, at the outset of what is considered the modern age of terror, the year of the Olympic massacre in Munich, he held that irregular warfare was a type of conflict

> in which the parties are not large units, but small and very small action-groups, and in which the outcome is not decided in a few large battles, but the decision is sought, and ultimately achieved, in a very large number of small, individual operations, robberies, acts of terrorism and

sabotage, bombings and other attacks. Irregular warfare is "war out of the dark."[11]

Here von der Heydte keys on the organizational element that defines this mode of operations—the dominance of small units of action—and links it to the three forms of violence embraced by irregular warfare. He even goes an important step further, associating irregular warfare with long, attritional struggles aimed at wearing down the enemy, rather than on short, sharp wars that may be won in a single decisive battle, or a few victories strung close together.

This emphasis on protracted, small-scale conflict may provide us with the most important clue to understanding what it takes to master irregular warfare. We are used to thinking of the great strategists and tacticians as squaring off against each other, after preliminary maneuvering, in brief, bloody, decisive battles between large armies or fleets: Scipio and Hannibal at Zama in 202 B.C.E.; Marlborough and Tallard at Blenheim in 1704; and, during the Napoleonic Wars, Nelson and Villeneuve at Trafalgar in 1805, with Wellington and Bonaparte at Waterloo ten years later. Alternately, when only one master was at work, we think of slashing campaigns like the series of battles fought by the heavy cavalry of the Byzantine general Belisarius, who in the sixth century restored much of the territory of the collapsed western Roman Empire, or the vast swift conquests of the Mongols under Genghis Khan in the thirteenth century.

But in irregular warfare there are virtually no set-piece battles; there is no armored, high-speed blitzkrieg. Far from quickly settling the fates of peoples, irregular campaigns are generally slow and cumulative. Think more of the example of Vietnamese general Giap who, for the most part, hewed to a strategy of slowly wearing down his opponents—first the French, later on the Americans—over a period of decades. Terror is intended to work in the same manner, gradually breaking the adversary's will to resist with continual small actions. This is surely al Qaeda's strategy today.

* * *

What then are the traits associated with mastery of the art of irregular warfare? Given the protracted nature of this mode of conflict, it seems clear that patience must be one of the virtues of the commander of irregulars. Beyond this there seems to be a rough divide between what one might label "operators" and "planners." Operators in irregular warfare are to be found out at the leading edge of the fight—like Robert Rogers, the pioneering ranger leader; John Paul Jones, the Revolutionary sea raider; or Nathan

Bedford Forrest, the great Confederate cavalry commander of the Civil War. Skillful planners of irregular warfare campaigns include the American Revolutionary leader Nathanael Greene, Vietnamese general Giap, and—it must be said—Osama bin Laden. Sometimes the operator and the planner are one person, as was the case with Cochise, the great Native American leader who inspired the Apaches to fight exceptionally effectively against near hopeless odds. T. E. Lawrence was another hybrid in that his strategic vision was as good as his desert survival skills and his demolitions expertise. As the modern phenomenon has unfolded over the past 250 years or so, the masters of irregular warfare have emerged from each of these three categories: the operator, the planner, and the hybrid leader.

Beyond individual qualities, how does one measure mastery? Is victory a prerequisite? This seems a sensible yardstick but does not account for the fact that most irregular warfare arises in situations where the material imbalance is great, the edge almost always to the conventional forces. That the more powerful side sometimes wins such wars, thanks to sheer weight of numbers and firepower—but not always, as Vietnam shows—should not be held against the skillful irregular who fights well and holds out for a long time against insuperable odds.

No, a victorious outcome alone cannot be the measure of mastery in irregular warfare, just as Hannibal and Napoleon are not removed from the ranks of the great captains of conventional warfare because they were ultimately defeated. Planning and fighting well, and demonstrating an ability to persist in the face of great adversity, are traits one must also associate with mastery.

Fighting well in irregular settings may still involve some of the canonical principles of conventional war, the ideas and maxims developed and refined over at least the past two millennia. The most salient conventional concept is that of mass. Strategy often demands moving the largest number of forces over the greatest distance in the shortest time. In the words of the rebel raider Nathan Bedford Forrest, victory goes to those who can get there "fustest with the mostest." A related point is to hit the enemy with as much of your force as possible at a point where he is the least concentrated and least prepared to absorb your blow. This formulation, perhaps the most important in conventional warfare, was the key to Lord Nelson's sea victory at Trafalgar as well as to the successful run of armored blitzkrieg campaigns by the Germans in the early years of World War II. Almost all conventional conflicts reconfirm the importance of massing one's forces at the decisive point.

But the commander of irregular forces is almost always heavily outnumbered and outgunned, often at the very point of contact with the enemy. Thus something other than expertise in maneuvering massed forces is required. In the irregular realm, this something else is stealth. Irregulars' small numbers often allow them to approach undetected, enabling them to strike by surprise—a key factor from World War II commando raids to the al Qaeda attacks on 9/11. Alternately, even when detected, the small size of the irregular force conveys an advantage in speed over larger, bulkier foes. For example, Robert Rogers and his rangers were detected on their approach to the village of St. Francis—a base for French-inspired terror raids against British colonists during the 1750s—and were soon pursued by large numbers of converging French and Indian forces. But the rangers had a speed advantage over their pursuers and were able to reach the target in time to inflict a stinging blow on the enemy. Their edge in mobility also served them well on the retreat afterward; only the reluctance of British regulars to come to their aid on the last leg of the march home caused most of the casualties the rangers suffered.

The edge conveyed by stealth, surprise, and speed has been described by one of the U.S. military's finest irregular warriors, the Navy SEAL (the acronym stands for sea-air-land) admiral William McRaven, as a form of "relative superiority" that must be exploited swiftly because it tends to erode nearly as quickly.[12] Thus a master of irregular warfare must understand that speed and stealth can to some extent substitute for mass. The small size of irregular units—whether they are special operators, insurgents, or terrorists—also allows them a much wider range of movements likely to go undetected. It is hard to move a brigade or a division very far under cover. But a dozen members of a Special Forces A-Team? Sixteen SEALS in a platoon? Nineteen terrorists boarding planes simultaneously? Much easier to go much farther undetected.

The irregular warfare strategist, knowing this, seeks to exploit the opportunity to force his adversary to spread his troops widely across the theater of operations, thus further enhancing his own side's ability to move stealthily. In some respects this is a photonegative version of the conventional military concept of the force multiplier, the notion that some tactics or technologies make one's troops far more efficient against an enemy that does not enjoy similar capabilities. For irregulars, the stealth advantage has some of this multiplier effect, but the real payoff comes in the form of what I would call a "force divisor" effect. That is, not knowing where and when a strike may occur, conventional forces must be dispersed to cover many points, making them more vulnerable to the irregulars' attack.

Among irregular planners, mastery may consist of integrating unconventional and conventional operations. In these hybrid campaigns, one side has both irregular and regular forces that operate simultaneously or sequentially. During the American Revolutionary campaign in the south, especially the period 1780–1781, Nathanael Greene had both types of forces operating at once against the British, almost completely confusing the Redcoats and exhausting them as they dashed from one crisis to another, finally compelling them to fall back on Yorktown, where they were trapped. Alternately, Vietnam's Vo Nguyen Giap provided an example of the use of the two types of forces in sequence, with periods of purely guerrilla operations giving way to conventional offensives in 1954 (against the French at Dienbienphu), 1968 (Tet), 1972 (the Easter offensive), and the final overrun of the South in 1975. Interestingly, Greene never won a conventional battle but ultimately triumphed. Giap lost two of his four major attempts to fight in traditional fashion, once against a primarily American force in 1968 but also to South Vietnamese forces, backed by U.S. airpower, in 1972.

But Greene and Giap seem to be exceptional, as most commanders of irregular forces have not had the option of going toe-to-toe with their more numerous and well-armed foes. Sometimes they have benefited from the looming presence of friendly conventional forces, as Lawrence did in the Arabian desert during World War I. The fact that General Allenby was engaging the Turks in a full-blown conventional campaign in Palestine no . doubt diminished their ability to focus on Lawrence's tribal irregulars. And before Lawrence, the Confederate cavalry leader Forrest enjoyed being able to operate widely and freely, with substantial friendly conventional formations serving to absorb most of the Union forces' attention and efforts. Although, at one point, the depredations against General William Tecumseh Sherman's supply lines grew so pernicious in their effects that about 80,000 of the 180,000 Union troops in the field during the drive to Atlanta in 1864 had to be diverted to thwart Forrest and his fellow raiders—a telling example of the "force divisor" phenomenon.

On balance, then, the mastery of irregular warfare relies upon some modification of the classical principles of war, particularly with regard to the notion of "massing at the decisive point." There must also be a willingness to recognize both the mixed nature of many military campaigns and, frequently, the just-off-stage presence of substantial conventional forces

The twenty-first century already shows clear signs that it will be a time replete with, if not dominated by, irregular warfare. Of the few dozen conflicts ongoing around the world as this book is being written, almost all feature insurgents and terrorists posed against harried militaries trying to learn the ways of irregular warfare to counter them. But even as the soldiers catch up conceptually, the insurgents and terrorists make new advances. In short, the age-old pattern of action and reaction in military affairs persists, placing a premium on those with the greatest aptitude for the unconventional. The chapters that follow recount the stories of many of the great masters of irregular warfare. The lessons to be derived from their campaigns retain a signal value in this new age of conflict.

2

FRONTIERSMAN:
ROBERT ROGERS

W hat Winston Churchill once described as the true "first world war"[1] was at its height some 250 years ago. The Seven Years' War (1756–1763) featured major field operations in Europe, where Britain's hard-pressed ally, Frederick of Prussia, strove to fend off Austrian, French, and Russian armies. In India, French and British forces vied for control of the subcontinent, each side augmented by large—and surprisingly well-armed—indigenous fighters. In each of these theaters the battles were for the most part traditional, with serried ranks on both sides standing to and unleashing massed volleys of musketry at each other, punctuated by artillery barrages that cut gaping, bloody holes in the ranks. It was war as it had been known for some centuries since the advent of firearms. But in North America, where British and French regulars squared off yet again, and each side also had colonial levies and Indian allies, something else happened to warfare: it became highly irregular. While there were some pitched battles and sieges, there were also countless small engagements across a wilderness land the size of Western Europe. An army operating here had to master bush fighting.

This meant, in the main, learning to move swiftly and stealthily over great distances through near-trackless forests, and by means of canoes and bateaux along lakes and rivers. In battle it meant setting ambushes and taking careful aim from covered positions, and staging lightning hit-and-run raids. How different this was from the set-piece massed field formations and the formal drill that attended the synchronized volley fire of proper European armies. Each side faced the challenge of this new mode of conflict, knowing from early on that mastery of the wilderness would decide the outcome of the war; but each met the challenge in different ways.

French army regulars never developed much capacity for irregular warfare, retaining to the end their reliance on conventional fighting. This served them well in early battles and sieges but quite ill in the crucially important defense of Quebec (1759), where the Marquis de Montcalm chose a stand-up fight and lost both the city and his life. When it came to irregular operations, the French relied on the efforts of their numerous Native American allies and, to a lesser extent, on their own colonists—who were few in number, compared to the British settlers,[2] but better schooled in the ways of the forests. Despite these skills, many French-Canadian settlers were siphoned off to augment the conventional forces as "colonial regulars."

Thus a kind of divided force structure emerged, in which the irregulars engaged in reconnaissance and terroristic raids, and also served as protectors and guides for the regulars as they moved about the wilderness, among and between the line of forts that defended New France, and out from them on offensives against the British settlements. In pitched battles their Indian allies and colonial woodsmen were sometimes used in a manner that accentuated their unconventional strengths; but on some occasions they were employed in conventional fashion and performed not as well. Montcalm's most grievous error was to deploy these troops to fight in the open at his last battle on the Plains of Abraham outside Quebec, where they simply could not volley as well as the Redcoats. And this misuse occurred after they had begun the battle from hidden positions and had done serious damage in sniping at the British regulars.

Early on in this bitter conflict, the French had made much better use of their irregular capabilities. Indeed, their bush tactics had worked spectacularly well. In one early action, a hundred or so French colonial regulars, augmented by perhaps six hundred Indian allies, inflicted a crushing defeat on a British column in brigade strength—just over two thousand troops when they set out, but down by several hundred after a month on the march, due largely to sickness. The Redcoats were joined by just a few hundred colonists and a half-dozen Indians, giving them little capacity for bush tactics. All were under the command of General Edward Braddock, slowly marching through the forest toward the key strategic point, Fort Duquesne (present-day Pittsburgh). When ambushed by the French and Indian force, Braddock tried to employ traditional field formations—all that he knew to do—massing his troops for volley fire, but this only made them more compact targets. The resulting slaughter saw Braddock mortally wounded and more than two-thirds of his force killed or wounded. The general's last words, however, foreshadowed a more supple strategic approach to war in the wilderness: "We shall know better how to deal with them another time."[3] Braddock would prove to be prophetic. But for the moment, complete catastrophe was barely headed off by the steady courage of the American colonial officer George Washington, who had come along on the expedition.

Other defeats would soon follow for the British as Montcalm continually exploited his ability to move conventional forces under the protection of a ring of irregulars during the campaigns of 1757 and 1758. His most notable success came with the capture of Fort William Henry, at the southern end of Lake George in New York, though it was tarnished by the atrocities committed by his Indian irregulars in the wake of the siege; the awful episode that has come down to us vividly through James Fenimore Cooper's account in *The Last of the Mohicans*.

At this point in the war it was hard to see how the French could be beaten, given their seemingly winning mix of conventional and irregular methods, and the far greater number of Native Americans who flocked to their side. But the British had learned from Braddock's defeat and other reverses, and if they had fewer Indian allies, they had far more colonists, many of whom were more inclined toward bush fighting than open-field battles. These were the men who would populate the ranks of the ranger companies, described by the historian Fred Anderson as "whole battalions of little wiry men able to move quickly through the woods."[4] They would eventually go well beyond merely providing security for the Redcoat regulars. Under the leadership of one of their own and of a British general of receptive mind, they would transform a field army and win control of a continent.

*   *   *

Robert Rogers was a New Hampshireman who loved the wilderness world and felt most truly alive there. In his youth he picked up Indian bush craft and almost certainly put it to use as a border smuggler, bringing in illicit goods to the British colonies from French Canada.[5] Some evidence indicates that when he was a child his family homestead was burned out by marauding Abenaki Indians, kindling an anger toward them that would never leave him. Aside from smuggling, Rogers is thought to have involved himself in other dubious activities, including forgery and counterfeiting. Francis Parkman summed up Rogers simply: "His character leaves much to be desired."[6] Nevertheless he became a folk hero for his exploits during the French and Indian War (as the struggle was known in America), as a leader of high-risk raids and countless long-range reconnaissance patrols deep in enemy territory. In an age when campaigning was limited to milder seasons, he and his small companies operated year-round, on snowshoes and ice skates in winter. He is still lionized today as the father of the U.S. Army Rangers, all of whom know virtually by heart the twenty-eight rules of his famous "plan of discipline" for irregular warfare.[7] Many of them instruct how to move in rough country without being detected, or how to react when ambushed.

But for all his codification of the rules of bush fighting, Rogers did not actually initiate the practice of "ranging" the colonial frontier to protect settlers from Indian and French-Canadian terror attacks upon the innocent. Ranger units had been forming and operating for many decades before Rogers, in a growing effort to curtail the increasingly bloody depredations that reflected a calculated French effort to deter the westward expansion of the British colonists. Indeed, from 1690 on, French policy in North America was driven by an effort to "scourge the borders and embroil the savages with the English."[8]

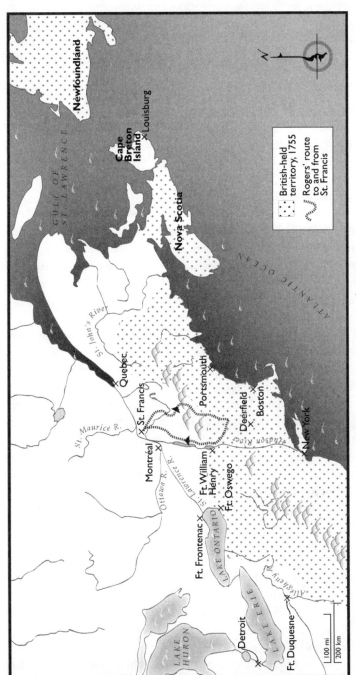

The Seven Years' War in North America

Perhaps the most infamous incident of this early terror war was the French-inspired raid, fomented by a fanatical Jesuit priest, that led to the Deerfield Massacre of February 1704. In this horrible action, fifty-three colonists were killed and more than a hundred taken captive and marched through the snow from their homes in Massachusetts to locations some hundreds of miles away in Canada. The raid and its aftermath were recounted in heartbreaking detail by a survivor, Pastor John Williams, ransomed after two years of captivity, in his tale *The Redeemed Captive Returning to Zion*. This atrocity, and countless others like it, drove the rise of rangers. What Rogers was able to do, half a century later, was to elevate bush fighting to a completely new way of war.

Where rangers had come into being largely for defensive and deterrent purposes—to protect frontier settlements—Rogers saw their offensive and punitive possibilities. He envisioned companies of green-clad woodsmen reporting every enemy movement, raiding small outposts, even striking deep into French territory to chastise the Indians for the atrocities they had committed. Throughout the war he and his rangers did all these things, their most famous action being the retaliatory raid on the Abenaki village of St. Francis, depicted so vibrantly in Kenneth Roberts's classic *Northwest Passage*. This attack required Rogers and his force of fewer than two hundred to infiltrate well over a hundred miles behind enemy lines, on foot and by canoe, then strike swiftly and make their way back. All this was done with French and Indian forces chasing them on the way to St. Francis—the rangers' canoe cache having been discovered at an early point—and harassing them almost all the way back. This action alone highlights two of the most important elements of modern irregular warfare today: "long-range penetration" and the ability to "observe, orient, decide, and act" more quickly than one's foes. Today this latter phenomenon is commonly called the "OODA loop" and is recognized as a key element in military effectiveness. Although it is generally associated with a twentieth-century fighter pilot, John Boyd, it may really have begun with Robert Rogers.

While British military leadership in this era has often been portrayed as hidebound and unwilling to innovate—Braddock being the iconic figure for this point of view—the truth is more complex. Braddock may only have stated the need for improvement with his dying breath, but other British soldiers had come to this conclusion earlier and had a far more complete grasp of the fundamentally irregular nature of warfare in the wilderness. The first senior officer to embrace bush fighting was a thirty-three-year-old general, George Augustus, Viscount Howe. British prime minister William Pitt had made him second-in-command of the force advancing on Fort

Ticonderoga in 1758, under Major General George Abercromby, an older and much more traditional officer. Pitt teamed them because Howe "had all the vigor, youth, and dash that Abercromby lacked."[9] Lord Howe was completely taken with the idea of an army replete with irregulars. He often went about in ranger garb, accompanying advanced patrols and joining in the thick of the fight. In one action, however, as his forces were reconnoitering in the vicinity of a small French detachment near Ticonderoga (Fort Carillon to the French), Lord Howe was shot dead in a confused firefight. Abercromby, his command no longer enlivened by Howe's presence, soon led his army—which outnumbered the French by about four to one—in a disastrous frontal assault that cost nearly two thousand dead and wounded in a single day.

This marked the low point of the war for Rogers and his rangers. After all his efforts to forge truly elite units—which two centuries later would become the model for the formal establishment of U.S. special operations forces—the command establishment had insisted on using them as cannon fodder in a fruitless frontal assault against a strongly fortified position. And so, as the 1758 campaigning season came to a close, there were few hopeful signs that the war against the French could be won.

But it turned out that Lord Howe was not the only British general to appreciate the need to develop greater capacities for waging irregular warfare. Others began to call for rangers as the need to counter the terror raids on English frontier settlements soon grew critical. For the French strategy early in the war of complementing their mannered conventional operations with a relentless irregular campaign was soon ratcheted up. Indeed, one of Montcalm's aides-de-camp, Louis-Antoine de Bougainville—better known to us today for his achievements as a scholar and explorer—went along with the raiders on one attack and was appalled by what he saw. As he put it in his *Journal* shortly after the Indian raid he witnessed:

> The ferocity and insolence of these black-souled barbarians makes one shudder. It is an abominable kind of war. The air one breathes is contagious of insensibility and hardness.[10]

If even French officers responsible for conducting such a campaign were horrified by it, the British sense of urgency should come as no surprise. At the start of the war there had been but one company of rangers, a few hundred soldiers. By the next year there were seven. All were under the command of Robert Rogers, and all had gone through his "ranging school." More were to come, as by war's end there would be ten companies all told. Selected

Redcoats too would study ranger tactics, the hope being that they would learn these new ways and take them back to their own regiments, spreading bush-fighting skills throughout the army. Thus the true genius of Rogers may have been made manifest in his role as educator and trainer.

Yet he must be given high marks also for seeing the many and diverse roles that his rangers could play in the field. Yes, they improved frontier defenses and deterred terror raids by paying French-aligned Indians back in kind with offense-minded punitive actions. And just as Native Americans acted as sensors for columns of French regulars moving through the wilderness, so too the rangers served as eyes and ears for the British and colonial conventional forces. But beyond these functions the rangers also began to undertake commando-style field operations in support of various campaigns.

They did this first in assisting amphibious operations in 1758 against Louisburg, a great island fortress and naval base that commanded the approaches to the Gulf of St. Lawrence. In 1759 it was rangers who found the path up the cliffs and spearheaded the advance from the St. Lawrence River to the Plains of Abraham outside Quebec. As the final campaign against Montreal began to unfold in 1760, a three-pronged convergent assault, Rogers would use his fertile brain to find even more uses for his rangers—at one point employing them as "combat swimmers" in a lightning attack on five French warships that were blocking the British advance along the Richelieu River.

More than all this, the rangers would point the way to transforming the British army in North America. No longer would the Redcoats be subject to the sort of ambush that had destroyed Braddock's force. No longer would they move so slowly, be so loud and visible. Instead of remaining in massed formation when under fire, they would come to respond to such new commands to take cover as "Tree all!" Soon Lord Howe's successor, Jeffery Amherst, found himself in command of an army that would scarcely have been recognizable as British had the king come to inspect it. As Fred Anderson has described this startling transformation:

> Since 1758 they had routinely cut the tails of their coats back almost to the waist; had trimmed the brims of their hats to within a couple of inches of the crown, and had worn them slouched, not cocked; had had their hair cut to a length of just an inch or two. At least one Highland regiment had given up their kilt in favor of breeches. Officers now seldom wore the gorgets and sashes that invited the attention of enemy marksmen; some had taken to wearing ordinary privates' coats. A few had even begun to carry tomahawks.[11]

Amherst himself was a highly deliberate general, almost Roman-like in his insistence on fortifying every position to which his army had marched, and on hacking out one stretch of road after another through the wilderness. Yet, like Howe, he saw the great value in cultivating a capacity for irregular warfare. He agreed with the colonial governor of New York, Lord Loudoun, whose view was simply that "it is impossible for an army to act in this country without rangers."[12] But this did not preclude rangers from acting without a regular army. And if Amherst's major field operations were achingly slow-paced, he was nonetheless willing to give Rogers his head by setting him loose upon the French and their Indian allies. It was Amherst who ordered the ranger raid on the Abenaki Indian village of St. Francis, still one of the greatest acts of long-range penetration in the history of irregular warfare.

Traditionally, military campaigning came to a halt during winter. This was certainly true in the harsh North American climate in the eighteenth century, and generally holds true even today in wintry places like the mountains of Afghanistan. But throughout the French and Indian War, as the main British and colonial American forces hunkered down during the months of snow and ice, the rangers remained active. Rogers led them in a series of patrols, raids, and skirmishes that saw them turn up in the least likely places, at the most inopportune moments—for the enemy. Snowshoes, a technology borrowed from the Indians, gave the rangers mobility overland, allowing them to do reconnaissance, take prisoners, and strike at supply columns. As rivers commonly froze over during winter, the French used sled convoys on them to move needed goods and ammunition between their forts and outposts. While they could move swiftly in this fashion, the rangers were able to outpace them by using their ice skates. Soon nothing became more ominous for those running the convoys than to hear the sound of blades scraping the ice, looming nearer and nearer. Given that it was often too cold for firearms to work, these were grim fights with knife and tomahawk.

But the rangers didn't have things entirely their own way. As the war dragged on, the French and their remaining Indian allies—the latter diminishing in number in the wake of the ranger raid on St. Francis, and as a sense of the impending British victory began to take hold—continued to mount patrols and raids of their own.[13] Rogers and his men found themselves, even at this late point in the war, engaging in some sharp fights and getting the worst of matters on more than one occasion. Returning to Crown Point with a dozen new ranger recruits the winter after the raid on St. Francis, Rogers was ambushed by a roving enemy war party that killed five and took four prisoners. Somehow he and a few others escaped.[14]

This wasn't the only time Rogers and his men had been in grave personal danger. From time to time throughout the war Rogers found himself cut off, pursued, or engaged in running fights on long retreats when patrols and raids went bad. In these situations his indomitability and endurance were the keys to survival for himself and his men. In this kind of war even a victorious action could quickly turn about. Coming back from the raid on St. Francis, for example, Rogers was pursued by large numbers of French and Indians for more than a hundred miles. Only his iron will and the fitness his drills and training had forged kept his hundred-odd rangers moving at a faster pace than the sizable groups of pursuers tracking them. That they eluded capture and were able to come back, albeit having lost about a third of the raiding force, is perhaps the most powerful evidence that Rogers had created truly elite troops, the first of such quality, purpose-built, that the world had seen.

Rogers, not yet thirty at the time of the St. Francis raid, had given birth to a type of military unit and enlivened a way of war that made possible huge improvements in British military practices. Even skeptics among the king's officers came to see this, and the British soon multiplied the number of "light" and "flank" companies of their own infantry units, arming many of them with the accurate, longer-ranging rifles that were coming into use and which a few rangers had employed during the war. Yet what Rogers had achieved in the realm of irregular warfare not only helped win a continent for the British Empire; he had also forged an instrument that would soon imperil much of the Crown's North American holdings in a full-throated revolution. The hard-pressed Redcoats, who would barely hold their own against an Indian uprising just after the fall of the French, would lose the war designed to maintain control over their American colonists—largely because of the colonials' masterful irregular operations. As to Rogers himself, the great architect of wilderness warfare, in middle age he would choose to become the enemy of his own people and end his days in defeat, exile, and ignominy.

* * *

The fall of Montreal in 1760 to Jeffery Amherst's converging columns—each of which Robert Rogers and his rangers had done so much to guide and empower—was a high point for the British. After that almost all the going proved to be downhill. Amherst, so patiently skillful in defeating the French, proved to be a colonial administrator of indifferent qualities. And in the immediate wake of the war the Native Americans quickly realized that without French backing their situation had worsened dramatically.

Only broad unification of the tribes and concerted action would give them any chance of holding on to their homelands. At this point in 1763—the same year the Treaty of Paris concluded the Seven Years' War—a broad insurgency erupted. Pontiac's War was named after the visionary, semi-mystic Ottawa leader who sought to unite the tribes by helping spread the idea, first advanced by Delaware Indian prophets, that the Almighty had brought down grave troubles upon them because of their consumption of alcohol. Purification of the people, via the embrace of abstemiousness, was the only way to rekindle past successes. The example provided by such personal discipline, it was thought, would so impress the king of France that he would send his forces once again to fight alongside the Indians.

Whatever their divine origins, these visions were of changes that most Indians, familiar with the disruptive, enervating effects of liquor, could accept, at least for a while, and their will to fight was only reinforced by ham-fisted British negotiating tactics. Soon the tribes were on the attack in many places. Every British outpost west of Detroit, all the way to Green Bay on the western shore of Lake Michigan, fell to the Indians. Detroit, Pittsburgh, and Niagara were in effect besieged as Amherst's road network was cut in countless places by raiding parties. In short, Pontiac conducted the very sort of campaign that Rogers had envisioned from the outset of the French and Indian War—coordinated, protracted, widespread raiding by small bands of highly mobile fighters.

Faced with these reverses and an almost entirely irregular enemy campaign, Amherst had to perform a kind of strategic triage. He focused on the idea of helping his three major forts withstand Indian sieges, and wrote to one of his subordinates about the need to employ any and all means at hand, including allowing blankets that had been used by smallpox victims to fall into enemy hands. In addition to waging a primitive form of biological warfare, Amherst also called for extreme brutality, including mass executions of warriors and their families.[15] But at this point in the war he had little ability to defeat the Indians in battle. The best he could hope for was to send relief columns and convoys to his besieged forces. Robert Rogers and his rangers joined one such force, heading off to Detroit in the fall of 1763. Unfortunately the British commander of the expedition, James Daly-ell, a man of high birth but of low capabilities, disregarded Rogers's advice and sent his massed force out to "hunt down" the Indians. The result was a predictable disaster. The British commander was killed and decapitated, and his head shown around triumphantly. Rogers fought heroically and fell back into Detroit with the other survivors of the rescue column. The fort held until further relief, under more prudent command, arrived.

Soon the British began to restore the equilibrium in the irregular fighting and were able to bring Pontiac to the peace table with offers of a renewed flow of goods and the implicit threat to unleash upon his people and his allies a terrorist swarm of Shawnees who were not members of the pan-Indian movement. Pontiac agreed to treaty terms. But the promised goods soon stopped coming, and the great chief was murdered by a disgruntled warrior from his own tribe. Without his vision and leadership, the Indians never again achieved meaningful levels of unity.

For his part, Rogers went to Britain to request permission to conduct explorations aimed at finding a route to the Pacific—the fabled Northwest Passage. His petition was denied, but he was given a command in the Great Lakes region that he used as a jumping-off point for extensive forays, including some that extended far beyond Crown territory. His detractors—and they were many—helped raise a charge of treason against him, which he successfully defended.

This experience seems to have soured him on British rule, and at the outset of the Revolution in 1775 Rogers sought service with the rebels. Given both his character flaws and his long service to the Crown, many among the revolutionaries worried he might be a British spy. Those suspicious of him included even George Washington who, in a letter to Congress, gave voice to his concerns about the loyalty of the great ranger. Although Washington made no direct charge, he referred quite insinuatingly to "the Major's reputation, and his being a half-pay officer."[16] This was enough for Rogers to be blackballed by the rebels, and he soon shifted his support back to George III.

Rogers quickly helped form and command units of "the King's American rangers," who fought with considerable skill and a desperate fury across much of the same ground Rogers and his rangers had traversed in the war against the French and their Indian allies. He remained a careful recruiter, at one point even catching the rebel spy Nathan Hale, who sought to infiltrate the force and report on British intentions.[17] Ironically, many of the Native Americans whom Rogers had fought in the previous war now allied themselves with the British against the rebels. They added significantly to the Crown's bush-fighting capabilities, the end result being the rise of an irregular war out of Niagara that for its ferocity made Pontiac's campaign seem pale by comparison. Indeed, the most savage battle of the Revolution was fought with irregular troops on both sides in 1777 at Oriskany, which featured perhaps the war's highest percentages of each side's forces killed or wounded in action.[18]

Rogers eventually alienated his British masters—who had become more enamored of another Tory ranger, one Walter Butler—and left their service while the war was still going on. He returned to the United Kingdom drunk, divorced, and despondent, dying there in 1795. The British erected no great monument to him, nor of course did the Americans. But the ultimate success of the Revolution had nonetheless been critically dependent upon Rogers's influence. He may have fought against his own people, but the troops who defeated the Redcoats and loyalist Tories grew from the earlier seeds he had planted. As one thoughtful account observes, "all the original rifle units of the Continental Army could be lumped into the ranger class."[19] These troops held their own in stand-up fights, fended off the irregulars they had to confront, and in the decisive southern campaign, blended traditional battles and insurgent actions in a manner and under a leader, Nathanael Greene, that the British could never effectively counter. For having inspired and helped enable such an innovative approach to war, Robert Rogers deserves an honored place in our memory—if not our sympathy.

3

FIGHTING QUAKER:
NATHANAEL GREENE

Painting by C. W. Peale, U.S. National Archives website

In one of military history's more ironic turns, each side began the American Revolutionary War (1775–1783) with considerable capacities for waging irregular warfare, yet both proved oddly reluctant to emphasize this mode of conflict. For their part, the Americans started with a citizen soldiery whose ranks were replete with fine marksmen who also had a great aptitude for operating in the wilderness. Their superiority in firefights, when allowed to aim freely at marks of their own choosing, was apparent in the early engagements in and around Boston and would surface time and again throughout the war. But for some reason rebel leaders from the outset chose to transform these fine natural soldiers into a "proper" (i.e., European-style) conventional army designed along classical lines, closely drilled in ordered movement and massed volley fire. The principal champion of "conventionalizing" the Continental Army, oddly enough, was George Washington, whose early experience with Braddock was apparently not searing enough to tarnish his dream of building a force that looked smart on the parade ground and fought well on the traditional battleground. As a supreme commander he proved quite hidebound about military doctrine.

Nevertheless Washington enjoyed the full confidence of Revolutionary political leaders and, save for the brief, futile plotting of the "Conway cabal," which sought to have him sacked, he was able to have his way. The military historian Russell Weigley has thus observed Washington's position in the early strategic debate with Charles Lee—not one of the Lees of Virginia, but a retired British officer with rebel leanings who had also served under Braddock—about how to wage the war:

> Washington rejected the counsel of Major General Charles Lee, who believed that a war fought to attain revolutionary purposes ought to be waged in a revolutionary manner, calling on an armed populace to rise in what a later generation would call guerrilla war. Washington eschewed the way of the guerrilla.[1]

Soon drillmasters like the imported Baron von Steuben were teaching soldiers to march, shoot, and die like automatons. This accorded closely with Washington's wishes, and the baron's influence rose all the way to the top of the rebel military as he brought to bear his insights from service as a staff officer to Frederick the Great of Prussia.

For their part, the Redcoats also had significant potential for conducting irregular warfare at the outset of the Revolution. Every unit had riflemen and flankers, and all held out the promise of making further tactical improvements over time, building upon the progress that they had made in the previous war. In addition, Britain's allies among the native tribes and the large number of American colonists who remained loyal to the Crown—the Tories, nearly a third of the total population—provided powerful augmentation in the tactic of bush fighting. Yet when given the opportunity to fight in a far more traditional manner—on open ground cleared for agriculture—the British too came to lean far more heavily toward the conventional.

Results in the field soon reflected the traditional cast of the contending armies, and not favorably for the rebels. George Washington's attempts to stand fast and fight on Long Island in 1776 nearly caused the loss of his entire army. Another near disaster was barely averted the following year in the vicinity of Philadelphia. To be sure, there were victories as well, in a surprise attack by a small detachment on Trenton the day after Christmas 1776, and at Saratoga in the fall of 1777. But both these battles had significant irregular elements, the former being a hit-and-run strike, the latter largely the result of weeks of highly accurate sniping and harrying of British general John Burgoyne's ill-supplied conventional columns.

After Saratoga, France entered the war on the rebel side, but this development reemphasized regular military operations as the expeditionary forces sent to America were almost all configured for conventional set-piece battles. In any event, by the time the French troops began to arrive in significant numbers, Washington had just about given up on the notion of winning a decisive pitched battle. After the hard-fought, drawn encounter at Monmouth in June 1778—in reality a near disaster—no further conventional fighting occurred in the north, where the war eventually devolved into something of a stalemate. The British held New York City but were unable to expand their control much beyond its immediate environs. The rebels held Boston and retook Philadelphia, and controlled more territory in the north overall. But they had little hope of dislodging the occupiers from New York.

It was at this moment of strategic stasis that the British sought to seize the initiative by shifting the focus of their operations to the south. Their naval capabilities made such a bold move possible, as French sea power was not concentrated in North American waters but was rather dispersed in other, ultimately ill-fated campaigns in the West Indies and in the Indian Ocean. So when the British struck south at the close of 1778, they were able to move without fear of interdiction. They seized Savannah, killing or capturing virtually all the rebel defending forces while suffering losses of only three killed and ten wounded.[2] Soon much of Georgia had fallen under their control. And even though a Franco-American counterattack on Savannah was mounted in 1779, British forces withstood the assault and siege, and the French expeditionary force and fleet under Admiral General Count d'Estaing soon left the Americans to their own devices—putting no small strain on the alliance. As the great American naval historian Alfred Thayer Mahan observed, the French withdrawal, by "abandoning the southern states to the enemy,"[3] ceded the initiative yet again back to the British, who soon put it to good use.

In 1780 the British moved aggressively once more, seizing Charleston, South Carolina, and trapping and capturing almost the entire rebel field force there—estimates of the total vary between three thousand and five thousand. Other victories would follow, especially in irregular encounters, where the British benefited from the services of two skilled bush fighters, Major Patrick Ferguson and Lieutenant Colonel Banastre Tarleton. Ferguson would organize and lead Tory rangers in several successful actions— but would die in the field at King's Mountain. Tarleton, commander of the British Legion, a mobile strike force, was a gifted cavalryman, one of whose early exploits of the war was to capture General Charles Lee while on a raid. In the southern campaign his troops won many victories against colonial irregulars and contributed heavily in conventional fights, especially at the great British victory in the Battle of Camden against Horatio Gates, the reputed hero of Saratoga—and the favored candidate of the Conway cabal to replace Washington. In the wake of the victory over Continental regulars, Tarleton was set loose to pursue and destroy rebel partisans. He soon won a resounding early victory against the guerrilla leader Thomas Sumter at Catawba Ford.

At this point, in August 1780, American fortunes seemed to have sunk as low as they possibly could in the southern theater. The British had seized the major cities of Georgia and South Carolina, defeated every field army that tried to face them in the open, and inflicted severe wounds on rebel irregulars. Only the victory of rebel "over mountain men" against Ferguson cast a ray of hope on the cause.[4] This was the moment when Washington gave the command of Continental forces in the south to a thirty-eight-year-old former Quaker from Rhode Island who had never held a commission before being appointed a general in 1775, Nathanael Greene. Self-taught in strategic matters—he had been closely questioned by members of his meeting when they found books on military affairs in his home library—Greene had by this time spent five years serving close to Washington. His errors in judgment had contributed to early defeats near New York and Philadelphia, but he had also fought bravely and led troops skillfully to better outcomes at Trenton and Monmouth. He had also served as quartermaster general of the Continental Army, a position well suited to his methodical brain. But Greene longed to return to an active field command, and when Washington offered him the South, he accepted eagerly.

Giving the matter deep thought before his departure for the theater of operations in October 1780, Greene wrote to Washington outlining the plan he intended to execute with every expectation of success, "I see but little prospect of getting a force to contend with the enemy upon equal grounds, and therefore must make the most of a kind of partisan war."[5]

Over the course of the following year, Greene's "partisan war" would turn the tables on the British. But it would not be simply a case of hit-and-run raids. Greene would blend these skillfully with conventional maneuvers, using lightning strikes by irregular forces alternately with pitched battles to keep his opponents off balance and always guessing as to his next move. More than this, he would exhaust the enemy, setting the stage for the British army's retreat to Yorktown, where it would finally be trapped.

* * *

That the campaign in the south would not be conducted according to classical military principles became apparent from the outset. Greene's first act as field commander was to divide his vastly outnumbered forces, giving half of them (about six hundred Continentals) to Daniel Morgan, one of the heroes of the victory at Saratoga. Advancing separately, Greene thought, they would both confound Cornwallis, the British commander, and maximize their militia recruitment efforts. Besides, if the Redcoats remained for the most part massed, and chased after one of the two American main forces, the second enemy formation would be able to run wild in another area—and the balky British columns would hardly be quick enough on the march to catch the Americans. Given that Cornwallis also had to worry about being able to come to the aid of the small garrisons of the many remote outposts he had created, and others of his ten thousand plus troops had to garrison Savannah and Charleston, Greene's opening decision to split his force seems inspired.

An aggressive, energetic commander, Cornwallis rose to the challenge by dividing his own force. Soon he sent Tarleton in search of Morgan while he went after Greene himself. This was a reasonable choice, given the problem the rebel general had posed. The only other viable alternative seemed to be to cede the initiative to the Americans and stand on the defensive. Neither Cornwallis nor Tarleton were inclined to do this; but their first countermoves played out badly. In a masterpiece of tactical battle management, Morgan defeated Tarleton at the Cowpens in January 1781,

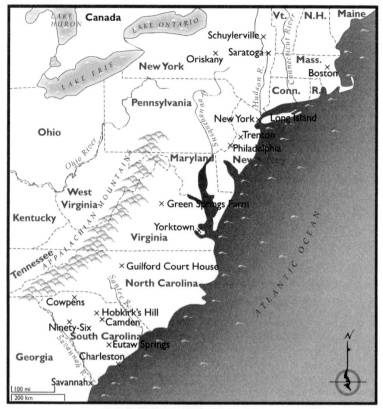

Nathanael Greene's Revolutionary War

while Greene stayed just beyond Cornwallis's grasp, retreating just in time across a series of northwest-southeast-running rivers. His quartermaster's brain had inspired him to make sure a sufficient supply of small boats was always at hand. And while the British were engaged in their own offensive maneuvers against the rebel main forces, guerrilla fighters were having their way with Tory militias and British garrisons at remote outposts. The first round clearly went to Greene. But the victory was somewhat Pyrrhic as Morgan's rheumatism was acting up seriously in the cold, wet winter weather, and he was invalided out of the army.

Bereft of his strong right arm, and without another subordinate in whom he vested similar faith, Greene now had but one conventional force with which to divert the British from their renewed offensives against the rebel guerrillas. Cornwallis caught up with the Continentals when Greene chose to stand and fight at Guilford Court House on the Ides of March in

1781. Greene tried his best to emulate Morgan's method of using militiamen as skirmishers and Continental regulars as his firm second line of defense. In this instance, however, a planned retreat of the militia went awry, and they failed to reform, leaving the regulars to fend off the Redcoats in a ferocious fight. They held on long enough to allow Greene to withdraw in good order, leaving the field to Cornwallis, whose army—even in victory—had lost more than a quarter of its men killed and wounded.

Soon after the battle, the British army retreated toward the North Carolina coast, where it could be replenished with fresh men and supplies, drawing succor from the Royal Navy. Cornwallis hoped to draw the Americans into a new battle where British logistical advantages would begin to tell, reestablishing the war's general pattern of victories won when in proximity to the sea. The historian Theodore Ropp described this strategic dynamic as a situation in which "the Continentals won no pitched battles in the open. . . . Most British attacks on seaports were successful. . . . Most of the rebels' successes were won in the back country."[6] Now, Cornwallis hoped, the campaign would continue on terms more favorable to British forces, as his move north would, he thought, compel Greene to follow and give battle. If Greene did not follow, the way would be open to conquer Virginia, where the American traitor Benedict Arnold was already leading a British raiding force and creating much disruption.

Yet Greene surprised Cornwallis again. As with his first move, dividing his army in the face of a far more numerous foe, Greene again violated the principles of conventional warfare by heading in the opposite direction from his main enemy. Instead of following Cornwallis, and before informing Washington, Greene took his army southward once more, aiming to set the backcountry ablaze and reclaim the Carolinas and Georgia. This move allowed Cornwallis to invade Virginia, where he prevailed against American forces that Washington had sent from New York under the Marquis de Lafayette. Tarleton, now working in tandem with other British raiding forces, caused considerable suffering among the populace. Nevertheless Greene stuck to his belief that the partisan war in the south was the best hope of achieving a strategic victory. Among the irregular formations fighting there, Greene's move resonated powerfully, energizing them to new levels of guerrilla activity.

Soon it seemed that no British or Tory patrol in the Carolinas could be undertaken without being ambushed. And no outpost was secure. In a series of hit-and-run raids, the rebels came close to compelling British withdrawal to Charleston and Savannah. When additional British troops were being distributed to shore up security in the hinterland, Greene's main force arrived on the scene, posing a whole new threat. So the British had to concentrate their forces once again, this time under the command of Lord Rawdon. Early on, in the spring of 1781, Rawdon bested Greene in a firefight at Hobkirk's Hill. Later Rawdon arrived on scene just in time to thwart Greene's effort to take the major outpost at Ninety-Six, so named for its distance in miles into the hinterland. The opposing forces met once more at Eutaw Springs on September 8, with the British again carrying the day in savage fighting—a characteristic of Greene's pitched battles—but suffering mightily.

While Greene engaged the main British forces, his irregulars went wild. As the historian Theodore Thayer notes, "while he was keeping Rawdon occupied, Greene's subordinates captured *all* the small forts in South Carolina except those in the vicinity of Charleston."[7] In this sort of fighting the partisan Francis Marion, the Swamp Fox, showed a special aptitude and a clear understanding of the larger purpose of the campaign. The historian Derek Leebaert rates Marion quite high in this regard, observing that "what elevated him above just being a guerrilla leader was his ability to accept authority and work hand in glove with Nathanael Greene."[8] Russell Weigley, who pioneered the concept of there being an "American way of war," went further in singling out Marion, noting that, when compared to other partisan leaders, he was "possessed of a superior sense of strategy and a superior willingness to cooperate with other leaders."[9]

Beyond Marion, Greene also enjoyed the benefit of a great cavalry leader, Henry "Light-Horse Harry" Lee,[10] father of Robert E. Lee, who would go on to write a brilliant account of the winning mix of conventional and irregular operations in his classic *Memoirs of the War in the Southern Department of the United States*. With just a few hundred riders under his command, Lee was often able to raise complete havoc with the vulnerable British communications and supply lines. Ironically, his famous son, who would come to command Confederate forces replete with skillful raiders during the Civil War, would choose to fight conventionally, viewing irregular warfare as "an unmixed evil."[11]

His supporting cast aside, it was to Greene's particular credit that he understood the fundamental dynamic of the campaign: he did not have to win conventional battles in order to prevail. Stand-up fights wore down the British and created opportunities for irregular actions that added to the enemy's physical and psychological fatigue. All Greene needed to do was keep his conventional force "in being," able to compel a fight or pose a new challenge when circumstances required. In his famous, fatalistic description of the conventional part of the campaign, Greene summed up matters: "We fight, get beat, rise, and fight again." This became his mantra, in the view of some historians making him more willing to accept tactical defeats, or not to press too hard when battles were in flux, in order to ensure the continuance of the overall strategy, which depended on keeping a conventional force in being. As Greene put it in a letter to Daniel Morgan, "It is not our business to risk too much."[12] Perhaps not. But these are odd words coming from a man who regularly risked his whole force in hard-fought pitched battles, and whose strategic moves—dividing his force, marching *away* from the enemy—were exceptionally bold.

In the end it was the British who were, to their amazement, beaten strategically. Without having lost a pitched battle after Cowpens, they nevertheless found their forces exhausted and worn down by attrition and constant marching and countermarching, and in 1781 they began withdrawing from all their backcountry forts and outposts. They holed up in Charleston where they remained until 1782, then made good their escape. As to Cornwallis, his fate at Yorktown is a best-known part of American lore, especially the grace note about his band marching out at the surrender playing a tune called "The World Turned Upside Down." What is less recognized is the crucial role that Greene's campaign played in his ending up trapped there.

* * *

When Lord Cornwallis turned his forces north into Virginia, he was emulating Greene's move away from him—so perhaps he should receive as much credit as his rebel opponent for creativity. Indeed, Cornwallis continued to win battles and, in conjunction with Arnold's and his successor's raiding forces, brought considerable suffering to Virginia and the prospect of renewed British control. Farther south, Lord Rawdon showed his ability to stand toe-to-toe with Greene's continuing operations and even to prevail tactically. The main British stronghold in the south, Charleston, continued to be virtually unassailable as long as the British held command of the sea, though it was briefly lost during the Yorktown campaign in the fall of 1781. But Greene's maneuvers had a peculiarly unnerving effect on the British high command in North America, which grew worried that the insurgency in the far south had to be dealt with in order to avert an overall disastrous outcome to the war. Cornwallis's superior, Sir Henry Clinton, took the position that the main Redcoat force "should have stayed in the Carolinas."[13] A bitterly contentious correspondence ensued between the two before Cornwallis complied with the order to retreat to the coast, pending redeployment of his forces.

Even on the retreat, Cornwallis lashed out successfully delivering a stinging blow to the Marquis de Lafayette's pursuing army at Green Spring Farm, where more than two hundred Americans died in a short, sharp action. The Redcoats were hardly a defeated force, as they were still able to rout American troops in battle, yet here they were withdrawing from occupied parts of Virginia. The only reasonable explanation for this was Clinton's concern about what Greene and his guerrillas were up to in the Carolinas and Georgia. He believed it imperative first to deal with Greene, then to return to campaign again in Virginia. In retrospect Cornwallis was probably right in assessing the chances of defeating Greene as low and the opportunities for success in Virginia as high, given that the terrain there was much less conducive to irregular warfare and Virginia militiamen less inclined to fight in an irregular manner. Which leaves us with one of those tantalizing historical "What ifs?" Had Cornwallis carried the day in his debate with Clinton, the close of 1781 might have seen Britain in possession of New York, Virginia, and, at the very least, Charleston in the south. As matters turned out, they held only New York, having lost Virginia. And even the occupation of Charleston continued only on borrowed time.

For this outcome Nathanael Greene deserves much of the credit. He had gone south and reversed a losing campaign. And he did so against skillful generals in command of veteran troops, in a theater of operations in which a third of the population actively supported the British and another third simply wished to stay out of harm's way. But it is the manner in which Greene achieved his results that is most distinguishing, in particular his masterful mixing of conventional and irregular operations. As a strategist he had an innate understanding that irregular warfare often demanded that the principles of war be violated, so in the face of a superior enemy he boldly divided his own forces. Later he would march away rather than toward the main enemy army, opening the door to Cornwallis's invasion of Virginia. The sheer audacity of these moves was further compounded by his willingness to face British forces in pitched battles time and again. Although Greene was careful enough to break off the fighting and retreat from the field when the risk was too great that his army might be broken, such judgments are hardly subject to precise calculation. The very fact that he took the field in this manner meant that, on any given day of battle, he could have lost all.

Without the willingness to take such risks, Greene would not have empowered the guerrillas working with him. Unless he could divert the British with his main force, his irregulars might be hunted down by Banastre "Bloody Ban" Tarleton and other well-practiced irregular hands among the empire's forces. That the British and their German mercenaries had developed a keen sense of the demands of counterinsurgency is reflected in the classic memoirs of Johann Ewald, who conducted many such operations during the war. In his *Diary of the American War: A Hessian Journal* and his *Treatise on Partisan Warfare* Ewald noted the potency of the insurgents but also their vulnerability to countermeasures when no friendly regular forces were nearby. Greene was well aware of this too, and no doubt was willing repeatedly to risk the loss of his Continental regulars because the failure to do so would almost certainly lead to the withering away of insurgent forces.

Nevertheless it took far more than cold-blooded strategic logic to follow such a campaign plan. It also required great courage, not only on the battlefield but in counsels of war. Greene had shown his fearlessness in firefights many times before and knew that a leader had to be an exemplar. On one occasion this duty led him calmly to continue writing dispatches sitting at his open tent while Cornwallis—who had just missed catching Greene at a river crossing—was in frustration bombarding the rebel camp with artillery he had drawn up right to the water's edge on the opposite shore. But it must have taken Greene just as much courage to make his daring decisions to divide his inferior force and to march away from Cornwallis, allowing the latter an open road to Virginia. It is Greene's strategic courage that stands out as exceptional in American military history. There has been no lack of brave field generalship over the past two centuries and more. But the kind of command boldness that he showed remains unusual and, when it comes to the irregular, in the words of Russell Weigley Greene, "remains alone as an American master developing a strategy of unconventional war."[14]

Do high-level British strategic disputes and errors diminish Greene's achievements? Not at all. The very fact that Greene persisted against superior forces and skillful enemy generalship was what drove Cornwallis to launch his own controversial move northward. His dispute with Clinton does not weaken the case for Greene's mastery, for it is the mark of a master that the enemy is placed in such uncomfortable positions in the first place. In any event, military campaigns that proceed without errors are nearly nonexistent. The true mark of mastery is the ability to recover from reverses and misjudgments, as Greene did again and again, and relentlessly to exploit the enemy's errors, which he also did.

It might be argued that Greene's achievements are diminished by the rebels' use of the American rifle, which gave an edge in the war, both conventionally and in partisan settings. It is true that American soldiers tended to be better marksmen. Many frontiersmen were skilled hunters, and rebel riflemen tended to train at longer ranges than their British counterparts. And in firefights, British losses were often higher, at the margin. But the Redcoats had many rifle units of their own to complement their smooth-bore "Brown Bess" muskets, they prevailed in many pitched battles, and they got much the better of the guerrillas on numerous occasions. No, Greene's success cannot be written off by overemphasizing the American edge in rifle fire.

Instead he won because of his conception of a superior strategy, which enabled him to prevail *despite* his tactical inability to win decisive conventional battles. He won because of the skillful blending of regular and irregular forces and operations. And he did so against some of the best field commanders the British employed in North America. In his time Nathanael Greene's contribution to victory was well and widely understood for these reasons, especially for how tactical defeats contributed to strategic victory. John Adams wrote of the ultimate strategic gains in the wake of Greene's loss at Eutaw Springs that the battle was "quite as glorious for the American arms as the capture of Cornwallis."[15]

Lacking Adams's more refined capacity for insight, the general public's instincts were nonetheless the same. Great crowds rallied and cheered at every stop as Greene made his way back to Rhode Island at war's end. Soon after, the state of Georgia voted to reward him for his services with the gift of a beautiful plantation outside Savannah called Mulberry Grove. Greene found running this operation in some ways more difficult than his campaign against Cornwallis. His situation was further complicated by the sizable personal debts he had accumulated during the war. Run down by years of campaigning in the field, unrelenting hard work, and loans coming due, Greene soon fell gravely ill and died in the summer of 1786. He was just forty-four. What may have died with him was an important strand of thought about irregular warfare in American strategic culture. As we shall see, however, many other cultures would soon demonstrate their consider-able capacities for waging unconventional warfare.

4

GUERRILLERO:
FRANCISCO ESPOZ Y MINA

Galleria de Militar

A million French soldiers died during the Napoleonic Wars, one-fourth of them in Spain. Of these quarter million dead, a bit more than half fell in set-piece battles against British, Portuguese, and Spanish regular troops, including losses incurred on the march to these fights or from wounds suffered in them. The rest of the French losses, amounting to somewhere between eighty thousand and one hundred thousand, came in the bitter "small war" that was waged for nearly five years (1808–1813) between Spanish guerrillas and French imperial regulars. It was characterized by an endless series of vicious, close-quarters clashes. French patrols, isolated small garrisons, and supply convoys were among the favorite targets of the guerrillas. But the insurgents' impact was also felt on the major battlefields of this war, as their very existence forced the French to disperse widely their troops in Spain—at one point numbering more than four hundred thousand—leaving them unable ever to concentrate overwhelming numbers against the coalition forces led by the Duke of Wellington. Thus British ability to hurt the French in the field, with a force of Redcoats never exceeding sixty thousand, was greatly enhanced by the power of the guerrillas to distract and disrupt their occupiers.

In recognition of the potent direct and indirect effects achieved by the insurgents, historians and strategists have ever since associated the modern concept of guerrilla warfare with this campaign. And it has turned into a mode of conflict that has manifested itself with increasing frequency in the ensuing two centuries, becoming since 1945 the world's most prevalent form of organized violence.

Beyond conjuring up an evocative image, the term "guerrilla" also offers a tacit homage to these early Spanish insurgents. It needs to be kept in mind, for the leading early historians of the war in Spain—and a few contemporary ones—have tended to downplay the contributions of the guerrillas to the British victory over the French.[1] To admit the insurgents' important role in the outcome of the Peninsular War could be seen as somehow diminishing the Duke of Wellington's own accomplishments, which even the French preferred to emphasize over their defeat at the hands of a largely peasant revolt. But, the modern historical consensus has come around to acknowledging that, working hand in hand—much like Greene's regulars and the southern rebel partisans did during the American Revolution—the two types of forces carved out a signal victory together. The military historian David Chandler has perhaps said it most succinctly: "Between them, the Spanish guerrillas and British redcoats were to make life intolerable for the French occupation forces."[2]

If the French were ultimately put on the run in Spain, this happened only after several years of hard, brutal fighting. The initial success of Spanish resistance against the small first wave French expeditionary force in 1808, led by Napoleon's subordinates, was soon followed by the appearance of the Emperor himself, who would swiftly defeat three separate opposing field armies and drive British expeditionary forces to a harried evacuation by sea. After these successes early in 1809, Bonaparte left Spain, never to return. Perhaps he had been let down because the Spanish riches he thought were there to be easily plundered proved illusory. Or maybe he was distracted by the resurgence of Austrian armed resistance to his empire and its continental system of attritional economic warfare against Britain. Then, by the time he had dealt with Vienna, the rumblings of a coming conflict with the Russians may have deafened him to his generals' pleas for help on the peninsula.

Whatever his disappointments or distractions might have been, Napoleon nevertheless chose commanders to remain in charge in Spain who were drawn from among his very best, including Marshals Soult, Victor, Ney, and Masséna. They would give respectable accounts of themselves in their pitched battles with Wellington, sometimes forcing him to retreat. And even against the guerrillas, they learned on the job some of the skills we have come to associate with counterinsurgency today: winning over the hearts and minds of the populace; creating smaller, more mobile forces; and even co-opting some elements of the occupied population to fight against their own countrymen.

In winning over the Spanish people, the French skillfully cultivated many local grandees by ensuring that their fortunes and prerogatives would remain intact. Abuses of power by Roman Catholic Church officials were publicized and punished, appealing to many—from commoners to aristocrats—who had come to resent Rome's heavy hand in Spanish society. The French occupiers also touted a host of social reforms aimed at awakening a desire for "liberty, equality, and fraternity," not unlike those set loose by their own revolution.

Further, some French generals showed a great sensitivity to the need to reduce the long shadow cast by military occupation—especially in the form of rape and pillage by their own soldiers—by trying to respect the personal security and property of the Spanish people. The French military's awareness of the value of treating the populace humanely may have grown from lessons learned the preceding decade when an anti-Republican guerrilla uprising in the Vendée, a coastal area of France just south of Brittany, was tamped down only when respect for basic rights accompanied skillful military action.

Perhaps the most accomplished French practitioner of this subtler aspect of the art of occupation was Louis-Gabriel Suchet, whose operations in Aragon and Catalonia provided a textbook model of this aspect of counterinsurgency. Under his command a large swath of Spain remained, for the most part, peaceful and secure. The historian Lynn Montross has described the situation:

> Suchet not only put an end to French looting . . . but actually refunded money extorted by his predecessors. Treating the conquered with scrupulous fairness, he created hospitals, orphanages and schools. By admitting Spaniards into a share in the government, he won their respect to such an extent that soldiers of the army of Aragon were able to go unarmed among the peasantry.[3]

Suchet was also a great field commander, defeating several British generals who sought to bring the successful methods Wellington employed on the Portuguese front to other parts of the peninsula. He encouraged the recruitment of Spaniards who were willing to join the cause against the guerrillas—as many of the latter, in the name of freedom, had simply seized upon the opportunity to engage in banditry. While Suchet's methods did not catch on completely throughout all of occupied Spain, his fellow commanders did strive at least in part to emulate his approach.

In short, the guerrillas were up against tough, smart occupying forces and sometimes had to fight other Spaniards. The conventional forces they tried to operate with were either far off or, when operating closer, beaten by the likes of Suchet. How then did the guerrillas come to prosper in the field and have such a powerful impact on the outcome of the war?

To be sure, the French occupation was resented, especially because both old King Carlos and his son Ferdinand were being held in France as hostages, with Napoleon placing his brother Joseph on the throne—the ultimate act of nepotism. But hard feelings about "overthrow and occupation" were not enough to make for a successful insurgency. That demanded the kind of charismatic leadership that could bring the people together, not only to rise up but also to fight effectively. The regency government in still-free Cádiz in southwestern Spain, wracked with its own byzantine infighting and performing poorly in the field, could not provide this sort of inspiration or even model military leadership. Instead it was left almost entirely to private individuals both to galvanize and guide the resistance.

Many of these insurgent captains arose from the peasantry in various parts of Spain. Some were struck down, others were beaten in battle. Still others either switched sides or seized the opportunity to resort to outright banditry. Some achieved small degrees of success simply by staying on their feet and fighting the French until liberation—like Juan-Martín Diez in Guadalajara, *El Empecinado* (the Indomitable).[4] But in the scale and strategic impact of his operations, one stood out from all the rest: a man who took the name "Mina." He was almost surely illiterate, a Basque-speaking farmer who was to become the most successful insurgent leader of the resistance. He would suffer stinging defeats and several wounds during the war years but would always rebound. Along the way he would improve his practices, exhaust and befuddle his more numerous French adversaries, and in the end, play a crucial role in their defeat.

*   *   *

In the beginning, he wasn't even Mina. Francisco Espoz was a common soldier among the Navarrese insurgents who had joined up to serve in a "land pirate" (*corso terrestre*) band of insurgent raiders led by his distant younger cousin, Javier Mina. Only eighteen at the time of the French invasion, Javier was a bright seminary student who came from a better-off branch of the family. He was an excellent speaker and organizer whose anti-French zeal soon became a rallying point for resistance in Navarre. Born in 1781, his cousin Francisco was twenty-eight at the time and was but one of many

The Peninsular Campaign and Insurgency

enthralled by the words and vision of Javier Mina. Later, in a clear example of guerrilla branding, Francisco would tack on his cousin's name onto his own, becoming Espoz y Mina. But he would routinely shorten it to Mina, allowing the venerated name to take its full effect.

The early actions of the Mina *corso* undertaken in the fall of 1809 were concentrated on striking at supply convoys and small detachments of French soldiers. The basic concept of operations was to hit and then run back into the mountains, where the insurgents could move more surely and swiftly, almost always eluding their pursuers. For months the insurgents stuck to this pattern quite successfully. But on occasion Javier would concentrate his forces against larger targets, as in an attack on a battalion of some eight hundred French troops deployed to the town of Los Arcos. In this action the smaller guerrilla force was augmented by hundreds of angry local peasants, from whom the French had been extorting money and requisitioning food. The locals eagerly joined in the attack. The French were driven out and Javier, flushed with success, decided against returning to the mountains. Instead he set up his headquarters in Los Arcos.[5]

This move proved to be a bit too impetuous: it drew the growing threat of Javier's force all too soon to Suchet's attention. The French commander dispatched a division (some ten thousand troops) to engage Javier, who quickly abandoned Los Arcos and had to stay on the run. He, Francisco, and the rest of the band gave a good account of themselves in the many running fights that ensued at the close of 1809; but by the spring of 1810 the French force had nearly doubled in size, and the guerrillas were forced to operate almost entirely in small, dispersed groups. In March of that year, Javier was traveling in company with a few others when they were ambushed by a French patrol. He was taken prisoner while Francisco remained on the run with six other fighters who would carry on in his name.

A heated debate among the French broke out next over what to do with Javier. One opinion, championed by Napoleon himself—such high-level attention being a sign that the guerrillas were already having an effect—was that he be publicly executed. Suchet and others in the field, however, sought to show clemency, then to use Javier to appeal to other Spanish insurgents to join with the French in bringing "true security" to their own country. This appeal had worked for Suchet in other areas; indeed, in some ways it foreshadowed the American effort two hundred years later to recruit Iraqi insurgents to the cause of countering terror in their country. But Javier would not allow himself to be used in this fashion.

Nonetheless by the time this attempt at turning him had failed, Napoleon's blood had cooled, and Javier was sent off to prison in France. He was freed upon Napoleon's abdication in 1814 and soon made his way to Mexico where he joined the rebellion against the Spanish monarchy that had been restored after Napoleon's fall. But Javier could not rekindle his soldier's luck. He was captured and later executed in Mexico City in 1817.

Meanwhile in the spring of 1810, Francisco headed a team of just six guerrillas fighting for freedom in a province that the French had now apparently pacified, and in which their occupying forces now numbered close to thirty thousand troops, including many cavalry and much artillery, the two areas in which the guerrillas were sorely deficient. Francisco's first step was to associate himself with his heroic cousin, taking his name and assuring his fellow Navarrese that Mina fought on. Soon new recruits began to join up. As the burden of requisitions and taxes to support the large French occupying force grew, so did Spanish resentment, and the ranks of the rebels swelled.

Still, Mina confronted plenty of problems. Perhaps the most pressing was the fractured nature of the resistance, whose members were enthralled at the time with a chaos-inducing concept they called simply "the Idea." Its basic point was that every man was the master of his own desires and could not be ordered around by anyone, French or Spanish. While the Idea helped enliven the resistance, it also encouraged freewheeling banditry. So Mina's first task was to rein in the men of the Idea as well as rival resistance leaders, a mission he undertook with a ruthlessness that was to become as well known as his bravery in battle and his fairness in settling disputes.

One of Mina's most dangerous rivals was Pascual Echeverría, who in the summer of 1810 commanded a force of guerrillas about half the size of Mina's, which was now about a thousand strong. Echeverría had established himself in the prosperous town of Estella, whose people bore the heaviest burdens imposed by his band. Mina went straight at him—but under the guise of negotiating an alliance. During their meeting, Mina arrested him on criminal charges, took him prisoner along with five of his most trusted lieutenants, and had them all sent off to a nearby monastery. Mina then seized the moment to recruit more than four hundred new troops, formerly under his rival's command, into his force—and then ordered Echeverría and his lieutenants shot. The people of Estella celebrated. The new recruits behaved.

Juan Hernández was another insurgent-gone-bad with whom Mina had to deal. He commanded a force composed almost entirely of cavalry and so could not be chased down, as Mina's force at this point was still made up mostly of light infantry. So Mina made overtures to Hernández, conjuring up images of a winning alliance in the making. The leader of the mounted bandits fell for the ruse, and he too was arrested at his meeting with Mina. After he was executed, his troopers joined the cause, and now Mina had cavalry.

Perhaps the greatest challenge to Mina's authority came from Casimiro Javier de Miguel, a former cleric who had been appointed a colonel by the Regency government that still held the southwestern strip of Spain and a few other cities. Father Miguel came to Navarre in August 1810 to take over from Mina, who at this point was still viewed with a mix of condescension and suspicion by the junta in Cádiz. For all his ruthlessness in pursuing power, Mina graciously handed over his forces to the colonel; but Miguel's military incompetence soon had the guerrillas surrounded by a fast-moving French force.

At this point Mina resumed command and extricated his troops from the potentially fatal encirclement. He arrested but did not execute the priest-turned-colonel, sending him back to the regents so that they could contemplate his shortcomings. In September the government in Cádiz formally recognized Mina as the leader of all resistance forces in Navarre, effectively ending his need—at least for the present—to do away with any more rivals.[6]

Mina's rough path to insurgent leadership was perhaps the first real test of his mastery of irregular warfare. The rivals he shunted aside were tough, wily men, and the softer Father Miguel was the favorite of the regency. Thus Mina had to thread his way carefully, tempering the brutal tactics employed against his competitors in the field with patient handling of the government's man. Future masters like Tito and Mao Zedong would face similar challenges, overcoming them in similar ways. But some, like the great Chechen leader Aslan Maskhadov, would fall short in terms of consolidating their command. Mina pioneered not only guerrilla field operations but the range of strategies associated with achieving command of guerrilla movements.

But while Mina was consolidating the French had not been idle. Although their forces in Navarre had shrunk by more than half after the capture of Javier Mina—a necessary reduction so that the burden of occupation would not weigh too heavily on the Navarrese people—a dynamic new general, Honoré Reille, arrived with a division of fresh, experienced troops to track down Mina. Soon the rebels were on the run once again. Throughout the late summer of 1810, French soldiers chased Mina and his men all over Navarre. But while the imperial troops exhausted themselves during the chase, the guerrillas struck back hard at targets of opportunity. Supply convoys were their favorite targets, especially ones that carried ammunition, the insurgents' essential need.

They also attacked other types of targets, one of the most important being a surprise assault on an entire brigade of Reille's force. To their great embarrassment, the French were sent running from the mountainous terrain around the Carrascal Pass, all the way back to Pamplona. In another key action, Mina struck at the French fort of Puente while Reille's main force was pursuing a small insurgent decoy detachment far to the west. Mina burned the fort down and killed or captured the entire garrison of three hundred troops. Perhaps two-thirds were taken prisoner, in these days to be marched to the Biscay coast where they would be placed on British ships and transported into captivity. Later, as the viciousness of the fighting intensified on both sides, prisoners would not be so humanely treated.

By this time, nearing the fall of 1810, the French realized that the capture of Javier Mina had brought them even more troubles with the rise of the new Mina. They decided to take fifteen thousand of Marshal Masséna's battle-hardened veterans from the fight against Wellington and redeploy them to Navarre. Mina was soon hard-pressed, escaping one trap after another thanks only to the steady stream of intelligence he received from friendly Navarrese, who also fed misinformation to the French—for which the natives were often brutally punished. Indeed, as Reille's frustration mounted, so did reprisals against the civilian population, including retaliatory executions, mass imprisonments, and the burning of homes whose families could not account for missing sons who, the local census said, ought to be living with their parents. If the war in Spain was a textbook example of irregular warfare, it was also a template for some of the cruelest counterinsurgency practices, many of which we have since seen again and again in a wide range of conflicts over the past two centuries.

Even while on the run, with most of his roughly two thousand fighters dispersed, Mina could still use his intelligence network to call many of them together for occasional counterattacks. In October 1810 he sought to replicate the success of his attack on Puente with a strike against another French garrison, at Tarrazona. But here the terrain was more open, the attack force was detected, and more than a thousand French hussars rode down Mina's massed force. The result was a slaughter, with Mina catching a bullet in the leg and barely escaping with his life.[7]

The following month, having recovered from his wound, Mina concentrated his fighters yet again—tying down forces that otherwise would have gone to the fight against Wellington—and was once again caught by the French, this time at Belorado. Mina lost more than five hundred of his men in this lopsided defeat.

As the year 1810 neared its close, the insurgency in Spain thus reached its low point. The bad news extended well beyond Mina's defeat at Belorado. Several other guerrilla leaders were being hunted down by French forces that had greatly improved their counterinsurgency tactics. In some places the insurgents even found themselves chased by their fellow Spaniards. Regency troops had never recovered from their catastrophic defeats of the preceding year and were able to hold on to the southwestern tip of Spain only with the support of British sea power.

Finally, prospects for coordinating guerrilla operations with Wellington's main force had also greatly diminished. The Redcoats, even after winning a hard-fought victory at the Battle of Busaco, had retreated from the Spanish-Portuguese border region all the way to the defensive lines of Torres Vedras in the hilly countryside around Lisbon. The best Wellington could now do was to send off some of his scouts to work with the insurgents. These were the kinds of irregulars depicted in C. S. Forester's classic of the Peninsular War, *Rifleman Dodd*, and in some of Bernard Cornwell's Richard Sharpe novels. Along the Mediterranean coast, the British frigate captain Thomas Cochrane showed some aptitude for raiding, sometimes in conjunction with rebel forces, but his superiors never fully seized upon the potential of this type of war from the sea.[8]

Thus the insurgents would have to bind up their wounds and return to the fight largely on their own. It would take Wellington two more years to prepare for and mount a lasting offensive into Spain, one whose success would be greatly aided by the French disaster in Russia in 1812.[9] As a leading historian of this era (and a descendant of Wellington) has put it, "Spain was to be saved . . . not by grape-shot . . . but by hardy guerrillas and the flash of the knife."[10] The sharpest of these knives was to be wielded by a resurgent Mina.

*   *   *

Even before the coming of the new year, Mina began rebuilding. His *nom de guerre* remained a magnet, and several hundred new recruits joined the cause. He called in his scattered cavalry units and executed their leader, Juan Hernández, who had allowed and engaged in many acts of banditry. In another brutal yet subtle move, Mina also executed—on trumped-up charges—a charismatic guerrilla leader of the borderlands of Navarre, known as Belza. Soon more than eight hundred new recruits came to him from these borderlands. By December of 1810 Mina was in command of almost three thousand men.

To his bloody clean-up operations Mina also added personal grooming: he ordered short haircuts for all his troops. Long hair, one of the hallmarks of the independent "men of the Idea," was no longer allowed. It symbolized defiance and hosted lice. Mina made sure that all those with long hair submitted to being shorn. Then Mina himself lost his locks in a public ceremony. If his men had been made to bend to his will, he had now shown that he was one of them, and the force was ready to take the fight to the French once more. In two firefights against French columns, on Christmas Eve and then again two days later, they killed some two hundred imperial soldiers and executed twenty captured Spaniards who were serving with the enemy. Mina was back.

The French responded swiftly, with a winter operation begun in January 1811 that saw some twenty-five thousand troops chasing Mina. In a move reminiscent of Nathanael Greene's trademark retreats after pitched battles, Mina ordered his forces to scatter and operate independently. And, like the British in the Carolinas, the French in Spain now dispersed their forces once more in a network of small outposts. A bitter "small war" ensued, with heavy casualties on both sides and the peasants becoming more and more the objects of French brutality.

To relieve the suffering of the people, Mina concentrated his forces yet again in the summer of 1811—a mistake that soon cost him dearly as a major part of his guerrilla army was annihilated in a pitched battle near Lerín. With more than four hundred killed and two hundred taken prisoner in this fight, Mina had no choice now but to disperse his remaining forces once more. It seemed there was no end in sight to the resilient French occupation and the hard fight ahead.

At this point, as sometimes happens in war, the enemy's very successes conspired to turn events. While Reille had been dueling with Mina, Suchet had been overseeing successful pacification operations in Catalonia and Navarre. Indeed, Suchet's moves had been so successful that surviving insurgent groups left these provinces and headed to Navarre to join Mina, swelling his ranks to their highest levels yet. Thus the guerrillas in Navarre, who had lost more than two-thirds of their three thousand fighters in the failing campaign of 1811, began 1812 with nearly four thousand men reporting in the ranks.[11]

During this rebuilding, Suchet, unaware of the covert exodus to Navarre, took the next logical strategic step after defeating the guerrillas in his area of operations: he besieged Valencia, the last great holdout city that resisted the occupation on the Costa del Azahar in eastern Spain. Here Suchet met a sizable opposing force under Captain General Joachim Blake, some forty thousand defenders. So he called for reinforcements from Reille's division in Navarre, a unit that became a key component in his successful offensive. Valencia surrendered in early January 1812. But the garrison occupying Navarre had by now been reduced to fewer than seven thousand troops, and France's Polish allies—mostly lancers, some of the best horsemen in the world—were recalled home, as preparations for Napoleon's invasion of Russia began. Always ready for aggressive action, Mina seized the initiative one more time. And this time he did not let go.

In his campaign of 1812, Mina was careful to avoid large pitched battles, so many of which he had lost in earlier years. Instead he mounted a swarming campaign featuring attacks on supply routes and remote small outposts. This shift away from pitched battles and raids on fortified bases, with the focus instead on attacking the lines of supply that sustained the French occupation, was Mina's key breakthrough—and the surest sign that he had finally mastered the nuances of this irregular war. No more would he run the risk of a decisive defeat in the field. Rather, he now placed the strategic burden entirely on the French, who suffered innumerable attacks on vulnerable supply convoys in the increasing costly effort to sustain their positions. Mina's innovation, aside from its impact on the war in Spain, would inspire future guerrillas, from Russia's Denis Davydov to T. E. Lawrence, and on to the Taliban in our time, to imitate his approach.

As his successes mounted, Mina's numbers increased. And even though Suchet sent a division and more back to Navarre after the fall of Valencia, by this time Mina had grown too strong to be defeated, especially since he refused to mass his forces and fight toe-to-toe.

This didn't stop Reille from trying, however. He was soon in command of some twenty-five thousand troops, the Army of the Ebro, against dispersed guerrilla forces under Mina amounting, in the summer of 1812, to just under ten thousand fighters. In a brutal struggle through the rest of the year, Mina kept the upper hand by remaining dispersed and continuing to strike "out of the dark." Soon the large French garrison in Pamplona was effectively under siege, as were a range of outposts that had not yet been overrun. When news came at the close of the year of Napoleon's disaster in Russia, the French began their retreat. Harried by Wellington, who had finally taken the offensive for good, the French would lose a major battle at Vitoria, in part because Mina's forces were still keeping over twenty-five thousand French troops from joining this big fight. By the close of 1813, Mina had been made a general and the war in Spain was effectively over.

A new fight now began for Mina, against the restored regime in Madrid and old King Carlos's son, Ferdinand. With fewer troops and reduced funds, Mina soon found himself in conflict with Madrid's politics. Decrees from Ferdinand calling for him to stand down enraged him, as did a new "constitution" which he famously had tied to a chair and shot.[12] Despite such acts of bravado, Mina knew he was operating on borrowed time.

His last trump card was to appeal to his fellow Spaniards along liberal political lines. Spain had been freed by its people from French dictatorship, he declared, and should not allow another autocrat—like Ferdinand—to rule. But the time was not yet ripe for such talk, and Mina was soon forced into exile, ironically, in France. But he would return to Spain with the coming of the reformist Queen Cristina and would play a role in the Carlist War during the 1830s, fighting for a more liberal constitutional monarchy. Thus his reputation was recovered some twenty years after the guerrilla war against the French. He died vindicated on Christmas Eve 1836.

If Mina had to wait decades for political rehabilitation, the ways of war that he had done so much to pioneer had not gone into eclipse at all. Even while Suchet and his colleagues were fighting the insurgents in Spain, Austrians were using similar tactics in the Tyrol against French forces. They would fail there, yet the irregular flame would kindle again in Russia during Napoleon's invasion in 1812—and would flare up to contribute mightily to his defeat.

5

HUSSAR POET:
DENIS DAVYDOV

Painting by George Dawe (before 1828)

The intellectual ripples radiating from the guerrilla war in Spain followed a decidedly eastern trajectory, arriving first in Prussia—itself recently beaten by Napoleon at Jena and Auerstädt—as the concept of *Kleiner Krieg* (small war). At the time, Carl von Clausewitz, who would later gain fame for his brilliant treatise *On War*, was teaching at the Prussian military academy and became intrigued by the subject. During the course of the 1810–1811 school year he gave more than 150 lectures on irregular warfare. With a particularly Prussian twist on the topic, he concentrated not on a rising of armed peasants, as in Spain, but on the potential for breaking regular forces into many small units and using them in unconventional ways. This approach was the most logical one for Clausewitz, given that he was speaking to professional military officers. As Walter Laqueur has observed, "He was, after all, addressing lieutenants and captains of the Prussian army, not Chouans [of the Vendée] or *guerrilleros*."[1]

Despite constraints imposed by the academy and concerns of the Prussian government over fostering a capability for arming the masses, Clausewitz's chief colleagues, Gerhard von Scharnhorst and August von Gneisenau, took the small-war concept further. They explored the rise of an armed citizenry, the *Landsturm*, drawn from among the general populace. In a curious policy turn, such a militia was actually created in Prussia. But when armed Prussian resistance to Napoleon was rekindled after his campaign in Russia, orders from the high command directed the *Landsturm* to eschew guerrilla tactics in favor of fighting alongside the regular army. In this way they would be joining with the other, better trained units formed from the general populace, the *Landwehr*, which were partnered in the field with regular infantry formations. As for Clausewitz, his interest in this early form of "people's war" waned. Only one part of one chapter in *On War* deals with irregular warfare.

But the ripples from Spain did not reach their end in Prussia. They continued eastward, where they freshened Russian strategic thought. The Russians soon formulated a synthesis of the Spanish notion of the armed masses and the Prussian preference for keeping irregular formations under the thumb of the regular forces. The Russian solution was to create a number of small, mobile military units capable of mounting deep strikes against invading armies while at the same time linking up with and directing the actions of local cells of popular resistance. Thus they came to enjoy both a "deep strike" military capability and a controlled form of people's war.

This answer to the problem posed by Napoleon and his incomparable *Grande Armée* was not arrived at ahead of time in military seminars or planning sessions. No, before the invasion of 1812 Russian strategic thought remained mired in conventional approaches to dealing with Bonaparte. After all, it was argued at the time, Russian forces had acquitted themselves bravely, if not outright victoriously, in their fight against the French in 1807 at Eylau. Its sequel, the Battle of Friedland, was a defeat, but one in which the Russian army nevertheless fought hard and avoided destruction. In the immediate aftermath of this losing struggle, the 1807 Franco-Russian Treaty of Tilsit was negotiated—in part on a raft in the middle of the Niemen River where Emperor Napoleon and Tsar Alexander I met.

The peace agreement, a treaty arrived at between near equals, seemed to confirm Russia's unimpaired strength. While Prussia was for the most part territorially dismantled and occupied by the French, Russia maintained a great freedom of action. In fact Napoleon urged Alexander to invade Finland in return for the tsar's promise to support the imperial economic blockade against Britain. As the French historian Georges Lefebvre observed, one view was that Alexander had "extricated himself from a nasty situation without loss."[2] He also retained his large, tough military along with the option to use it at the time and place of his choosing, treating Tilsit as but a truce.

But this big Russian army and its generals had not been shaken sufficiently to change their approach to battle, and they would go into the next fight with the French much as they had the last. The only difference this time was that the war would be fought on Russian soil. Napoleon had no intention of ceding the initiative to Alexander. As tensions rose sharply in the first years after Tilsit, the French emperor resolved to invade Russia.

In June 1812 he massed more than half a million French, Polish, and other allied troops for a march on Moscow.[3] Russian field and reserve forces were divided and dispersed, somewhat smaller, and still saddled with their largely conventional battle doctrine. The only new wrinkle was the idea of retreating into the Russian hinterland, a delaying strategy to wear down the French and wait for the right moment to launch a counterstroke, whenever that might be. In the event, the Russians retreated some four hundred miles before making a brief stand at Smolensk under the command of Barclay de Tolly, a Livonian of Scottish descent who was a principal architect of the plan to trade space for time.

Popular Russian outrage over the loss of Smolensk led the tsar to sack Barclay; but the new commander, the sixty-seven-year-old Mikhail Kutuzov, soon retreated yet another two hundred miles without a fight. Some seventy miles west of Moscow, at Borodino, he finally made a stand early in September. Once again Russian soldiers acquitted themselves very bravely; but they retreated from the field after a tremendously bloody fight that saw each side suffer tens of thousands of casualties. And then Moscow itself was the French target.

At this point it seemed that the only Russian hope lay in the "scorched earth" policy that had been implemented during the French advance in the hope of denying sustenance to the *Grande Armée*. Crops and homes were burned as people in the path of the invasion evacuated; even Moscow was abandoned and put to the torch. This tactic created many difficulties for the French but was not about to defeat them. Clausewitz, who had gone over to the Russians and was with the army in the field at and after Borodino, noted in his account of the campaign that "there prevailed at this time a condition of grief and despondency."[4] Clearly, the Russians would need something more.

It came in the form of a synthesis of insights from Spanish guerrillas and Prussian strategic thinkers, crafted by a brilliant cavalryman, Lieutenant Colonel Denis Davydov. In August, just a month before Borodino, Davydov had proposed the creation of a long-range raiding force of one thousand riders who would strike at French logistics and communications. They would also be employed to link up with the peasants, most of whom were eager to fight the French and their allies after the rape, pillage, and general brutality the invaders had visited upon them.

Davydov took this proposal to one of his immediate superiors, General Pëtr Bagration, whom he had come to know after serving as his aide-de-camp. For his part, Bagration respected Davydov as a fighter and for his many intellectual gifts. In addition to his skill in the saddle, Davydov wrote popular poetry that idealized the hussar's life of courage in battle and the pursuit of excess in every other area. Leo Tolstoy in fact used Davydov as his model in later crafting dynamic characters like Denisov and Dolohov for *War and Peace*. Alexander Pushkin, who knew him well, wrote of Davydov in a beautiful poem as "my marvelous rider."

In any event, Bagration was impressed and took the plan to Kutuzov. A veteran commander whose record had been besmirched by Russia's humiliating defeat at the Battle of Austerlitz in 1805, Kutuzov was ill disposed toward the notion of setting loose a thousand horsemen at a time when he needed every musket and saber close at hand for the looming battle with Napoleon. But he was prevailed upon to give the plan at least a tentative try, and in a fateful moment a bureaucratic compromise was reached: Davydov would be given a force of fifty regular hussars and eighty Cossacks with which to conduct an irregular raiding and insurgent campaign against the French. He took them and immediately rode off to strike swiftly at the enemy—but also to be already gone in the event Kutuzov had a change of heart.

Within a few weeks of Davydov's setting out, he learned of his mentor Bagration's death in battle while commanding the Russian army's center at Borodino. Davydov and his men, operating far inside French-occupied territory, were filled with sadness and rage. They determined to strike the enemy immediately in retaliation for the loss of their beloved leader. Soon a scout came with word of an approaching French infantry column of some four hundred soldiers. An ambush was laid, then sprung by Davydov's smaller force. Some of the French were killed and the rest, about three hundred, sought to surrender. For a brief moment the lust for revenge competed with Davydov's military code of conduct, then the Frenchmen were taken prisoner. As Davydov wrote in his memoirs, he was "convinced that the greatest tribute I could show to the memory of my heroic benefactor was to be merciful."[5] He held a memorial service for Bagration later that day.

Over the next ninety days the "hussar poet" mounted a whirlwind campaign with his irregular forces, which Tolstoy would label Davydov's "terrible weapon." It was a weapon destined to play a crucial role in the ultimate, utter destruction of the invading army. The impact of this relatively junior officer on such a major campaign impels us to ask, "Who was Davydov?"

* * *

Born in 1784, Denis Davydov was a career military officer whose family background and apparently liberal leanings made his authority-loving superiors suspicious of him. His father, also a serving officer, had been compelled to resign his commission under a cloud of pending charges, the family suffering financially and in loss of reputation. Denis himself briefly left the service in 1804 but returned two years later and fought bravely in the campaigns leading to the climactic struggle for Russia. Just before Eylau, he first tested his light cavalry skills in rearguard actions against the French, almost losing his life in the process.[6] But he learned a lesson about the need for a defensive rearguard sometimes to take the tactical offensive, moving from position to position and striking out, not just sitting in wait for the approaching enemy mass. After the Tilsit treaty—during the negotiations he saw Napoleon close up and exchanged a glare with the emperor—Davydov fought in Finland in 1808, learning from the Finns' use of small, dispersed raiding forces and incubating ideas of his own.

Central and Eastern Europe in Napoleonic Times

In the time between Tilsit and the French invasion in June 1812, Davydov cut a dashing figure in Russian society when he wasn't off in the field. As he described himself, he was, "a company commander in the Hussar Life Guard Regiment, with two crosses around my neck and two other decorations on my gold-braided red jacket. I was drowning in delights and, as is customary, was in love up to my ears."[7]

The conservative Russian court remained concerned about his father's sullied reputation and about the seriousness and political reliability of the hussar poet who, even in these days—fifteen years before the rising of the liberal Decembrists—seemed to view the ruling regime with an alarming insouciance. Whatever the concerns at court, in the darkest moments of the campaign after Borodino his energy, confidence, and intelligence proved most welcome.

Davydov's basic mission was to cripple the *Grande Armée* with deep raids far behind the lines against security outposts and supply lines. He was little concerned with the small numbers that had been allotted to him, as he knew that he could rely on the fighting spirit of the Cossacks, many of whom were already roaming about and attacking targets of opportunity wherever they could find them. The great French eyewitness chronicler of the campaign, Napoleon's aide Armand de Caulaincourt, noted in his account that, from the very outset of the war until Smolensk, for the most part "we were faced only by Cossacks."[8] After Borodino, Clause-witz observed that their role increased hugely. The Cossacks, he recalled, "swarmed in every direction."[9]

These amazing natural horse soldiers had been living in southern Russia and Ukraine for centuries, banditry and raiding being at the core of their way of life. The best-known portrayal of the Cossack style remains Nikolai Gogol's *Taras Bulba*, a novel in which Cossacks are seen, in many respects, as the heroic personification of Russia itself.[10] It was no surprise that, though nominally under the command of their *hetman*, Matthew Iva-novitch Platov, Cossack riders soon swelled the ranks of Davydov's force once he got moving.

In imitation of some of the "people's war" aspects of the insurgency in Spain, Davydov also reached out to villagers living deep within the area of Russia controlled for now by the French. At first the villagers mistook him and the other hussars for Frenchmen or their allies because of their showy uniforms. So, in an act of "branding" of his own, Davydov and his men let their beards grow and put on peasant caftans. For Mina in Spain branding had been achieved by adopting his cousin's name and cutting his men's (and his own) hair. For Davydov, branding consisted of dressing down, looking scruffy, and speaking in peasant dialect.

Once he gained the confidence of the various villagers, Davydov pro-ceeded to instruct them in resistance methods that he had conceived. The basic idea was to get the occupiers drunk, wait until they passed out, then kill them. Dayvdov went on to advise that the Frenchmen killed at the end of these bacchanals had to be hauled deep into the forest and buried, along with their uniforms. No clothes or trophies were to be taken, as these might be spotted by French soldiers investigating their comrades' disappear-ance, and would bring retributive violence upon the village.[11] It appears that, for all his other traits, Davydov was meticulous about his insurgent tradecraft. His thoughtful dissemination of these procedures led to the es-tablishment of what might be called "resistance franchises." The imprint of this innovation may still be seen today in the al Qaeda network's effort to mobilize and train widely dispersed terrorist cells along common lines of instruction. This notion of armed franchises truly began with Davydov.

From his first combat experience as a rearguard before the Battle of Eylau, Davydov had been impressed by the need to keep moving and stay on the attack. He soon proved to be a high-energy guerrilla leader, raiding French supply convoys and freeing prisoners taken by the French at Borodino—many of whom joined him, making a mockery of the manpower limit Kutuzov had set. When his depredations caused growing concern among the French, the emperor sent a flying column of some two thousand troops to chase down Davydov. But friendly villagers and scouts kept him apprised of French movements, and soon the hunters became the hunted.

Meanwhile, Napoleon and the roughly one hundred thousand troops he had brought to Moscow remained there for a fateful month, in the hope that the tsar would capitulate after the impact of Borodino. But Bonaparte had completely misjudged Alexander, who took this time to begin drawing together fresh forces with which he sought to form a giant pincers to close on the *Grande Armée*. All this time, Russian irregulars were giving the French fits. As Caulaincourt observed, the raiders "were harrying our foragers daily and seizing prisoners almost at the very gates of the city."[12] Given that Moscow had been evacuated, stripped of supplies, and largely burned, foraging had become a critically important function. But the raiders made this nearly impossible. Napoleon knew he would have to retreat well before the weather turned.

By the time the French withdrawal began on October 19, Davydov's irregular campaign plan had been fully embraced by the Russian command. Not only had his raiding force grown in size and spread further its area of operations, others had sprung up as well. More and more Cossacks came from the south, and villagers throughout the French-controlled area of Russia were covertly killing their occupiers. For the most part, these other insurgent activities grew even without the charismatic leadership of a Davydov in command.

An important exception was in the area of operation of Alexander Figner, another natural guerrilla fighter. Like Davydov, he was an intellectual, his particular skill being a gift for foreign languages and accents. But Figner had a far darker side than Davydov: he reveled in killing the French even after they had surrendered. On one occasion Figner tried to murder Frenchmen captured by Davydov who recalled in his memoirs that "as soon as he [Figner] learned about my prisoners, he came running to beg permission to have them shot."[13] Davydov would have none of this and tried to prevent such atrocities whenever and wherever possible. But he could not be everywhere, and the brutality of the raiders and other insurgents in Russia rivaled, perhaps surpassed, what was happening at the time in Spain.

As Napoleon's forces left Moscow—still an army of somewhat more than a hundred thousand effectives at this point—they had a retreat of many hundreds of miles before them, and they were to be harried every step of the way by raiders and partisans. At the same time sizable Russian forces were moving to block the French withdrawal by seizing fortified points that Napoleon had left in the care of lighter formations.[14] Kutuzov would just miss trapping the emperor. No further great battles were fought, though sharp skirmishes occurred from time to time with the vanguards of the main Russian forces.

In the main, perhaps due to Kutuzov's caution, it was left to the irregulars to strike a multitude of small yet cumulatively terrible blows. In the three weeks it took to cover the roughly 270 miles from Moscow back to Smolensk, Napoleon lost more than two-thirds of his remaining troops. Not all of these tens of thousands of casualties were caused by Davydov and the other raiders, but most were. The weather remained mild until November 6, when the first snow fell, thus exposure to the cold cannot be considered the principal cause of this heavy rate of attrition.

But after Smolensk the weather turned severely cold, further weakening the roughly thirty thousand French troops who were still capable of fighting. They were hurried along by Napoleon's fear of being caught in the Russian pincers, and hounded every step of the way by Davydov and a swarm of other irregulars. Philippe-Paul de Ségur, another senior French officer who wrote a memoir of the campaign, summed up his frustration with the Russian raiders—and not just the agonizing final stretch—by describing a typical encounter:

> We saw them calmly reloading their muskets as they left the field, walking their horses between our squadrons. They relied on the slowness of our picked troops as much as on the swiftness of their own mounts. . . . Their flight was accomplished without disorder. They turned around several times and faced us. . . All this made us think. Our army was fought out, and here was war being born again—fresh and undiminished.[15]

Thus the French had to absorb an unending series of stinging blows, at best beating off the partisans only briefly. All the while they had to race on through the cold, trying to outrun the pursuing Russian field forces that hoped to cut them off at the Berezina River crossing. Only some five thousand French soldiers who made it that far were still in organized units. Stragglers added several thousand more. But this was all that remained out of more than half a million French and allied soldiers that had begun the war six months earlier.

*   *   *

For Davydov, the great victory was to have a bittersweet aftertaste. When he finally came to field headquarters just before the end of the campaign, he found that his call to allow raiding forces to strike ahead, deep into Poland—cutting off the last of the *Grande Armée* and perhaps even capturing Napoleon—had fallen on deaf ears. He was even chided by staffers who claimed he had been avoiding risk by fighting so far away from the main actions. In his memoirs, Davydov noted that "the duties of a partisan were poorly understood in our army."[16] He who had actually seen Napoleon during the retreat—too well protected by the Old Guard to be taken that raid—was now tethered to the slow-moving regular Russian army.

Still, the raiders had done their work, mortally wounding a French military machine that had been the scourge of Europe for two decades. The military historian David Chandler has concluded: "The contribution of Russian soldiery was only of secondary importance; the raids of Cossacks and partisan bands did more harm to the Emperor than all the endeavors of the regular field armies of Holy Russia."[17]

Moving now in tandem with the regulars, Davydov could nonetheless interpret his orders in ways that allowed him to advance well ahead of them, scouting the way, seizing important posts, and continuing to inflict sharp blows on the enemy. In the weeks and months after the French were driven out of Russia in December 1812, the tsar was convinced that he should give Napoleon no time to rebuild his forces. The pursuit was to continue.

So Davydov drove ever forward, always on the heels of the French, engaging in one sharp cavalry fight after another. But fresh enemy formations were coming from the west to stiffen the resistance, particularly at the Elbe River. Here the brutal Figner would die trying to cross, last seen on his horse splashing in the river, surrounded by Polish lancers still fighting for Napoleon and the waning life of the "Duchy of Warsaw" he had created. Davydov would have his own problems at the Elbe, though his greatest moment of danger would actually come at the hands of his own superiors.

Showing his usual energy, Davydov had advanced up to the outskirts of the new section of the city of Dresden, on the right bank of the Elbe. He was vastly outnumbered by French troops under the command of a General Durutte, but by various deceptions—like building far more campfires than he had troops—he made his opponent believe that major formations of Russian troops were nearby. Davydov now took boldness a step further, trying to bluff Durutte out of Dresden by offering him a cease fire while the French evacuated the new section of town, crossing from the right bank of the Elbe to Old Dresden. The ruse worked. The French withdrew and blew the city's bridges. And when Davydov began to assemble boats to give the appearance of an impending amphibious assault, Durutte began evacuating the old city, heading off to Leipzig.

The Dresden city fathers wanted to canonize Davydov. Instead his superiors court-martialed him for the "crime of state" of having "entered into negotiations with the enemy" and for allowing the opposing army to escape.[18] Davydov was relieved of his command, but the testimonials of the Dresden city fathers—grateful for having been spared the horrors of fighting in the streets—provided reason enough for the charges to be quietly dropped. Yet, Davydov was not given back his command, and the general who sacked him claimed credit for the liberation of Dresden, a credit that would last only until Napoleon returned, briefly, to win one of his last battles there in the summer of 1813.

Before Bonaparte's counteroffensive, Davydov was seconded to the Prussians, with whose cavalry he rode. He fought with distinction over the following year, later with Austrian troops, then finally back among his fellow Russians, right up to Napoleon's abdication in 1814. By this time he had been promoted to major general, finishing his campaign by returning a teenaged French drummer boy—one Vincent Bode, whom he had captured on a raid back in Russia, and kept with him ever since—to his father in Paris. Davydov had promised that he would see the boy home. And so he did.

After Davydov came home to Russia, he settled for a while in Moscow to write poetry. Returning to work, now as a general officer, he was saddled with staff supervision, something he found distasteful. But at last he had time to develop a deep love for a young woman whom he married in 1819. His happy family life and writing soon seemed to overshadow all else, and in 1823 Davydov resigned from the Russian army.

Yet there may have been more behind his retirement than the lure of family and poetry. Davydov had grown sympathetic to some of the radical reformers who sought an end to the oppression of the Russian serfs, whose hard lives many had seen up close during the war. It is certain as well that Davydov was unhappy with Alexander's growing authoritarianism and support for reactionary regimes. In December 1822 the tsar had attended the Congress of Verona and offered to send Russian troops to Spain to suppress social reformers there, Mina among them.[19]

While Alexander's offer to intervene in Spain was rebuffed, the tsar continued his reactionary ways until his death in December 1825, when confusion over succession led to a near revolution in Russia. The Decembrists, a group of reform-minded officers, supported the accession of the tsar's brother Constantine, who it was thought would support a reform constitution. But Alexander had wanted his much younger brother, Nicholas, a very strong conservative, to succeed him. As the crisis mounted, the Decembrists' ranks thinned and, in the final confrontation in the streets of St. Petersburg, most of their more dedicated followers were killed by grapeshot fired from loyalist cannons. Many of the survivors were exiled. Davydov, who was on friendly terms with a number of the conspirators, was investigated but never charged with wrongdoing. As for Nicholas, he would serve as a bulwark against change for the next thirty years.

In a show of loyalty to the new tsar, Davydov returned to active service, campaigning in the Caucasus in response to a Persian incursion into Georgia. This region would see the rise of Shamil, the great insurgent leader of the resistance to Russian rule and one of the forerunners of a rising tide of Muslim fighters that would reach its peak in the campaigns of Abd el-Kader. For Davydov, now in his mid-forties, life in the field was growing harder, and he soon took ill and was invalided home. The campaign in the Caucasus went on, and Shamil was ultimately defeated. Yet the echoes of his stand resonate in Tolstoy's classic novella *The Raid* and can still be detected in the Chechen insurgency that bedevils Russia today.

Ever the soldier, Davydov saddled up one more time, in 1831, to put down yet another Polish insurrection. The Poles had seen their country wiped off the map of Europe at the end of the Napoleonic Wars and were determined to continue fighting for their freedom. Davydov was placed in command of the cavalry vanguard of the Russian army that was marching to put down the rebellion. As usual, he roamed far ahead of the mass of Russian troops—so far that he encountered the main Polish force that greatly outnumbered his troops. Instead of retreating and reporting, Davydov engaged the entire Polish army for half a day, allowing the rest of the Russian forces to envelop the Poles from the flanks. A signal victory was won and, for his heroic stand, Davydov was promoted to lieutenant general.

Soon after, he returned to his family in Moscow and then went on to settle at his wife's family's estate at Verkhnyaya Maza in central Russia. Now the country gentleman, Davydov spent his last years writing bawdy poems, insightful memoirs and reflections on irregular warfare before dying in 1839 of a sudden illness. In his "Essay on Partisan Warfare" he crystallized a concept of military operations that prefigured the course and conduct of many of the insurgencies that were to arise over the following two centuries. More than this, Davydov caught a glimpse of future wars—including those of our time and those yet to come—that would be dominated by small, swift groups of irregulars. He saw the power of such partisan-like formations:

> By making continuous attacks and turning up at different points, they distract both the enemy's attention and part of his forces and force him to follow one single route and to grope his way forward, with no hope of wiping out the indestructible swarm of light troops or even of catching up with it, cutting it off, or driving it up against some obstacle that would make it possible to surround it. He [the enemy] therefore has no choice but to retreat, preceded and surrounded by partisans.

As we shall see, these "indestructible swarms" have truly had their innings since Davydov's time. We have already observed them in the insurgencies that overthrew colonial rule in so many parts of the twentieth-century world, and in places like Vietnam, where even American super-power was humbled. We see them again now in the form of the net-worked, globally dispersed guerrilla/terror movement that has confounded the leading nations of the world since 9/11. If Davydov was right, the prospects for mastering the challenge posed by these swarms are not bright. Their similarity to earlier Muslim resistance to Western control is profound and deep, as will be seen in the next chapter.

6

DESERT MYSTIC:
ABD EL-KADER

While this is a book about the great captains of irregular warfare, it also indirectly concerns the countries that have had deep experience with this form of conflict. By now it should be clear that France is one of these countries. We have seen in preceding chapters that French soldiers fought against Rogers, on the same side as Greene, and then once again were opposed to Mina and Davydov. In later chapters the French military will also be seen in action against Giuseppe Garibaldi in Italy and Vo Nguyen Giap in Vietnam. But immediately next is the seventeen-year struggle (1830–1847) to impose French rule upon Algeria, a land from which one of the great Muslim insurgent leaders arose. In this long war French forces, by dint of their extensive experience with irregular warfare, would once again prove formidable opponents. Their insurgent adversary would thus have to demonstrate the highest level of skill simply in order to remain in the field against them, much less to prevail—as he very nearly did.

Exactly why Charles X, the restored Bourbon monarch of France, sought to conquer Algeria remains a subject of debate. The king's stated goal of ending piracy, the international terrorism of that age, was unconvincing even then, as Algeria had already curtailed the operations of its corsairs by 1815. There was also some talk of bringing Western morals and governance practices to a benighted people, a theme that resonates with our era's nation-building mantra. But France could hardly be seen as a paragon of governance, given the Revolution, the Terror, Bonapartism, and the shaky Restoration. Indeed, Charles's efforts to reimpose strong monarchical rule in France would lead to yet another revolution, just as the invasion of Algeria was getting under way. His successor, Louis-Philippe I, the last king of France, would rule with an ever-weaker hand over the next two decades. France could hardly have been seen as an appropriate ambassador for the spread of good governance. At best, an Algerian war was a temporary diversion from domestic French woes.

This leaves us to consider baser motivations. Chief among them was the financial dispute that arose when Algerian commercial grain interests sought repayment from France for shipments that had kept the French people fed during the long years of the British naval blockade against Napoleon. The Algerians' dunning irritated the French, and the dispute grew more bitter, leading to the 1827 "flyswatter incident." The Turkish satrap, Dey Husayn of Algiers, fed up with the French consul's dismissive attitude toward the debt—which amounted, with interest, to more than twenty-four million gold francs at this point—apparently slapped him with his fly whisk, a terrible breach of diplomatic form that outraged the French and made them still more reluctant to pay their debt.

In the following months Husayn ratcheted up the pressure by closing down French trading posts in Algeria. The French in turn imposed a naval blockade of the country. At this point Husayn seems to have authorized piratical action against French merchant ships plying their trade in the Mediterranean, which stoked French anger, some of it now righteous. A kind of strategic logic also came into play, the belief that France's naval position would be greatly strengthened by obtaining bases in North Africa.

Lastly, in terms of securing a "green light" from the other great powers, the post-Napoleonic Concert of Europe acquiesced in the French action. It may have appeared to many in Europe that an adventure in Algeria would be a useful diversion of resurgent French strength. Keeping Paris's attention elsewhere, far from the hurly-burly at the center of European power politics was, it seemed, a good idea.

Thus in May 1830 Charles shipped off more than thirty thousand troops to invade Algeria. The French were confident that resistance would be weak, given the disunity of the Arab tribes and their broad resentment of the corrupt and inefficient rule of the local representative of the Ottoman Empire in Constantinople, or Stamboul.[1] At the outset all went well. Under the command of General Auguste-Louis de Bourmont, French forces captured Algiers in a few weeks. The Dey's treasury had been seized with enough gold to pay for the invasion's cost to date. The general was well pleased, so much so that he sent a triumphal message to his monarch: "The whole kingdom of Algeria will probably surrender within fifteen days, without our having to fire another shot."[2] Mission accomplished.

A week after this predicted end to the fighting, a strong French column was ambushed about thirty miles from Algiers and nearly wiped out. To this continuing, and growing, resistance was added confusion about whether the mission would be sustained once Charles fell from power in July. The situation soon righted itself, however, as the French Chamber of Deputies acclaimed Louis-Philippe I king—or, as he was to be known, the citizen king. The new monarch had fought heroically in the early battles of the Revolution, leaving France only after the king and queen were executed. He was not the man to walk away from this small war.

But the war soon got bigger, for the Algerians were not as disunited as the French assumed. Partly this was so because the very act of invasion had given the Arab and Berber tribesmen common cause—the goal of expelling the infidel occupier. Another catalyst was to come in the form of a young, charismatic leader, one Abd el-Kader (Servant of the Almighty). The son of a respected Sufi mystic,[3] Muhi al-Din, he was only twenty-five at the time. But he had already made his pilgrimage to Mecca, and during the journey he had met Shamil, who would soon lead Muslim resistance to Russian expansion in the Caucasus. Abd el-Kader was equally well schooled in theology and the military and diplomatic arts, as his father had foreseen that Algeria would one day have need of a great leader who combined the spirit and the scimitar.

But even Muhi al-Din, whom the great social observer Alexis de Tocqueville described as "saintly,"[4] did not think his son's time had come. Instead he called for the Algerian tribes to ally themselves with the sultan of neighboring, independent Morocco, who he thought was the appropriate authority for leading this defensive holy war, or jihad, to protect the people. Muhi al-Din's faith was misplaced, however, as it seems that the sultan may have felt better about having French rather than Turkish rule in Algeria, and the Moroccan troops he sent under his son's command were soon fighting against the very tribesmen who had sought his assistance.

At this point Muhi al-Din reconsidered his son's readiness for command and, out of necessity—he himself was too old and frail to take charge—used his moral authority to gain acceptance from the tribes for Abd el-Kader's accession to leadership of the resistance against the French. It helped greatly that his son's natural modesty and courtesy appealed strongly to the independent-minded tribal leaders. It also helped that, despite his small stature—being just over five feet tall—Abd el-Kader was a masterful horseman and swordsman, with a magnetic gaze and a quiet but eloquent manner of speech.

In his very first proclamation, made in Mascara on November 22, 1832, Abd el-Kader conjured a vision of broader unity among the people than they had ever imagined. As he explained the purpose of the war of liberation,

> it may be the means for uniting the Muslim community and of preventing dissensions among them and of affording security to all the inhabitants of the land, of putting an end to lawlessness, and of driving back the enemy who has invaded our country in order to subjugate us.[5]

With such words he lit a flame in Algeria that would never be fully extinguished, despite his ultimate defeat and the century of French occupation that would follow. The insurgents who would finally win Algeria's independence in 1962 were inspired and guided by the remarkable campaigns of this great jihadi general.

*   *   *

At the outset of the war for Algeria, the French were unprepared for the level of unity the tribes were able to achieve, and were completely befuddled

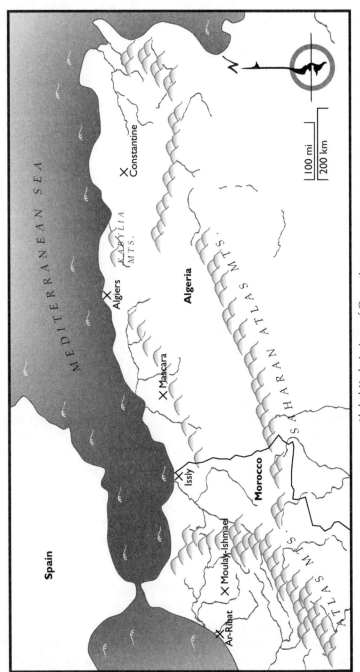

Abd el-Kader's Area of Operations

by the tactics they employed. Basically Abd el-Kader relied on the tribes' abilities to conduct classic Bedouin raids, or *razzias*. His forces had greater mobility—in terms of speed of movement and (thanks to camels) an ability to move great distances off road. And, due to the support of the increasingly oppressed and outraged Algerian public, they had excellent intelligence about French dispositions. For their part, the French relied upon mass and firepower, especially artillery, to cow their opponents. But the tribes fought in small bands, picking and choosing when they would strike, whether at balky French columns on the march or against isolated outposts. Initially, the insurgents had a field day against French forces, whose own frustrations led them to commit atrocities that only further alienated the populace.

Compounding these problems, General Bourmont also made the mistake of thinking his principal problem was with the Turks in power, so he proceeded to "de-Turkify" the Algerian civil administration. This soon left him with no one who understood how to make the society work—much as "de-Ba'athification" would cause chaos in Iraq some 170 years later.

General Bourmont was sacked soon after Charles X fell and was replaced with a somewhat more competent but far more brutal successor, Pierre Boyer. A veteran of some of the toughest fighting against the insurgents in Spain, Boyer inflicted great punishment on the innocent because he could not come to grips with the tribal raiders. Pierre the Cruel, as he came to be known, was also Pierre the Conventional, remaining slow, clumsy, and road-bound in his efforts to confront the guerrillas. The insurgency thrived, and by 1833 Abd el-Kader and those allied with him controlled about two-thirds of Algeria, all but a few strips along the country's northern coast.

The French now brought in a new commander, General Louis-Alexis Desmichels. He was a cavalryman of repute, having fought heroically in some of the major battles of the Napoleonic Wars. From the start he understood the need for swift, light forces that could catch the insurgents unawares and pursue them with some hope of making captures. His forces began to engage the enemy more often and, on occasion, came off the better. Abd el-Kader had his first serious opponent, and the two men sparred for some time.

During this period the jihadi leader's father passed away. Suspicion remains to this day that Muhi al-Din was assassinated—and the French general's home government in Paris, riven with dissent, deprived him of resources. Both leaders were thus concerned about their ability to maintain the fight, Abd el-Kader worrying mostly about preserving unity, Desmichels driven to distraction by deficiencies in men and arms. This situation led them, by a kind of tacit consent, to begin peace negotiations using Jewish Algerians—who understood both Arab and French cultures and languages—as intermediaries.

The result of these negotiations was the Desmichels Treaty, signed February 26, 1834, which recognized and accepted the French presence in Algeria but at the same time gave de facto consent to Abd el-Kader's rule over the tribes and control of much of the territory and commerce of Algeria. But this peace, so carefully arrived at between Desmichels and Abd el-Kader, was to prove short lived. As it turned out, the French translation of the treaty gave rather greater colonial control to the occupiers while the Arab version sharply limited the Europeans' encroachments on Algerian sovereignty.[6]

Perhaps even more important, French merchants—both those returning to Algeria and new waves of traders—deeply resented what they saw as Abd el-Kader's monopolistic control over the markets. They pressured the French government to renegotiate the treaty. As this lobbying intensified, secret codicils to the treaty were produced, to the grave discredit of Desmichels, who was called home at the close of 1834 under a cloud of suspicion and growing concern. His replacement, General Camille Alphonse Trézel, was yet another Napoleonic veteran but, like Bourmont, very conventional minded.

Seemingly more aware of his limitations than Bourmont, Trézel devised a plan to woo some of the tribes to work with French forces—an initiative not unlike the "awakening movement" in Iraq undertaken in 2006–2007 to bring Sunni tribes over to the side of the American forces fighting the insurgency there. The French made some headway with this strategy, which Abd el-Kader swiftly sought to curtail by means of punitive action, lest his power base erode.

Matters came to a head in June 1835 when insurgent tribesmen were set loose to mount small attacks throughout French-occupied Algeria. This had an immediate and crippling effect on colonial rule as, in Abd el-Kader's words, "no bird will fly without my permission."[7] Trézel's response was to set off with about three thousand troops on a march to Mascara, which he regarded as Abd el-Kader's critical center of gravity, with the idea that defeating the jihadi decisively there would end the insurgency and consolidate colonial rule.

What ensued was a disaster for the French. Although Trézel and his troops acquitted themselves well in the first ambush set by Abd el-Kader, in the forest of Moulay-Ishmael, the next one at the Machta River crossing was their undoing. Abd el-Kader placed a force of snipers in front of the

French there, holding back some cavalry ready to strike from the rear. The result was a slaughter that saw some four hundred of Trézel's men killed and a similar number wounded. The rest of the force was widely scattered, losing all capacity for cohesive action. All the artillery and the baggage train were lost. The French were humiliated, much as the British had been under General Braddock in the American wilderness eighty years earlier. Abd el-Kader's, authority among the tribes was reaffirmed by this display of military skill. The French would either have to send more troops to Algeria or treat with him.

Initially they tried to fight, sacking Trézel and replacing him with General Count Bernard Clauzel, who came with reinforcements and promised immediate action. His notion of "action," however, was of the most unimaginative sort—a series of punitive raids against innocent Algerian tribes, which left men, women, and children dead and flocks scattered in the name of what he called "total occupation." These atrocities only kindled a hatred of the occupier that shored up Abd el-Kader's support.

Clauzel, keener on reactions in Parisian salons and Parliament than among Algerians, next sought to win a big pitched battle, so he marched his army against the holdout city of Constantine. He hoped that a great victory there would gain approval for his request that an additional thirty thousand troops be sent to Algeria so that he could "finish the job." In the event, his big, balky expedition suffered much the same fate as had Trézel's, save that Clauzel's losses mounted to more than three thousand. He was recalled in November 1836, to be replaced by one of the other generals who had been serving in Algeria, Thomas Bugeaud. A veteran of the war in Spain who had served under Suchet, Bugeaud had many new ideas he wished to put into action against Abd el-Kader, whom he had earlier beaten at Sikkak, the one conventional battle the emir ever fought.

Bugeaud thus came into command with a remarkable reputation as the only man who had bested Abd el-Kader. He inspired confidence also because of his ability to articulate the strategy he intended to use against the insurgents: the *razzia*. That is, Bugeaud intended to break the French forces, which included the Foreign Legion, into countless flying columns that would raid the raiders. But it would be a while before this strategy could be attempted. The king and Parliament, tired of the costs of fighting a seemingly interminable insurgency, instructed Bugeaud first to try to negotiate another peace treaty with Abd el-Kader. This he accomplished, the result being the Treaty of Tafna, signed on May 30, 1837, which was in most ways a replay of the Desmichels Treaty, right down to its secret codicils. Bugeaud and Abd el-Kader then met on June 1st to declare peace and friendship publicly. For now the fighting was over. A few months later Bugeaud headed home to France, told King Louis-Philippe that he was no longer needed, and retired, at fifty-three, to his estate in the Dordogne.

The peace, however, would be edgy. Many of the Algerian tribes were unwilling to live with permanent French occupation of even a part of their country, and they were held in check only with difficulty by the authority of Abd el-Kader. Indeed, as John Kiser has assessed the situation, "peace was more harmful to the emir than war."[8] An ongoing conflict gave the tribes an external enemy against which to unite. Peace left them with the unrequited lust to mount their traditional *razzias* and a growing sense of resentment toward the man who was, in the name of building a nation, trying to control tribes who had always been their own masters.

The French were almost as unhappy, given that the treaty limited them to a few coastal settlements and left Abd el-Kader still largely in a position to exercise control over Algeria's commerce. In addition, a scandal broke when the secret codicils were revealed, as Bugeaud had agreed to deport some of the tribal chiefs opposed to Abd el-Kader and had sold the emir thousands of French firearms, ostensibly for keeping the peace against recalcitrant tribes. Aside from concerns about selling weapons that might be used against French soldiers and settlers, there was outrage when it was learned that a side payment had been made to Bugeaud of nearly two hundred thousand francs. While he did not personally benefit from the bribe—about half went to subordinate officers, the rest was used for road improvements in his home district in France—Bugeaud had nevertheless tarnished his reputation and undermined the treaty.

The peace too continued to be fragile, with both sides engaging in activities that stretched the terms of the treaty to the near breaking point. The French were determined to open up land routes to connect their coastal holdings more directly. Abd el-Kader was making trade overtures to the Americans, which greatly aggrieved the growing French commercial interests. And there were inevitable small clashes involving forces on both sides. There was also an inadvertent escalation of suspicions about Abd el-Kader's true intentions, the standing army he was building—which he claimed was needed to keep the tribes in line—was approaching a size that could be viewed as threatening to the survival of French settlements. There was more truth than paranoia in this view: the stronger the Algerians became, the more the tribal leaders wished to renew the jihad against the Europeans.

Near the close of 1839, after two and a half years of peace, Abd el-Kader convened a council to hear the complaints of the tribal leaders. Their resentment of continuing French encroachment had reached a boiling point, and the emir knew that he could either go along with their call to war or risk losing his leadership and the national unity that had so far been achieved. He agreed to renew the conflict with the French.

War broke out again with a fury that the colonizers could not contain. In the early days and months of the insurgency, when small attacks were being mounted at or around nearly every settlement, the French saw little hope of victory. In Paris during 1840, Parliament debated what to do, and there seemed a growing sense of resignation about both the inevitability of war and the horror it would bring. The great French strategic thinker, the Baron Jomini, yet another veteran of the war in Spain, summed up the nature of a national uprising that takes the form of an insurgency: "There be in it something grand and noble, which commends our admiration [but] the consequences are so terrible that, for the sake of humanity, we ought to hope never to see it."[9]

In the midst of the parliamentary debates, the views of the deputy from the Dordogne, Thomas Bugeaud, came to the fore. A decade earlier he had opposed the very notion of colonizing Algeria. Now he argued that the only way ahead was complete conquest. He called for eighty thousand troops to be sent and for his raiding concept of operations to be employed. King Louis-Philippe and the Chamber of Deputies called for him to again take command in the field. He did, returning to Algeria early in 1841. Abd el-Kader was about to face his sternest challenge.

*   *   *

The strategic situation that Bugeaud surveyed on his arrival was desperate. Abd el-Kader and his mobile, well-informed light forces were able to strike at settlements whenever they chose. The French response had been largely defensive, with most troops being tied down in or near settlements—which then made them vulnerable to raids on their supply and communications lines. When the occupying army did try to take the offensive, it could not move swiftly enough to catch the raiders, as such efforts were bogged down by the sheer size of the expeditions, their logistical requirements, and a fanatical devotion to dragging along artillery. In lieu of engaging the insurgents, the suffering troops often vented their rage on innocent villagers and farmers, with their atrocities fueling the rage of the Algerians against the French.

Bugeaud swiftly put an end to much of this folly. After a relatively brief period of retraining and morale building, he launched a campaign that, in large part, emulated the raiding style of Abd el-Kader and his forces. The basic concept was to move from a military approach based on taking the offensive with a few large units to one characterized by many small detachments swarming about, keeping the enemy on the run, at times even catching up with and engaging his forces. With this shift to small units of action, Bugeaud also gave the lie to the notion that harsh terrain—this war was fought mostly in deserts and mountains—always gave the insurgent an enduring advantage. The military historian Douglas Porch has elegantly summed up Bugeaud's basic tactics:

> Mobile columns numbering from a few hundred to a few thousand men, shorn of artillery and heavy wagons, could fan out over the countryside to converge from different directions on a previously selected objective. In this way, Bugeaud was able to penetrate into areas that before had been immune to attack, carry the fight in to the very heart of the Kabylia Mountains, and give his enemies no rest.[10]

Abd el-Kader adjusted to the new French approach as best he could, abandoning the fixed positions he had allowed to harden during the peace and redeploying his forces in counterattacks where least expected. The French never gained the same degree of mobility as the insurgents; so in their frustration, and as part of Bugeaud's use of terror tactics to cow some of the tribes back into submission, they burned crops, killed the men they found, and raped the women. Abd el-Kader, his forces still in being but unable to face the French in open battle, began to see some tribes going over to the enemy. His sources of intelligence began to dry up, his movements became constrained.

Yet his sense of humanity never left him. In the midst of this brutal fighting, Abd el-Kader proposed regular prisoner swaps, a clever way to counter French propaganda that to be captured by his forces was to be tortured and killed. The jihadi general even offered to allow Catholic priests to be sent to live among the prisoners he was keeping, sustaining their spirits until the war ended. And if an allied tribe went over to the French, Abd el-Kader thought carefully about whether to attack them. If in his view they had switched sides due to the heavy punishments the French had inflicted upon them, he let them alone. If, however, they had turned out of opportunism, they soon felt the lash of his still considerable power.

The war went on in this fashion until the spring of 1843, each side landing punches, neither seemingly capable of a knockout blow. But on May 19, 1843, a French "flying column" stumbled upon Abd el-Kader's *smala*, the mobile home base of the tribe's families, flocks, arsenals, and administration. With French raiding parties operating throughout the country, it was probably inevitable that the *smala* would be found at some point. It was a large, soft target—it contained almost twenty thousand people, mostly women, children, and old men—but with about five thousand fighters too. The French raiding column consisted of about six hundred cavalry under the command of the Duc d'Aumale, King Louis-Philippe's youngest son. He was greatly outnumbered but had the advantage of surprise, so important in irregular warfare. The duke's boldness won through as the defenders were disorganized and set to flight. The British expert on irregular warfare, C. E. Callwell, captured the irony of the situation: "The most decisive reverse suffered by Abd el-Kader . . . was inflicted upon him in what was almost an accidental manner by a few troops of horse."[11]

Abd el-Kader's family narrowly escaped this disaster. He himself had been away, shadowing another French detachment. In the wake of this huge victory, the French picked up the tempo of their operations. Abd el-Kader soon felt the need to seek haven across the border in Morocco. But Bugeaud came and chastised the Moroccans, winning a great battle over them—a dukedom and promotion to marshal too—at Issly. His haven imperiled, Abd el-Kader was kept constantly on the move, occasionally striking back at the French. But he had apparently lost the initiative, fighting on now with an ever-narrowing circle of tribal allies, constantly hounded by Bugeaud and his flying columns. All Abd el-Kader could do was to continue the struggle, hoping other small resistance cells would arise and that the French popular will to continue the war would finally break.

This was indeed his best chance, and in 1845 the Bou Maza movement did arise—something that looked a lot like what we would call a network today, and which John Kiser has labeled a "hydra."[12] Soon the number of insurgent attacks began to rise again, and Bugeaud's greatest concern was probably that French war weariness would set in. This fear may have led him not only to tolerate but also to endorse some of the worst atrocities of the war in the hope that the Algerians would be terrorized into giving up the fight.

Thus in June 1845 one of his subordinates, a Colonel Pelissier, personally set a fire at the mouth of a cave where more than five hundred men, women and children were sheltering. All but ten of them were asphyxiated. Pelissier claimed to be proud of his action. In August a Colonel Saint-Arnaud, eschewing fire, instead chose to entomb three times that number of insurgents in another cave. Showing that he had some sense of the evil he had done and the outrage that wide knowledge of the atrocity would spark, Saint-Arnaud sent a private message to assure Bugeaud that all was done in secret: "No one went into the cave. Not a soul but myself."[13] But word did get out, and soon the world came to call Bugeaud the "Butcher of the Bedouins."

Yet these French actions were for naught. The atrocities may have terrorized some into submission, but they galvanized others to action. Abd el-Kader himself soon showed his fangs again too. In September 1845 he ambushed a French flying column of more than four hundred cavalry. Only seventeen avoided death or capture. The insurgent leader then went after a supply convoy, taking its goods and more than two hundred prisoners. In response, Bugeaud unleashed eighteen flying columns simultaneously, the goal being to flush out and track down Abd el-Kader. They failed to do so. Bugeaud authorized more atrocities, as well. But the French government and people finally grew sufficiently outraged to relieve Bugeaud of his command in June 1847. He was replaced by Louis-Christophe-Léon Juchault de Lamoricière, an officer who had served in Algeria since 1830, rising from captain to general.

Lamoricière was about the same age as Abd el-Kader and shared his deep interest in theological matters. He had been appalled by French excesses and, soon after taking command, put out peace feelers. Abd el-Kader, who respected his opponent's skills honed over many years in the field, accepted the offer to negotiate peace one more time. He even agreed to surrender if it would bring an end to the suffering and allow his fellow Algerians to live in decent conditions under French rule.

In December 1847, Abd el-Kader went willingly into captivity in France. His stay there was supposed to be brief, as King Louis-Philippe had promised him a comfortable exile in Alexandria. But the king abdicated in February 1848, in the wake of a social revolution, and Abd el-Kader was held in custody. It would take much lobbying by many of his former adversaries—including his bitter foe Saint-Arnaud, now minister of war for the new government of Louis-Napoleon Bonaparte, the nephew of the great conqueror—to obtain his release. But by December 1855 he was living in exile in Damascus.

During this last phase of his life Abd el-Kader returned to the religious meditations that had so interested him as the son of a Muslim holy man. He also entertained visitors and made friends among those from the West who admired his life and accomplishments, notably the British explorer/adventurer Richard Francis Burton. His only return to "action" came in the summer of 1860 when anti-Christian riots in Damascus saw hundreds of Europeans being massacred. Abd el-Kader rescued many, giving them sanctuary in his compound and standing up against the raging mob, trying to calm and disperse them. He saved thousands of lives.

In the following years Abd el-Kader resumed his life of quiet contemplation, shared his thoughts with others, and reflected ever more deeply on the common values that lay at the heart of all major faiths. But the world did not forget his accomplishments in the field. When he died on May 25, 1883, the obituary in the *New York Times* called him "one of the ablest rulers and most brilliant captains of the century." Algeria would remain under French rule for another eighty years but the next time brutal methods were used to try to defeat insurgents there, the French people would be so appalled by their own military's behavior that Algeria was finally set free. As Abd el-Kader always believed it would be.

7

NATION BUILDER:
GIUSEPPE GARIBALDI

Gustave Le Gray (1820–1884), *Portrait de Giuseppe Garibaldi (1808–1882) à Palermo en 1860*

Perhaps the most powerful force unleashed upon the world by the French Revolution was the notion of nationalism. The millions who were mobilized to fight for France did so largely out of a sense of commitment to country. And those who resisted Napoleonic invasion and occupation, especially in Spain, Prussia, and Russia, were imbued with much the same spirit. Certainly the idea of nationhood also inspired a measure of the resistance to colonial control that energized so many of the peoples that the great powers sought to bring under their influence during the nineteenth century. Most of these resisters fought heroically in the names of their actual or hoped for national identities, like the Poles who were crushed by Davydov, and the Algerian tribes led by Abd el-Kader. Yet almost all of them failed to stem the rising tide of imperialism—which would not ebb until the aftermath of World War II, when the empires had either been toppled or were exhausted, and a series of successful "people's wars" arose around the world to throw off their rule.

Before then, however, there were few points of light. Empires dominated nations so greatly that by 1900, as Lenin observed, more than 90 percent of the land mass of Africa (up from just 10 percent in 1876) nearly 60 percent of Asia, and 99 percent of Polynesia had been subjugated by imperial powers.[1] South America was to some degree insulated from colonialism by the Monroe Doctrine, but the more localized empires that were forming there sought to crush nascent nations—like Uruguay and the various republics trying to break free from Brazil—whenever they could. Only a few places successfully resisted imperialism. In Asia, Siam would remain free, as would Ethiopia in Africa—the latter at least until the 1935 Italian invasion.

In Europe perhaps the greatest exception to imperial control arose in Italy, a land over parts of which France, Spain, and Austria had been fighting for hundreds of years. From the sixteenth-century Italian Wars during Machiavelli's time—the cynical master of realpolitik actually concluded *The Prince* with an idealistic exhortation to free Italy from foreign rule—to the post–Napoleonic hodgepodge of spheres of influence that ran from the Alps to Sicily, here were lands and peoples that had not been truly unified since the fall of the Roman Empire.

In the decades after the fall of Napoleon, unification in Italy seemed little short of impossible. Direct Austrian control in the north was only partially offset by more subtle French influence, under their restored monarchy, in other parts of Italy, including Piedmont and the papal territories around Rome. While Spain had long left the great game for Italy behind, France and Austria more than made up for this absence by vying for influence with the many independent principalities and dukedoms that had emerged over time. In sum, Italy seemed one of the least likely places in the world where nationalism might triumph over well-heeled, highly motivated imperialism.

Even in the unlikely event that the great powers could be driven out militarily, local rulers—like the House of Savoy in Piedmont, the pope in Rome, or the proud Venetians—would strongly resist ceding their power to a new national authority. Yet none of these obstacles deterred a whole generation of grassroots resisters—drawn from peasant farmers, fishermen, and students—from coming together in the Young Italy organization and fighting for their imagined country.

The roots of this resistance lay in yet another organization, a more secret one known as the *Carbonari*. The name was chosen to make a symbolic connection with carbon as it is found in coal—a hard substance that is slow to ignite but is a great source of energy. This secret society was organized along very networked lines, with small cells and nodes communicating for the most part in the Austrian-occupied parts of northern Italy—though the original aim of the group was to push out the French. The basic strategy for liberation was to foment unrest in the hope of provoking France and Austria into fighting each other, with Italians seizing the opportunity to escape their grasp and declare independence.

What followed, then, were simultaneous small uprisings in 1830 and 1831, during which the *Carbonari* found that the Austrians knew how to network as well. Insurgent cells throughout Italy soon found they had been infiltrated, and many of their members were killed or captured. Austrian secret police even followed the links between group members into France, where their "hit squads" kidnapped or assassinated many more. Indeed, the whole Austrian campaign against the *Carbonari* offers a textbook-like example of how to take apart a network by means that might be described as infiltration followed by exploitation.

Out of the ashes of the *Carbonari*, survivors fled to several other European countries, and many made their way to South America as well. One of the most important refugees was Giuseppe Mazzini, a lawyer, writer, and revolutionary who became the principal architect of the new, reshaped resistance to be mounted by Young Italy. He realized that the great powers could not easily be played off against one another to Italy's benefit. Instead he called in his manifesto for the organization to focus single-mindedly on waging an "insurrection by guerrilla bands."[2]

Mazzini's call to arms was enthusiastically greeted, and soon the ranks of resisters were swelling once again, not only in Italy, for nationalists in several other countries were drawn to the notion of mounting armed resistance against the ruling empires of the Concert of Europe. It made the early 1830s a tense time. The wrath of the masses had been truly kindled, and now they had received a practical guide to action from Mazzini. The defenders of the existing order felt so threatened that one of their leaders, Prince Metternich of Austria—the Henry Kissinger of his time—went so far as to decry Mazzini as "the most dangerous man in Europe."[3]

Metternich may have been right conceptually, but in practical terms Mazzini, the gaunt intellectual, was badly miscast for the role as a man of action who could lead his movement to victory in the field. Even his strategic vision was limited, and it would be left to others to flesh out the general notion of *guerra alla spicciolata* (war little by little) that Mazzini had in mind. While there was no lack of good ideas among Italians about how to wage irregular warfare—particularly as articulated by the school of thought led by Carlo Bianco, Guglielmo Pepe, and Cesare Balbo—there was yet no "man on horseback" to lead them to victory in battle. Instead their and Mazzini's particular contributions were conceptual. As Walter Laqueur has put it, they were the first to make "the link between guerrilla warfare and radical politics"[4] that would inspire so many people's wars over the next 150 years.

Initially Mazzini thought that such an inspirational leader might not be necessary; but the savage defeats suffered in 1830–1831 had made him more sensitive to the need for a charismatic commander. And so he began to look for leadership potential among his recruits. In a back-alley lodging in Marseilles, at a secret meeting of Young Italy there in 1833, Mazzini met a new fellow who had come to the cause, Giuseppe Garibaldi. Already at this first meeting, Mazzini speculated that this bluff merchant sea captain might have the qualities he was looking for. Physically imposing, Garibaldi was also inspiring in his comments about how Italians would drive out their occupiers. Other Young Italy cell members at the meeting were equally impressed with Garibaldi's potential as a man of action. His biographer Nina Baker characterized the meeting this way: "Mazzini, the Head, and Garibaldi, the Arm, had come together, and the revolution had begun its thunderous course down the corridors of history."[5] Perhaps so, but the thunder would roll for a very long time before the storm broke in its full power.

*   *   *

Only two years younger than Mazzini, Giuseppe Garibaldi was born in 1807 in Nice, which had been the Italian Nizza until French annexation by conquest in 1792. It was returned to the House of Savoy after Napoleon's abdication in 1814. Garibaldi's father was a fisherman, and the son soon followed the father's path to the sea, learning his trade as a merchant seaman on voyages throughout the Mediterranean and the Black Sea. He first learned of Mazzini from a fellow trader, and Italian nationalist, whom he met when both were in the Crimea on business. The meeting between Garibaldi and Mazzini that soon followed in Marseilles sparked a close relationship between the two that was sometimes roughened by serious conflicts over strategy; but neither ever questioned the other's commitment to their noble cause.

In the beginning Mazzini was clearly the man in charge, Garibaldi the obedient recruit. So when asked to infiltrate the Sardinian navy—the kingdom included the island of Sardinia and the coastal territory and Alpine foothills of the Piedmont—then foment mutiny and take over the warship in which he was serving, Garibaldi agreed immediately. Mazzini's idea was to topple the French-leaning monarchy in this part of northern Italy with a guerrilla campaign launched from Switzerland that would culminate in a popular rising and a siege of the key city of Genoa. Garibaldi was to captain the seized ship and use it to bombard the great port from the seaward side.

It was a grand plan that floundered from its outset in February 1834. Mazzini had recruited a retired general to lead the popular army, which amounted at the beginning to a thousand men. The old general promptly ran off with the money that Young Italy had given him to purchase arms and equipment. Half the force was intercepted by Swiss border patrols, the other half soon scattered. As for Garibaldi, after the betrayal of his plot he narrowly escaped capture. He was thus put on the run, assuming a new identity and moving from one ship crew to another. He was tried in absentia and sentenced to death. It was a dark time.

At this point Mazzini temporarily gave up on this early version of what in the twentieth century would come to be called "people's war." Well aware that a period of rebuilding was needed, he did his best to guide and inspire his surviving cadres, and to recruit new members. As many old *Carbonari* had fled to South America, Mazzini encouraged Garibaldi to go there and reach out to them. On this advice, Garibaldi sailed to Brazil, arriving at Rio de Janeiro on New Year's Day, 1836. About the same time that Abd el-Kader was at the height of his success in Algeria, Garibaldi was at one of his lowest points.

But things began to brighten for him as he made his way in the maritime trade and soon had a vessel of his own. In this way he both eked out a living and made many connections with the Italian diaspora in Brazil and Uruguay. Still, he was restless for action. And when an opportunity arose to support a rebellion against the newly formed "empire" of Brazil, which had won its independence from Portugal just ten years earlier, Garibaldi eagerly accepted a naval command in the service of the "free republic" of Rio Grande do Sul. All he could hope to do at sea was engage in commerce raiding, the age-old weapon of those with weaker naval forces.

Garibaldi enjoyed some small successes but was eventually hunted down and cornered in a running fight. He fled up the Rio de la Plata, his ship being interned in neutral Argentina. Garibaldi himself landed in a hospital, as he had taken a bullet in the neck during the battle. It was the first of several serious wounds he would suffer over the course of his long life as an insurgent leader. Eight months later he was well enough to make his way back to Rio Grande do Sul, where he was greeted as a hero and given command of the republic's small regular navy of coastal and riverine craft.

Over the next few years Garibaldi fought numerous small-scale battles in coastal waters and often went upriver to support the army of the republic with his cannons. In some respects his actions resemble those of Lord Cochrane, who occasionally provided support of this kind to insurgents during the Napoleonic occupation of Spain. But even this was not enough action for Garibaldi; from his crews he formed mounted raiding parties that went out between naval actions to harass the advancing Brazilian forces. It turned out that Garibaldi was a magnificent natural horseman in addition to being a superb sailor.

The cause of Rio Grande do Sul, however, was a losing one. Not only were the Brazilians more numerous, they were better led, and they further benefited from the attractiveness of their young emperor's (and his regent's) lenient reconciliation policy toward the rebels, which prompted many defections. But as the end neared in Rio Grande, another small republic, Santa Catherina, declared its independence. Rio Grande could spare no troops, but Garibaldi was sent with some gunboats to help these new allies at sea.

It was in the course of sea and land operations on behalf of Santa Catherina that Garibaldi met Anita, the woman who would leave her quiet, comfortable life—and the wealthy older man to whom she was at least betrothed, more likely already married—to live with and bear the children of the insurgent leader. She proved the perfect match for him. As Garibaldi noted in his memoirs, with some assistance from his editor, Alexandre Dumas, she "looked upon battles as a pleasure, and the hardships of camp life as a pleasant pastime."[6] Anita rode and fought at Garibaldi's side even when pregnant. By this time his little navy had been lost and Garibaldi had become a leader of irregular cavalry, fighting and then constantly shifting locations to avoid the pursuing imperial forces.

When the couple's first son was born in September 1840, the cause of the two rebel republics was already nearly lost. For all the gallantry of the guerrilla forces, the combination of Brazilian blandishments and brute force simply could not be overcome. Garibaldi and Anita left the battle and settled in the remaining free republic, Uruguay. There they sought domesticity and married in March 1842, when they received word that Anita's husband might have passed away.[7]

They were not destined to live peacefully. Uruguay soon came under attack from Argentina, whose dictator Juan Manuel Rosas had grand designs for enlarging his territorial holdings. Rosas had interned Garibaldi early on in his career as a privateer, in the wake of the battle in the Rio de la Plata. Now the former sea raider was to show the dictator his skills as a leader of irregular forces. In 1843, after Rosas had destroyed the regular Uruguayan army, Garibaldi formed an Italian Legion from among the large expatriate community living in Montevideo. Over the course of the next five years he would lead a vigorous defense of the great Uruguayan city, closing breaches made by the forces of Rosas, raiding the enemy at the most unexpected times and places.

Anita bore him three more children during these years, and Garibaldi became famous throughout the world as a freedom fighter, thanks partly to Mazzini's energetic publicizing of his achievements. During this time Garibaldi also began to cultivate his own particular "brand," the red shirt that he and all his fighters wore in battle. The origin of the Redshirts was a burnt-down warehouse from which the only significant salvage was a huge amount of rough red cloth. But Garibaldi's mystique had to do with more than just color. He had also become renowned for his skillful guerrilla tactics, which relied on speed and stealth, minimal firepower, and the maximum shock of an assault at close quarters. These doctrinal trademarks grew in part from chronic deficiencies in arms and ammunition; but they also conformed closely to Garibaldi's character, which in its essence was a combination of cleverness and ferocity.

Another reason for his global popularity was his personification of the ideals of individual and national freedom. In Garibaldi people could see in practice something that all might strive for. Even in defeat he fought on and, by persisting, gave hope of victory. Certainly this was the case in his long defense of Montevideo, where the thwarting of Rosas's design for conquest for just long enough finally led Britain, France, and even Brazil to call for an end to the fighting and formal recognition of the Republic of Uruguay. By the time this was formalized, Garibaldi had left with his family for Nice, where he arrived in June 1848, at a moment when Europe seethed with social revolution.

* * *

Garibaldi had returned at Mazzini's urging, with sixty of his most loyal fighters from the Italian Legion and several black slaves whom he had freed. One of them, named Aguyar, a masterful horseman, always rode a black horse immediately behind Garibaldi, following him like a familiar spirit. He too became a part of the brand. As to the conviction and death sentence that had been pending for fifteen years, both were quietly forgotten by the authorities, as the Piedmontese populace would never have stood for their hero's arrest. The growing feeling that this was the time to strike for Italy's freedom from foreign rule now reached as far as their king, Charles Albert.

A hastily formed expedition was soon planned in support of the newly declared Republic of Milan, whose people had risen up and ejected the local Austrian occupying force. But the threat of retaliation loomed, and Charles Albert, Mazzini, Garibaldi, and other volunteers from as far away as Rome all converged on Milan. It was the first time that Mazzini and

Garibaldi's Struggle to Unify Italy

Garibaldi has seen each other in fourteen years, and each showed some signs of wariness toward the other. Charles Albert had little respect for either of them and made sure that Garibaldi held a very subordinate command. The tension was unhealthy.

Thus when the Austrians did return during that summer of 1848, Garibaldi was off in the country organizing a new legion of guerrilla fighters while King Charles Albert's regular army was being demolished at the Battle of Custoza. The king quickly sued for peace, which enraged Garibaldi, who led his irregulars on a fighting retreat to and across the Swiss border. Mazzini was with him, and this latest defeat somehow served to remind them both of their old bond that had been born in such adversity. For these two, the question now was not of giving up the struggle but, as Garibaldi asked Mazzini, "Where do we fight next?"[8]

The answer, as it turned out, was Rome. When some of the men who had traveled up to fight with the Milanese returned, in defeat and frustration, they began to agitate for more democratic rule in the papal states. They also demanded that Pope Pius IX, who in this era exercised both great spiritual authority and temporal power, declare war on the Austrians. Given that Pius seemed to harbor pro-Austrian feelings, this was hardly likely. Tensions rose during the autumn of 1848, stoked in large part by the arrival of Mazzini, who openly called for the declaration of an independent republic. In November the pope fled.

In the following months the Romans drafted a democratic constitution with a triple executive, the "triumvirs," an echo of ancient Rome. By April 1849 Mazzini was ensconced as the dominant executive, with Saffi and Armellini subservient to him. But the enemies of the republic had not been idle. Pius, who was sheltering in the Kingdom of the Two Sicilies under the protection of Ferdinand II—also know as "Bomba" for his relentless shelling of Sicilian rebels—was whipping up Catholic fervor in Spain, France, and Austria for a military expedition to restore him to power. France got off the mark first. The newly elected French president, Louis Napoleon, acted with great energy. He may have been dilatory about releasing Abd el-Kader into exile, but when it came to fighting the republicans in Rome he showed no hesitation.

Mazzini knew that he needed Garibaldi for the coming fight, and summoned him to Rome, where he arrived with some five hundred fighters, now known as the Garibaldini. More volunteers were coming in to serve under him every day, among them about three hundred art students. What they lacked in training they hoped to make up in zeal. But even with their ranks swelling, the defenders of Rome were outnumbered by General

Oudinot, who arrived at the end of April in command of more than seven thousand French solders.

Instead of waiting passively behind the walls for the siege to commence, Garibaldi took the offensive with his much smaller force, catching the French completely by surprise. The bitterest fighting took place in the Corsini Gardens, among flowerbeds and rows of cypresses. The French numerical advantage meant less on a battlefield broken up by trees, hedges, and watercourses; after six hours of heavy fighting, Oudinot's forces broke. Garibaldi had won the Battle Among the Roses but had taken a bullet in the side. It hardly slowed him. But French operations came to a complete halt. Rome was safe for the time being.

The republic's respite was short, however, as Ferdinand had finally gotten his force of ten thousand men under way from Naples. Garibaldi surged out of Rome with his men and immediately harassed Ferdinand's army with constant raids. At Palestrina the Garibaldini caught a large portion of the enemy in a disadvantageous position and hit them hard. At this juncture Louis Napoleon sent an emissary, Ferdinand de Lesseps—who would go on to build the Suez Canal—to treat for peace with Mazzini. Negotiations went so well that Mazzini released the entire Republican Army to join up with Garibaldi against Ferdinand. They soon drove him from the war, but meanwhile the French were readying a new offensive—in complete violation of the treaty just negotiated.

Garibaldi barely made it back to Rome in time to engage the now massive French force, which exceeded thirty thousand troops. He suffered heavy losses and a sharp tactical defeat; but strategically he had prevented a French *coup de main* capture of Rome. The war now settled down to a siege, which Garibaldi resisted with all the skills he had honed in the defense of Montevideo. His red shirt was seen everywhere. As the historian George Macaulay Trevelyan described it, Garibaldi "constantly went the rounds, visiting the places where the fire was hottest, and restoring the enthusiasm of the defenders, now by a word of personal sympathy, now by standing like a statue above his prostrate companions while a shell was bursting in their midst."[9]

In this manner Garibaldi kept Rome from capture for a month. During the siege, tensions between him and Mazzini erupted again when the latter refused Garibaldi's heated requests to allow the defenders to break out and engage in guerrilla warfare against the French. Mazzini thought that by staying in Rome he would win more of the world's sympathy. Perhaps so, but sympathy has seldom stopped a siege. Yet when Mazzini did decide to negotiate surrender terms, Garibaldi and those who wished to do so were authorized to break out. With Anita by his side—she had joined him just before the siege, leaving their children with his parents—and without Aguyar, who had been killed by an artillery shell, they and a small band rode out of Rome to the last cheers of the republic.

What followed was the most harrowing time in Garibaldi's life, as he and Anita were chased across Italy with the loyalists. It was a time when, as Trevelyan wrote, "those who donned a red shirt . . . and faithfully wore it during the next month, deliberately chose a dress which, from one end of the Peninsula to the other, exposed the wearer to be hunted like a wolf and shot on sight."[10]

Anita, whose constitution had been worn down by the rigors of the siege, died during their flight. Garibaldi managed to escape with the help of members of the insurgent network throughout Italy, many of whom were found out by his pursuers and killed. Mazzini accepted exile to England. Once again he and Garibaldi were estranged. A decade later they were to join forces one more time, with far better results.

* * *

After almost a year on the run, Garibaldi landed in New York in the summer of 1850. He went there in part because Margaret Fuller, the proper Bostonian and friend of Ralph Waldo Emerson and Henry David Thoreau who had been in Rome during the siege—and had nursed wounded Republican fighters—had told him of the beauty of freedom in America. Fuller had also charmed Garibaldi with her assessment of the Roman republic as "the visionary country of her heart," and he wanted to see the land from which such a wonderful woman came. Early on, however, all he saw was boiling tallow in the course of his work as a candle maker, the only job he could find.

Garibaldi worked the tallow for just under two years, then went back to sea for the next two, traveling first to Peru as a mate, then gaining a captaincy of his own for voyages to China, the Philippines, and finally, in 1854, to England. There he connected once more with Mazzini. Whatever their personal differences, Mazzini had been writing polemics about an Italian *risorgimento* (resurrection) that had caught the fancy of most of the world's idealists. He had been particularly fulsome in his praise of Garibaldi, who was greeted in England as a great hero.

When they met, Mazzini convinced Garibaldi to return to Sardinia, simply to wait on events. Mazzini believed that French and Austrian interests would inevitably clash, providing yet one more opportunity for Italians to win their independence. Garibaldi was persuaded and made his way back. Charles Francis had abdicated some years before; his son Victor Emmanuel was made of sterner stuff. Indeed, he seemed quite the liberal and showed little concern about Garibaldi's return. Perhaps this was because the great rebel settled on a farm on the small, rocky island of Caprera, off the coast of Sardinia.

For five years Garibaldi farmed. His children, who had been settled with cousins, stayed with him while he worked and waited. In 1859 the break came. Tensions between France and Austria reached a boil, and Victor Emmanuel contrived an alliance with Louis Napoleon, now Napoleon III, dictator of France. Their joining brought swift victory in the Battle of Solferino, the first in history in which both sides were armed almost entirely with rifles, the accurate infantry weapon that would change the face of nineteenth-century warfare.[11] For his part, Garibaldi had agreed, at the request of the king, to form an irregular corps, the Alpine Hunters, who performed skillfully.

In the wake of the war, the House of Savoy gained Lombardy from the Austrians, but at the price of giving Nice, Garibaldi's birthplace, back to the French. Although troubled by this, Garibaldi agreed to serve as the king's emissary to the people in several of the dukedoms that had been propped up by Austrian power. Garibaldi brought them all in. Central Italy was now unified, and greater gains were in the offing.

Garibaldi's willingness to work with Victor Emmanuel in the name of the emerging Italian nation created yet another rift with Mazzini, one that never really healed. The aging revolutionary still could not stomach monarchy. But however this issue frayed their friendship, they remained in touch. And the next year Mazzini convinced Garibaldi that the time was ripe for a revolution against the Two Sicilies. Bomba's son Francis now ruled every bit as harshly as his father had. The people yearned for a leader. Out of loyalty to Victor Emmanuel, Garibaldi discussed the matter with him and his chief diplomat, Count Cavour. Out of this meeting the notion arose of having Garibaldi travel to Sicily as a private citizen to help the suffering people there.

In May 1860 Garibaldi and other concerned citizens—about a thousand, indeed they would come to be known as "the Thousand"—landed on the west coast of Sicily at Marsala. They were greeted with great enthusiasm, but few Sicilians actually joined their ranks. The Thousand, more than a hundred of them medical students, were lightly armed and vastly outnumbered by Francis's forces, and now had to plan their offensive in the absence of a massive popular uprising. Their first battle came at Calatafimi, where the king's forces, more than two thousand, were dug in on a terraced hill. Garibaldi broke his force into a number of small units and assaulted the summit from every angle, taking advantage of the slight cover offered by each terrace. After a hard fight, Francis's men were routed, and Garibaldi began his march on Palermo.

Because the numbers he would soon face were in the tens of thousands, Garibaldi resorted to some of the tactics he had employed as a guerrilla fighter in South America. He feigned a retreat with elements of his force while most of his men closed in on Palermo. The enemy was duped, sending almost five thousand troops on a chase into central Sicily. Still, a garrison of more than sixteen thousand remained in Palermo, backed up by warships that could provide fire support. Despite these odds, Garibaldi drove on into the city with perhaps seven hundred of his original Thousand and a slightly larger number of Sicilians who had joined the cause after Calatafimi.

Here at Palermo Garibaldi would enjoy both a tactical and a strategic victory. Once inside the city, he dispersed his Thousand in small bands, attacking the enemy everywhere simultaneously. The far larger defending force fell back on the city center and port, the warships indiscriminately bombarding the parts of the city that had been occupied. Still Garibaldi pressed on, pioneering the mode of operations that the great Chechen fighter Aslan Maskhadov would employ against the Russian army in Grozny in 1996, when he drove them out against similar odds. But where Maskhadov gained momentum against the Russians as the struggle wore on, Garibaldi's force was coming apart. They had little ammunition, so most of the raids featured hand-to-hand combat. Losses were high, and the Thousand were dwindling dangerously low in number.

At this moment Garibaldi struck a psychological blow: he offered a ceasefire and an opportunity to discuss terms of withdrawal for the king's men. They accepted. And left. Soon Garibaldi overran the rest of Sicily with lightning raids, landing thereafter at Melito on the toe of Italy's boot. From there he began his campaign against Naples, the king's great stronghold. Francis panicked and fled, leaving the city to Garibaldi, who arrived there in September 1860.

Mazzini had also come to Naples, to give Garibaldi the green, white, and red flag that had flown over the Roman republic during its short life. When they met, Garibaldi told him that the flag would also be adorned with the coat of arms of the House of Savoy. Mazzini expected this but was nonetheless crushed, as he had held out hope to the last that Garibaldi would turn antimonarchist. He parted from Garibaldi and left for England. Mazzini spent the last twelve years of his life in self-exile from the Italy whose modern emergence he had done so much to bring about.

After Mazzini's departure, Garibaldi finally met in direct battle against Francis, who had cobbled together a new army and tried to march on Naples. Garibaldi beat him in a pitched battle at the Volturno River, and the threat was ended. Victor Emmanuel had been campaigning at the same time in central Italy, freeing the papal states. He entered Naples as the first king of Italy on November 7, 1860, making it clear that he was to be the constitutional monarch of a democratic nation.

Soon after Victor Emmanuel's entry into Naples, Garibaldi sailed for his farm on Caprera with a bag of seed corn, all he took for his labors.[12] He lived there with his children, remarried and had two more children in his old age. Occasionally the trumpets sounded a call to arms. During the American Civil War, when Union prospects were at their lowest, an aide to President Lincoln made an overture to Garibaldi to come help. Nothing came of it as both the government in Washington and Garibaldi had second thoughts.[13] At about the same time he launched an ill-advised campaign against the last papal holding, Rome itself. This "Aspromonte Affair" ended badly, with Victor Emmanuel's troops stopping the march, and wounding Garibaldi in the process.

But there was no deep rift with the king. In 1866 Victor Emmanuel asked Garibaldi to command an irregular force once more against the Austrians, which he did with distinction. The following year he led another disastrous, unauthorized march on Rome, this time losing about a thousand of his followers in battle with the French forces still protecting the city Louis Napoleon had so brutally taken from the republic nearly twenty years earlier.

Garibaldi's last foray into the field came in the Franco-Prussian War in 1870, when he joined the side of the French republic that was declared in the wake of Napoleon III's abdication. Victor Emmanuel took the opportunity to seize Rome for Italy, but Garibaldi, now sixty-three, led a force of irregulars drawn from many nations to fight the Prussians in France. Of his last battles in the Vosges Mountains, his opposite number, General Edwin von Manteuffel said of Garibaldi that he admired "the great speed of his movements" and his "energy and intensity in attack."[14] The old lion still had some fight in him, it turned out, and the novelist Victor Hugo went so far as to claim that Garibaldi was the only general on the French side that the Prussians had not beaten.

But the Vosges campaign was his last lightning. Garibaldi returned to Caprera after the war and spent the last decade of his life on the farm he had come to love. He enjoyed being known as the "man of the age" but seldom left the island. His life grew ever simpler; after he finished his memoirs there was little left to do in explaining the course and purpose of his life to his fellow Italians and to the world.

The only item that remained tantalizingly out of reach was Garibaldi's philosophy of irregular warfare. Where Mazzini had mounted something of an offensive of platitudes and generalizations in his treatise on guerrilla operations, Garibaldi remained mostly mute about the idea of there being principles of irregular warfare. Perhaps this is because his great campaigns already speak so eloquently about the power of the few, when properly employed. Even in defeat, as in Rio Grande do Sul and in Rome, Garibaldi's small, swarming detachments and relentless pursuit of the offensive achieved remarkable results. But it is in his victories, on the defensive in Montevideo and in the amazing city fight for Palermo, that Garibaldi left us monuments to the art of irregular warfare that should stand as long as soldiers have memories.

8

REBEL RAIDER: NATHAN BEDFORD FORREST

Just months after Garibaldi's great triumphs in Sicily and Naples, which did so much for Italian nationhood, the American Civil War broke out. It grew from a long-simmering dispute over the appropriate extent of central government, and from a deep-seated belief on the part of many Americans that the constitutional right to life, liberty, and the pursuit of happiness required an end to the enslavement of African Americans. It is interesting that both sides in these disputes looked to Garibaldi for inspiration. As Derek Leebaert has observed, he was "a nation-builder to Federals (with New York's 'Garibaldi Guards'), who saw themselves preserving a country, and to Confederates, who were confident that they were bringing one to birth."[1] Thus nationalism once again sparked conflict. On this occasion, however, the scale was to dwarf the size of most other nationalist wars—save for those of the Napoleonic Era—and it would be the first truly modern war. That is, during all its four years the Civil War was waged with mass-produced rifles and artillery, and troops regularly moved by rail, with their actions coordinated by telegraph.

Nationalism also bred ferocity. Coupled with accurate weapons and wedded to large forces, this meant huge casualties. Over a quarter million Confederates died in battle or from their wounds, of just under nine hundred thousand who served. Union fatalities exceeded 360,000 of the roughly 2.2 million who fought. This remains the bloodiest war that Americans have ever waged—and it was against their own countrymen. But these terrible losses were not simply the result of concurrent leaps in weapons, and information technologies; their root cause lay in the belief of generals on both sides that, despite all these changes, Napoleonic methods could still be applied to this Napoleonic-sized war. Thus Union and Confederate soldiers were often condemned to march shoulder to shoulder into heavy fire, in formations most resembling Wellington's thin red line or the columns of the French Old Guard, employing a battle doctrine that has been labeled by some Civil War historians "attack and die."[2]

In the main, generals on both sides adhered stubbornly to notions of massed assaults against well-armed defenders. If tried frontally, blunt-edged attacks of this sort led to such disasters as the Battle of Fredericksburg in December 1862, when Union forces suffered thirteen thousand casualties—to fewer than five thousand rebels—in a single day of battle. The Confederates showed just as much bullheadedness in Pickett's Charge at Gettysburg in July 1863, when losses mounted to half the fourteen thousand men employed in that attack alone, over just a few hours. Even when linked to flanking movements, as Ulysses S. Grant repeatedly did in his campaign against Robert E. Lee in the spring and summer of 1864, the results were just as dismal. In the Wilderness, Grant lost almost eighteen thousand troops in two days, against Lee's forces' casualties of about seven thousand. At Cold Harbor just a month later, the proportion of losses was even worse, with Union casualties at seven thousand against just over one thousand for Lee's forces in a day's action.

Most generals on both sides shared this retrograde view of how to conduct their battles, reflecting the influence of the Baron Jomini's great lesson from his study of Napoleon: strike with the greatest mass at a single "decisive point."[3] Their perspective might also have grown from having participated in successful frontal assaults during the war with Mexico (1846–1848), in which so many had served as junior officers.[4] As things turned out, it was the Union commander-in-chief, Abraham Lincoln, who would eventually overcome his generals' predilections by calling for major offensives mounted simultaneously in all theaters, sustained by the railroads and coordinated by telegraph. But it would take Lincoln nearly three long years of jawboning, coaxing, and coercing before the strategy that would ultimately overwhelm the Confederacy was finally adopted in full.[5]

By the time the Union offensives were at last underway in earnest in 1864, the South had formulated a powerful response that combined fighting largely on the tactical defensive with regular troops while taking the offensive with guerrillas and deep-strike cavalry. A key champion of the tactical defensive was General James Longstreet, one of Lee's chief subordinates and a man who had argued strongly against continuing to batter away at Union forces fighting from well-prepared defensive positions at Gettysburg. Beyond Longstreet, General Joseph E. Johnston also had a considerable appreciation of the superiority of the defensive in pitched battles, as he would skillfully demonstrate in his delaying actions against Union general William T. Sherman during the latter's drive for Atlanta in 1864.

As to leaders of irregular forces, the Confederacy enjoyed the great benefit of having several commanders—mostly cavalrymen—who thought strategically in terms of waging a wholly different kind of war. Some favored the idea of guerrilla operations. The darker version, as practiced by William Quantrill in the west, looked quite a bit like terrorism, as at the burning of Lawrence, Kansas, and in the various depredations of the James brothers. These sorts of operations attracted a lot of riffraff, leading to more heinous acts and reinforcing a trend toward banditry. This devolution in behavior and goals contributed strongly to the repeal in early 1865 of the Confederacy's Partisan Ranger Act which had been passed in April 1862 to legitimize and regulate irregular warfare practices. But as Lee ultimately put it regarding the guerrillas: "I regard the whole system as an unmixed evil."[6]

A somewhat more acceptable form of guerrilla warfare was practiced in the Shenandoah Valley by John Singleton Mosby. His campaign
unfolded on friendly territory where the people aided and abetted the
Confederate cause. Mosby's rangers—never amounting to more than a few
hundred riders—caused no end of mischief for Union forces operating in
the area. At one point Mosby even abducted a Union general. But none of
these actions ultimately rose to the level of achieving truly strategic effects.
Still, one can see in these operations in what came to be called "Mosby's
Confederacy" at least a foreshadowing of the kind of resistance and insurgent movements that would one day arise in Nazi-occupied France, and
later in American-occupied Iraq.

But to throw a real monkey wrench into the works of Lincoln's great
"cordon offense"[7] it would take much more than terror raids and kidnap-
pings. Out in the western theater of operations, west of the Appalachian
Mountains, a number of rebel commanders arose who took the irregular
offensive against the advancing Union masses. One who made a tremendous mark in four long-range raids was John Hunt Morgan. Usually operating in brigade strength—roughly two thousand to four thousand riders—he
struck hard and inflicted great damage in Ohio and Indiana. His forays
were, however, in the words of one historian, "spectacular but pointless."[8]
They were too disconnected from the overall campaign.

In his last Ohio raid, Morgan and his men were tracked down by
Union cavalry troopers who had finally become adept at "tip and run"
operations themselves. They killed or captured almost all the rebel raiders.
Morgan himself was taken and imprisoned in the Ohio state penitentiary
but worked with other prisoners to dig a tunnel and escape. Once loose,
he evaded recapture and made his way back south. Soon he was leading
another raid; but his forces were detected, tracked, and cornered once
again. This time Morgan was killed. His great skill as an irregular fighter
had never been fully realized.

There was however one Confederate military leader possessed of similar skills who did figure out how to employ the raid and the *coup de main* in
a manner that was well integrated with the overall Confederate strategy in
the west: Nathan Bedford Forrest. A man with a total of about six months'
formal education—he always said pens made him think of snakes—and no
prior military experience, Forrest entered the Confederate Army a private.
He would rise to the rank of lieutenant general, and along the way he would
prove that the rail and telegraph technologies that so empowered Union
forces also imperiled them. For a modern industrial army is highly dependent
on secure logistics and communications. To make both insecure was For-

rest's goal, one he repeatedly achieved for significant periods of time at crucial moments during the war. His record was so good that Ulysses S. Grant
himself, the best Union commander and later on president of the United
States, judged Forrest "the ablest cavalry general in the South."[9]

* * *

Growing up on the frontier in Tennessee during the early 1820s, Forrest became tough, resourceful, and independent-minded. For that era he was big
too, being over six feet tall and well muscled. His father died in 1837 when
he was sixteen, so Forrest as the eldest son took on the burden of providing
for his mother and five younger brothers. But as he came into manhood his
desire for adventures farther afield came to the fore. He joined a group of
volunteers who intended to enlist with Sam Houston in Texas and, when
the group disbanded before arriving, he continued on anyway. But a severe illness followed, and he never did serve in the army of the Republic
of Texas. Instead he eventually made his way home after recuperating. He
stayed only briefly, for about this time his mother was remarrying, which
allowed him to strike out on his own once more. He joined the mercantile
and livestock business of his uncle, Jonathan Forrest, in Hernando, Mississippi, soon demonstrating a skilled eye for cattle and horses.

It was a period of fierce commercial competition, and Forrest was
soon embroiled in bitter disputes on behalf of his uncle, a kindly man
with little business aptitude. On one occasion in 1845, two men came to
see Jonathan—it seems to collect on a debt—and in the ensuing argument
one of them shot down the elder Forrest. Bedford, showing his penchant
for swift action, immediately gunned down the two assailants, establishing
what his peers called a "reputation for volatility." Nevertheless he had on
balance more redeeming qualities, including gallantry toward women and,
in an age of very hard living, abstinence from both tobacco and alcohol. Just
months after Jonathan's death, Forrest courted and wed Mary Ann Montgomery, a woman from a fine family. He also began to involve himself
more deeply in the slave trade, where he could apply his merchant's insight
to more than just horses and cattle.[10]

For any aspiring slave trader, Memphis, Tennessee, was the place to
be, as it featured the most vigorous market for African Americans. By 1852
Forrest had moved there and soon grew quite prosperous. By the time the
Civil War broke out in 1861, he was a millionaire. He was also a respected
citizen and member of the city council. When Tennessee seceded from
the Union, Forrest volunteered as a private, but he soon rose to lieutenant colonel, no doubt in recognition of the fact that he had used his own

funds to raise and equip a battalion of cavalry (some seven hundred riders). Thus the self-made man, lacking in formal education and previous military experience, went to war.

Given his thin credentials for command, one might expect Forrest to have failed early on; but it soon became clear that he had a natural instinct for soldiering. He quickly grasped the importance of seizing and holding the initiative, and understood that firepower was now more important to cavalry than the saber. Throughout the war he would use horses basically for mobility while his men would, for the most part, fight on foot. The one-fourth of his troopers who held the horses during the initial battle became his reserve, remaining fresh to mount and sustain the pursuit of a defeated, disorganized enemy force.

Forrest's other traits included an extremely innovative tactical approach to battle and a farseeing strategic sensibility. In an age when his colleagues—and most of his Union adversaries—sought victory through the shock of frontal attack, Forrest pioneered a concept of operations based on mounting simultaneous attacks on flanks and rear—what we today call swarm tactics. At the more strategic level, he understood that the farther Union forces advanced, the more vulnerable their communications and supply lines became—much like the situation Napoleon had faced in Russia. Indeed, in striving for some antecedent to Forrest's prowess in irregular warfare, the historian Walter Laqueur made the analogy explicit, noting that Forrest's campaigns "resembled those of Denis Davydov in the (Russo-French) War of 1812: deep-penetration raids into the enemy's rear rather than guerrilla warfare."[11]

If some of Davydov's practices reemerged half a century later in Forrest's raids, Forrest's own imprint on later mechanized operations was to be felt just as strongly among the tank commanders of the 1920s and 1930s, for whom a study of the rebel raider's campaigns was viewed as mandatory.[12] One of the greatest masters of the blitzkrieg, Erwin Rommel, carefully examined Forrest's methods.[13] Thus, in addition to his insights into irregular warfare, Forrest would provide some of the inspiration for the rise of modern maneuver warfare.

Forrest became famous for his relentless pursuit of the offensive, but he began his military career with retreats, though skillful ones. The first occurred at Fort Donelson in February 1862, where Grant trapped about thirteen thousand rebels. Almost all ended up surrendering, save for the five hundred or so troopers who escaped with Forrest, who had requested and been granted permission to try to break out. In his next big fight, at the bloody battle of Shiloh in April, Forrest commanded the Confederate

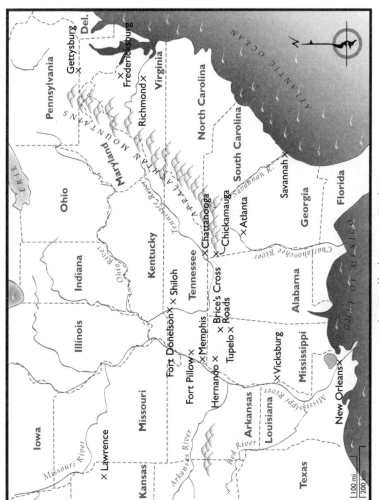

Nathan Bedford Forrest's Civil War

rearguard against the Union pursuit mounted by Sherman, Grant's great comrade in arms. In the savage fighting that ensued, the rearguard held on long enough for the main rebel force to withdraw safely, but Forrest suffered a bullet wound—the first of four he would receive during the war—and barely escaped being killed or captured.

After a brief period of recuperation, Forrest returned to the field, this time much more on the offensive. Over the summer and fall of 1862 he honed his growing mastery of the bolt-from-the-blue raid, striking at small Union detachments as well as at rail and telegraph lines. But it was his characteristic simultaneous attacks on flanks and rear—swift, slashing, and completely disruptive of the Union forces' cohesion—that became a true hallmark of his raiding style. His operations contributed mightily to disrupting Union operations after Shiloh, so much so that the South seized the strategic initiative. But under the clumsy generalship of General Braxton Bragg, the Confederate offensive that began in Kentucky soon fizzled.

At this point Forrest took his raiders west, where Grant was now trying to march overland toward the key Confederate river fortress of Vicksburg. With Union forces intending eventually to come upriver from New Orleans, which had been taken by David Farragut at the end of April, the loss of Vicksburg would split the Confederacy in two. But Grant didn't reckon with Forrest's tremendous energy, mobility, and fighting spirit. In a relentless series of raids on Union telegraph and rail lines, along with strikes against supply depots, Forrest completely halted the Union advance on Vicksburg.

As 1862 drew to a close, Union forces had to fall back on Memphis for, as Bruce Catton noted, Forrest's raids "brought Grant's army to a standstill. All hands were put on half rations, and to keep his army from starvation, Grant sent his wagons out into the country to seize supplies."[14] Tens of thousands of tough Union troops, led in the field by their most effective general, had been thwarted by the comparatively tiny irregular force—never more than a few thousand riders—led by Nathan Bedford Forrest.

Grant, however, was not a man to quit on an important objective. He soon renewed his efforts, this time relying heavily on the Union Navy to move much of his force by river most of the two hundred miles between Memphis and Vicksburg. For this campaign Grant had slightly more than a hundred thousand troops under his command, and he used them brilliantly in maneuvers, first away from the river and then back toward it—and Vicksburg. Forrest pestered him every step of the way, striking all over the map, sometimes riding for days nonstop so he could hit a target a hundred miles from where he had last raided. The only way Grant coped with Forrest was by allocating nearly two-thirds of his force—more than sixty thousand troops—to the protection of his lines of supply and communications.[15]

Vicksburg fell in July 1863, just as Lee was losing the Battle of Gettysburg back east. But Forrest had shown precisely how disruptive a tiny force could be when used skillfully against a modern army's transportation and communications infrastructure. While Davydov and Abd el-Kader had demonstrated the effectiveness of such small-scale raids, they had operated against slow, wagon-drawn logistical systems. Forrest demonstrated that similar, even greater results could be achieved against railroad-based supply organizations despite the presence of telegraphic links that allowed the alarm of his presence to be spread swiftly. He just had to hit hard and run, for pursuit from multiple directions was never far off.

After the Vicksburg campaign Forrest once again served with the main Confederate force operating in southeastern Tennessee and northwestern Georgia. It was still commanded by Braxton Bragg, who was now trying to prevent a Union advance beyond Chattanooga. Bragg and Forrest had what can only be called a toxic relationship. Bragg could barely tolerate the irregular cavalryman: "The man is ignorant, and does not know anything of cooperation."[16] Forrest viewed Bragg as "a damned scoundrel."[17] This hardly formed a basis for fruitful collaboration.

Nevertheless in the late summer of 1863 the two men and their forces were able to catch the Union commander in this area, General William Rosecrans, in an awkward spot that imperiled his whole force. The place was near Chickamauga Creek, not far from Chattanooga but already in Georgia. Bragg struck Rosecrans there in September, in one of the bloodiest battles of the war. While Confederate casualties were higher than the Union's during the two September days of battle—some twenty thousand versus sixteen thousand—Rosecrans was clearly defeated, a catastrophe being averted only by the stand of General George Thomas, the "Rock of Chickamauga."

Determined to exploit this opportunity, Forrest lobbied Bragg hard to follow up the victory with a relentless pursuit, a view that was supported by Longstreet, who had come from the east with fresh forces to assist in the campaign. But Bragg would have none of it, wanting instead to reconsolidate his force after all the carnage. Forrest argued that the suffering would be in vain if Bragg did not take quick advantage of his victory. Bragg would not budge, and Forrest exploded against him, asking of the staffers at the meeting, "What does he fight battles for?"[18] Less polite things also were said, and Forrest had his troopers taken away from him. Soon he was transferred to Mississippi, where he was ordered to mount raids to keep the federals from making further incursions there.

In this manner Forrest was shunted aside on the eve of the great Union offensive against Atlanta, the campaign that many historians believe truly sealed the Confederate defeat. For its capture in September 1864, just two months before the presidential election, ensured that Lincoln—whose prospects were shaky—would have a second term, and that there would be no peace short of victory over the Confederacy. Forrest, who had completely thwarted two major Union offensives already during the war, would almost surely have delayed Sherman's advance (Grant had now moved east to take command of all federal forces), likely long enough to have thrown the election into doubt.

Even if his coming to Georgia had brought more federal troops in pursuit, as historian Albert Castel has suggested,[19] they would have had to rely upon the same rail lines as Sherman's forces, increasing the impact of any disruptions Forrest would have caused. Nor is it clear that Union leadership would have been willing to strip the Mississippi theater of troops, given that Napoleon III had just set up a "Catholic empire" in Mexico. The possibility that tens of thousands of French troops might engage in further adventurism—on American soil—encouraged the maintenance of a substantial military presence in the trans-Mississippi region.

The South, however, took advantage of none of these favorable factors, and Forrest was relegated to fighting far to the west of the decisive area of operations. He did so against ever greater odds, as there were almost no other important Confederate formations left in the west, leaving him to build his own new force from scratch. Still, he achieved remarkable results. They were just not the results that the South most needed at this critical juncture.

*   *   *

During 1864 Forrest would grow as proud of his handful of newly recruited raiders as he was disappointed in his superiors. These troopers were quick to imbibe the spirit of his operational concepts, sometimes riding out on their own for days and weeks. On these independent raids they showed great cleverness in using the power of the Forrest "brand," claiming their leader was with them when they demanded the surrender of a Union outpost. This *ruse de guerre* often worked; but increasingly, even when Forrest was with them, he was made to show himself in order to convince skeptical federals he was indeed present. Then they would generally surrender.

In April 1864, at a place now quite far behind Union lines on the Mississippi River called Fort Pillow, some forty miles north of Memphis, this need to show himself caused Forrest to have two horses shot from under him while he reconnoitered the post and tried to intimidate its garrison of about six hundred soldiers, just over half of them African Americans, into surrendering. The defenders felt their position was secure enough to mount a resistance, even in the presence of Forrest, as there was a Union naval gunboat right there at the fort. Even so, once the battle was on, with Forrest typically striking from several directions simultaneously, the rebels overran the fort and began to slaughter the Union soldiers. Some ran away along the river but most were taken prisoner, and many were forced to kneel and were shot execution-style in the head. African American prisoners were particularly singled out in this manner.

Fort Pillow proved to be the darkest day in Forrest's career. An abundance of eyewitness evidence, including from Union soldiers, confirms that, once he became fully aware of what was going on, he put a stop to the killing. But even though the madness was ended, in less than half an hour, more than a hundred federals were murdered. Forrest was responsible for this horrible war atrocity, something that would nag him for the rest of his life. It would also tarnish the U.S. military's memory of him and impair efforts to distill the lessons from his advanced concepts of field operations as European military leaders were doing. The American armed forces averted their gaze from Forrest and even went so far as to name the great base that is home to the majority of their special operations forces Fort Bragg, memorializing instead the military hack who did so much to keep Forrest down.

After Fort Pillow, Grant and Sherman began sending flying columns after Forrest. The first major effort consisted of more than eight thousand troopers who came to grips with him in June at Brice's Cross Roads in northern Mississippi. Forrest scraped together every man he could find, which amounted to little more than three thousand. Yet, he seized the initiative and mounted another multidirectional attack. This favorite battle tactic of his worked again, and the federals suffered more than two thousand casualties. Forrest's own unit lost about five hundred killed and wounded. The battle was something of a masterpiece of swift movement and misdirection of the enemy, perhaps Forrest's best.

Union leaders were stung by this reverse; but in their coldly calculating way Grant and Sherman decided to continue after Forrest in the same manner. In part they did this to keep him busy far away from the decisive area of operations around Atlanta. A month after Brice's Cross Roads, a much larger Union force, more than twelve thousand, induced the rebels to attack them as they were advancing near the town of Tupelo, Mississippi. In this battle the federals also benefited from Forrest's Achilles-like decision to stay out of the fight. He was fuming about having been passed over for command in this theater in favor of Stephen Lee, a distant relative of Robert E. Lee. Forrest insisted that his new superior lead the troops into battle, which Lee did in a most clumsy, direct fashion. The rebels were badly beaten, losing well over a thousand men—a third of the force—to Union casualties of fewer than seven hundred. Forrest approached his superior after the battle and said, "I'll tell you one thing, General Lee. If I knew as much about West Point tactics as you, the Yankees would whip hell out of me every day."[20]

Eventually Forrest's exile from the main action was ended—but too late, as Atlanta had already fallen. Now, instead of using his skills to bedevil Sherman's sprawling army of freebooters rampaging across Georgia—easy pickings for a raider like Forrest—he was sent along on General John Bell Hood's kamikaze-style offensive into Tennessee. Hood was soundly defeated, as he had been in the clumsy attacks he mounted against Sherman's forces outside Atlanta after he had replaced the more skillful defender, General Joseph E. Johnston.

That any Confederates made it back from the catastrophe in Tennessee had much to do with Forrest's heroic conduct of rearguard operations. As one of Hood's staff officers reported, when the rebel army was finally out of harm's way, "I heard General Hood heartily thank Forrest . . . saying to him that without his aid he should never have brought his army [back] across the Tennessee River."[21] Even in the midst of an outsized military debacle, Forrest had fought effectively, in this case winning time. But his skill in such an awful situation should prompt us to ask how much more effective he would have been had his talents been employed months earlier in thwarting Sherman's advance, which was already slowed by Johnston's sturdy defense of Atlanta.

During the last months of the war Forrest kept on fighting hard and succeeded in holding his command together. When the end finally came for the Confederacy, it was the idea of linking up with Forrest and fighting on that animated President Jefferson Davis's abortive attempt to escape from besieged Richmond. Davis, who had brought in Bragg as his senior military adviser during the last year of the war, admitted that Forrest's worth was "not understood at Richmond."[22] It was the understatement of the war.

Upon his return to private life, Forrest found that his knack for commercial success was gone. He failed in one venture after another, from mercantile to agricultural enterprises, and in an attempt to start a railroad company. His health also began to fail, with the cumulative effects of four years' rough living, four major wounds, and what may have been undiagnosed diabetes all taking their toll on him. As he declined financially and physically, however, yet one more opportunity to serve came to him—or so he thought. He was invited to lead a secret Southern resistance society whose goal was to throw off the yoke of Northern occupation and control. He accepted, becoming the first grand wizard of an organization called the Ku Klux Klan.

Forrest's dalliance with these terrorists did not last much beyond the elections of 1868, when Klan threats and violence probably swung a couple of Southern states away from Grant in the presidential election. But it was not enough to prevent the Union general's victory. Soon after, Forrest repudiated the Klan and its ideology and tactics, spending the last years of his life a penitent. His health finally gave out in 1877, when he died at the age of fifty-six.

In the near term Forrest was much remembered for the massacre at Fort Pillow and his Klan affiliation. But his military reputation grew despite these blots, receiving a major boost in a famous article published in 1892 in the *New Orleans Picayune* by the great British expert on irregular wars, Field Marshal Joseph Viscount Wolseley, who praised in particular Forrest's "acute judgment and power of perception."[23] Ever since, he has become a central character in American folklore—racist demon to some, military genius to others, and, even more, a tragic hero of the South's "Lost Cause."[24]

These views, each of which has some merit, nonetheless fail to get at the heart of his contribution to the evolution of irregular warfare: his emphasis on simultaneous multidirectional attack and his belief that the greater the size of the enemy, the greater his vulnerability to disruption of his communications and transportation infrastructures. Instead of being remembered by his aphorism about getting there first with the most, Forrest—who almost never had a numerical edge over his opponents, save for brief, very localized tactical situations—should be known as one of the fathers of swarm tactics. He demonstrated, for the first time in modern war, that whatever new power industrial advances conveyed to militaries, they also opened a host of new vulnerabilities. That should be seen as the insight that has informed insurgents, commandos, and terrorists ever since.

Whatever his personal flaws, Forrest was a quintessential master of irregular warfare, one who built substantially on the methods pioneered by Denis Davydov and Abd el-Kader. He should also be seen as the progenitor of a number of skillfully conducted irregular campaigns waged in the 150 years since he and his troopers held sway. One does not have to look far to pick up the trail of his intellectual legacy. Another American master of irregular warfare, George Crook, would soon be relying regularly on Forrest-like ways in the final series of campaigns launched against the Indians of the West who stood in the way of American "manifest destiny" during the decades immediately after the Civil War. That the Native American resistance also relied on irregular tactics and strategies would make for a compelling clash, testing the skills on each side to the limit.

9

GRAY FOX:
GEORGE CROOK

As the American Civil War was winding down, the final phase of the Indian Wars was gearing up. While federal forces had been focused on fighting the Confederates, the still-free Native American tribes west of the Mississippi River had been able to stem the tide of white settlement—and in places had reversed it, as the Apaches did for several years in Arizona under their great leader Cochise. But once the Union was fully restored, the fundamental strategic problem of the Indians resurfaced: they were simply too few against too many. This numerical inferiority drove the Western tribes to fight in irregular ways, with hit-and-run raids and ambushes their most common tactics. There was clear precedent for this in American history, as we saw in the brutal wilderness war waged by Native Americans and whites during the eighteenth century. In the first half of the nineteenth century the pattern continued, with the Seminoles of Florida mounting a heroic, protracted guerrilla resistance under Osceola that lasted into the early 1840s. But their defeat was inevitable, especially once the American military began to target crops and villages, a brutal success formula.

The Indians of the West may not have been aware of all this history, but they quickly learned that the coming of white settlers meant the end of their way of life. Cochise, for example, had at first tried to live peaceably with the settlers during the 1850s, even having his people contract to provide firewood to them. For decades he had been able to hold off the Mexicans who tried to make incursions into his people's lands; but the Americans who displaced them after the 1846–1848 war seemed likely to pose a tougher challenge. So he decided to begin relations with the new interlopers in a more conciliatory manner.

But cultural misunderstandings, cupidity, and mutual mistrust all contributed to the outbreak of violence in Arizona. As did treachery, the most egregious instance occurring in February 1861, when a young and inexperienced federal officer lured Cochise and several family members to a meeting, ostensibly to talk about cattle rustling and the recent kidnapping of a white child, but then attempted to arrest him on the spot. Cochise escaped the trap, though wounded in the process, and several of his family members were taken prisoner. He retaliated with a raid on a wagon train and the taking of hostages, which he killed when his own people were not released. In retaliation Cochise's brother and two nephews were executed. The war had begun.

Cochise and the Apaches mounted punishing raids throughout the Civil War years and persisted even after. And they were hardly alone in resisting white incursions. Other Indian tribes farther north were also beginning to come into conflict with homesteaders who wished to settle on their lands, prospectors looking for precious metals, and still others who passed through on their way west, cutting a swath of environmental degradation along the way. So the Sioux, the Cheyenne, and other tribes began to fight for their lands and their ways of life. Inevitably their resistance prompted the coming of the American military, whose job was to protect the innocent—and also to subdue the Indians. All too soon, to use the military historian S. L .A. Marshall's phrase, this part of the West became a "crimsoned prairie."[1]

Initially the Indians got the better of the whites on virtually all fronts. The Apaches were better desert and mountain fighters, taking every advantage of familiarity with their home terrain. The Sioux, Cheyenne, and other Plains tribes were magnificent horsemen who were able, again and again, to combine speed of movement and stealth to their advantage. White settlers offered a wide range of slow-moving, often static targets, not unlike their eighteenth-century forebears who first began to push inland from the East Coast. Further, while the Native American tribes were still basically Stone Age peoples, thanks to illicit arms traders they soon possessed advanced weapons, especially the quick-firing repeating rifles now coming into production. Thus it was not unusual for the Indians to outgun the bluecoats in battle.

The tribes also had several great insurgent leaders. In the harsh desert-and-scrub environment of the Southwest, Cochise was joined by other Apaches like Mangas Coloradas (Red Sleeves) and Geronimo, among others. Mangas was his father-in-law; Geronimo was with Cochise from the start of his campaign in retaliation for the trap that had snared his family. Their brilliance as hit-and-run raiders was demonstrated over many years of hard fighting, scarcely dimmed by the reverse at Apache Pass where they once tried unsuccessfully to engage in a toe-to-toe, massed fight. Mangas's reputation remained untarnished even in death, as his fall came from a desire to negotiate peace. He fell into a trap similar to Cochise's—but Mangas didn't escape.

Farther north, the Plains Indians were also brilliantly led. Their great leaders included the mystic Crazy Horse and the visionary tribal unifier Sitting Bull. Together they would bring about the spectacular downfall of George Armstrong Custer in the summer of 1876 at the Little Bighorn. In the mountains and forests of the Pacific Northwest another remarkable leader was Chief Joseph of the Nez Perce, who would one day confound his bluecoat pursuers during the course of a magnificent thousand-mile fighting retreat that very nearly saw him and his people escape to Canada.

In short, the terrain, the weapons technology available to the tribesmen, and the high quality of their chiefs were factors that all pointed to the need for exceptionally skillful leadership on the part of federal forces. Instead, at the outset the Indians confronted a foe who featured a mixed bag of conflicting traits. Many of the government soldiers were battle hardened, but just as many were war weary. Even with post–Civil War reductions in forces, their numbers were quite large enough for the tasks at hand, and securing the frontier was virtually the only mission of the U.S. Army. But its leaders' tactical notions, reflecting their dominant Civil War experiences, were far more oriented to stand-up fights than to irregular operations.

All these factors combined to keep the initiative with the Indians for several years after the Civil War. In the North the signal event was the slaughter of a small force that had ridden out of Fort Kearny in the Wyoming Territory under an impetuous officer, one Captain William J. Fetterman. He had bravely earned a colonelcy during the Civil War and held the Indians in contempt, particularly what he regarded as their cowardly hit-and-run tactics. He was fond of saying that with just eighty troopers he could ride right through any opposing Indian force. Naturally he soon fell into a simple false retreat trap, and he and his eighty men were killed just days before Christmas 1866.

Throughout 1867 desultory fighting continued, and the bluecoats began to learn from their hard experiences against the Sioux and the Arapaho on the Plains. But not fast enough for President Andrew Johnson, who sent a peace commission to Wyoming in the spring of 1868 to try to end the fighting. The agreement signed in May required federal forces to close their forts along the Bozeman Trail, which ran right outside the gate of Fort Kearny. The Indians burned the forts immediately after they were abandoned. The tide of white settlement had been stemmed.

In the Southwest, the situation was just as bad. The Apaches were able to move about and strike small communities and wagon trains at will, for a while breaking the trail links between Texas and California. Federal forces had little luck engaging the Indians or protecting the settlers. This despite the fact that from 1865 to 1868 Cochise had his hands full on another front, fighting the incursions of the Tarahumara, Yaqui, and Opata Indians who were being pressured northward by Mexican forces into Apache territory.[2] Cochise dealt with this problem, then turned his full attention once again to the whites, unleashing an absolute reign of terror.

Many settlements and mining operations were soon abandoned, as none seemed beyond the reach of Apache raiders, and the federal soldiers were almost never able to prevent an attack or to mount a successful pursuit. The one officer who did show some aptitude for fighting the Apaches, Howard Cushing, was lured into a trap and killed in May 1871. Thus the situation in Arizona and New Mexico was as dire as that of Wyoming.

Ulysses S. Grant, who had been elected president in 1868 to succeed Andrew Johnson, had finally had enough. During his first years in office he had tried to follow Andrew Johnson's peace policy toward the Indians. But the humiliation of the Indian attacks eventually impelled him to renounce the conciliatory approach in favor of renewed military action. The only questions now were about how to fight smarter, and who might be able to conduct a more effective campaign.

Grant reached out to an officer with considerable experience fighting Indians in the Pacific Northwest, both in the 1850s and again later in the 1860s, and whose combat record in the Civil War had been sterling: George Crook. In the years following the war, after having earlier subdued the Paiutes and pacified much of Idaho, Oregon, and northern California, Crook was sent to hold an administrative post in San Francisco. His job there was to determine which soldiers should be retained and which released from service during this period of overall force reductions. Grant knew there were better ways to use him and wanted to make him commander of federal forces in Arizona. Once that territory was tamed, Crook was to be placed in command in the northern plains. But William T. Sherman, who now headed the army, opposed the appointment on the grounds that Crook, a lieutenant colonel—he had temporarily held general officer rank during the war—was too junior. In this dispute the president asserted his authority as commander-in-chief, and Crook got the job.

Thus in the summer of 1871, beginning in Arizona, the government instituted a whole new approach to the conflict with the Indians: federal forces were to keep the tribesmen on the move. Instead of hunkering down in their forts or moving only in heavily armed convoys, U.S. troops would be called upon to move swiftly in small detachments, to master the terrain and the tactics of their enemies, to take the fight to them. Crook and his troops would have to accomplish this, if such a scheme were to work, against a host of highly skilled adversaries fighting with the indomitable will of those protecting their ancestral homelands. To defeat them would require the highest level of mastery of the art of irregular warfare.

* * *

The man Grant chose to assume this challenge grew up a quiet Ohio farm boy whose father had volunteered him when the local congressman had asked whether one of his many sons might wish to go to West Point.

Theater of the Western Indian Wars

George was put forward and accepted to the U.S. Military Academy, attending during the years immediately after the war with Mexico. He graduated in 1852, ranked thirty-eighth in a class of forty-three cadets, and was immediately sent off to the Pacific Coast—by ship to Nicaragua, overland to its west coast, then at sea again for the final leg of the journey. Crook's initial duties were to keep the peace in northern California and southern Oregon. During this time he developed a great love of the wilderness and much respect for Native American peoples and cultures. Intellectual curiosity and his uncanny empathic ability to see the world through Indian eyes would serve him well.

One of Crook's closest friends during these years was John Bell Hood, who was to join the rebel cause in 1861 and would come to be known for conducting his battles with much dash but little subtlety during the Civil War. The two spent countless days hunting together. But where the wilderness soon gave Crook a great appreciation of stealth and swift raiding tactics, Hood was barely moved to question his basic notions of straightforward soldiering. Then and later, as Robert E. Lee once said of

Hood, he was "all lion, none of the fox."[3] Crook, on the other hand, very quickly showed his aptitude for bush fighting. This cleverness, along with his wise compassion, led the Native Americans to give him the sobriquet *Nantan Lupan*, the Gray Fox Chief. We shall see that he also had his share of the lion.

The first glimmers of Crook's genius for irregular warfare came in the Rogue River War in Oregon in 1856. In this fight against elusive Indian foes, he realized that the fundamental dynamic in this kind of warfare was not the clash of mass on mass but rather the challenge of finding, then engaging the enemy before he could disappear once again. It is the same challenge that counterinsurgent leaders have faced from the French fight against Abd el-Kader in the 1830s–1840s to the American struggles against the Vietcong in the 1960s, and more recently against al Qaeda and its affiliates. The lesson Crook drew from Rogue River was the value to be found in subdividing one's own force, however small it might be, so as to have many small units of maneuver hunting for the enemy rather than just one or a few big strike forces.

It was a concept of operations that worked well for Crook in the remote Far West, where he grew adept at swarming the Indians from several directions simultaneously. In a series of victorious fights he brought order to the region, albeit at the cost of an arrow in the hip whose head would stay in him the rest of his life. After Rogue River, Crook was sent farther north, taking his methods to the Columbia River basin and beyond, where he enjoyed similar successes. By 1859 he was back in southern Oregon and soon worked his way down again to San Francisco in preparation for a return trip east. He was in New York at the outset of the Civil War.

Given that the army was expanding rapidly, even a junior officer could hope to be given serious responsibilities from the start of the conflict. This was certainly the case with Crook, who was made a brevet colonel and placed in command of the Thirty-sixth Ohio Regiment, which was already deployed to West Virginia. In this area of operations the principal threat came from Confederate guerrilla fighters working in small bands, combining to mount raids and then dispersing afterward. Crook found the challenge they posed to be much like that of fighting the Indians, and his response was much as it had been on the Rogue River: break his command into a multitude of smaller units that kept themselves and, more important, the enemy on the move.

He had very good results with this approach. Rebel insurgents were kept on the run, often blundering into one of Crook's flying columns. The tactics resulted in a lot of small-scale, vicious fighting at close quarters, instead of stand-up pitched battles. But they assured that the guerrillas were in no position to terrorize the people. And West Virginia stayed securely in the Union.

The only real problem Crook had during this period was with prisoners. When trapped by his flying columns, insurgents increasingly chose to surrender rather than fight. They knew they would likely be released on parole, which they would promptly violate. This infuriated Crook and his men, who sometimes found themselves capturing a guerrilla for the second or third time. Their brutal, unethical, but practical solution to the problem was to take no more prisoners. In his autobiography, Crook described the policy this way:

> By this time every bushwhacker in the country was known, and when an officer returned from a scout he would report that they had caught so-and-so, but in bringing him in he slipped off a log while crossing a stream and broke his neck, or that he was killed by an accidental discharge of one of the men's guns, and many like reports. But they never brought back any more prisoners.[4]

Crook's counterinsurgent methods in West Virginia—which have much in common with the kind of savagery often seen on both sides in other irregular wars, from the eighteenth century to our time—troubled some of his superiors. But his results impressed them, and he rose in rank and responsibility. By the summer of 1862 he was in command of a full brigade and was drawn deeply into more conventional fighting. He was soon chagrined to see his superiors' seemingly unbounded faith in the efficacy of frontal assaults, despite the fact that they were usually hurled back with appalling loss of life.

Crook was particularly angered by events surrounding the Battle of Antietam on September 17, 1862, a terrible, bloody day in American history when nearly twenty-five thousand soldiers from both sides combined were killed or wounded. Crook fought in the battle with great distinction that day, but could not conceal his disgust for Union generalship at the higher levels. He put his view of the senior commanders' conduct in this battle quite bluntly: "Such imbecility and incompetency was simply criminal. . . . It was galling to have to serve under such people."[5]

Since Crook didn't hold these thoughts for his memoirs but actually said them out loud, including to his superiors, he soon found himself transferred back to West Virginia. Later, by the summer of 1863, he was part of the campaign in the Western theater, where he was a brevet brigadier general in command of a division at the Battle of Chickamauga. Like his Confederate counterpart Nathan Bedford Forrest, Crook saw the brief opportunity the rebels had to exploit the opportunity gained in this battle. He noted: "If the enemy had followed up his victory vigorously, I don't see how it would have been possible for the army to escape disaster."[6] (Recall that Forrest broke with Bragg over this missed opportunity. From Crook's point of view, the great rebel raider had every reason to do so.)

In 1864 Crook went east again at the request of Grant, who was taking command in the field there and of overall Union forces. Crook had caught Grant's eye, and the chief wanted smart, hard-fighting generals under him. Soon Crook was in command of a cavalry corps operating in the Shenandoah Valley under General Philip Sheridan, whom he knew from West Point and had served with in the Pacific Northwest in the 1850s. At a key battle near Winchester, Virginia, Crook employed one of his surprise flanking maneuvers that totally unhinged the Confederate position, giving the day—and more than a thousand Confederate prisoners—to the Union. Sheridan took credit for crafting the maneuver in an official report, enraging Crook. So it went.

This would not be Crook's last brush with self-aggrandizers. In another action, he came to the rescue of George Armstrong Custer, who had mounted an impetuous frontal assault on a strong rebel position. Custer was in dire straits, suffering heavy casualties, when Crook in his seemingly patented way struck the enemy from the flank, compelling them to capitulate. But it was Custer who then rode up to the enemy position himself, collecting Confederate battle flags as trophies to show his superiors. This episode and the one involving Sheridan led Crook to believe that it was "not what a person did, but it was what he got the credit for doing that gave him a reputation."[7] Such comments hardly endeared him to his military colleagues and even bothered members of government whose ears his grumbling reached.

One night, two months before the end of the war in February 1865, a Confederate guerrilla team threaded its way behind the lines and was able to capture Crook and General Benjamin Kelley at their lodgings in Cumberland, Maryland, then make good its escape. The generals were brought to Richmond, where the rebel government sought to use them to enable a prisoner exchange on favorable terms. But Edwin Stanton, the Union secretary of war, indicated that he had no intention of bringing the troublemaker Crook back. Fortunately General Grant interceded, and Crook was returned. He was soon in action again, commanding in one of the final blocking battles that prevented Robert E. Lee's escape from Grant's grasp a few days before the surrender at Appomattox.

In the wake of the war Crook returned to the Pacific Northwest, after marrying in August 1865 at the age of thirty-six. Oddly, his wife Mary's brother was one of the Confederate raiders who had captured him. The couple never had children and lived apart for long periods. Crook spent much of his time in the field during the last quarter century of his life while Mary remained at her family's estate in Oakland, Maryland. For Crook it was to be seemingly endless years of long rides on muleback—he preferred mules to horses—and camp life, punctuated by bursts of intense combat. As good as he had become at fighting the various tribes of the Pacific Northwest he grew tired of his work in this region.

When President Grant asked him to turn around the disastrous situation in Arizona, Crook's initial reaction was one of bare, grudging acceptance. But he soon realized that he would have a chance to learn about an entirely different Native American culture and would have the opportunity to test himself against irregular warriors who had confounded every single bluecoat general that had come up against them. For a thinking soldier like Crook, it was an opportunity not to be missed.

*   *   *

George Crook was something of a military mystic. A quiet man, he was given to long periods of study, reflection, and solitude. When he arrived in Arizona he camped outside the military installations he was visiting, hunted in the countryside, and spent the evenings making word lists of the Apache language. These were the things he had done to help him understand the terrain and the tribes of the Northwest, and he believed they would work in Arizona as well. He moved about with no retinue, was seldom in uniform—though he always carried a shotgun—and was once even mistaken for a common laborer and was offered a job as a mule-train packer. He politely turned down the opportunity and went his way. Like Nathan Bedford Forrest, Crook was abstemious. If he had a "brand," it was rooted in his simple ways and contemplative silences.

After some weeks of orientation and meditation, Crook was ready to act. He realized that he needed to improve his forces in two areas in order to defeat Cochise, Geronimo, and the other Apache insurgents: mobility and scouting. To increase his troops' speed of movement, he decided to operate without artillery, which he judged only slowed down a column and was of little use against enemies who refused to form up or fight from fixed positions. Crook also figured out how to strip down supplies to the bare minimum, so much so that his close colleague John Bourke said of him, "He made the study of pack-trains the study of his life."[8]

As to improving scouting, Crook realized that his bluecoats would never have sufficient ability to track the Apaches on their own, so he reached out to those who lived in and knew the country best. He first tried Mexican settlers who had learned to survive in Apache country, but they proved insufficiently aggressive in pursuit. At this point Crook had a great insight that Apaches could, and should, be used in the fight against other Apaches. He soon courted and won over the Coyotero and White Mountain tribes, who had long feuded with Cochise's Chiricahuas, promising them that whites and Indians would work together to create a secure, peaceful land. It was the kind of message and method that would be used again by American troops in Iraq during 2006–2007, when many Sunni tribal insurgents were convinced, in the name of peace, to work against al Qaeda cadres.

Crook's overture to the "enemy" generated a firestorm of criticism among white settlers in Arizona, who hewed more to the line of General Philip Sheridan that "the only good Indian is a dead Indian." Crook's superiors in the military and the government were also skeptical. But Crook persisted and soon had a force of friendly Apaches able to track their foes speedily and unerringly. At first Crook simply wanted them to point out where the Chiricahua bands were, so that his now fast-moving bluecoats could engage them. But it proved difficult to hold his scouts back, so Crook let them start the fights as well—with excellent results. This teaming of outstanding native allies and better bluecoats, operating in hard-charging flying columns, soon brought the insurgent Apaches to heel. As to Crook's insight into peeling off portions of the enemy populace to join the counterinsurgent cause, Martin Blumenson and James Stokesbury observed: "He was perhaps the first man in high places to recognize that the divisions separating groups of Indians could be used as a weapon."[9]

By the close of 1872 most of the increasingly harried Chiricahua had chosen to make peace and were on a reservation. They had no solution to the concept of operations that Crook had pioneered, which took away their sanctuaries and allowed them no respite from pursuit. Cochise, terminally ill, probably with cancer, made his sons promise to keep the peace. Geronimo also reconciled himself to reservation life. Yet his desire to raid remained strong, and it seems he sometimes went off to attack Mexican settlements south of the border. For Crook this was a time of mopping up, establishing reservations for tribes that wanted to be off on their own, and striving hard to deal justly and humanely with the many administrative details of overseeing a conquered people. It was a peaceful interlude that would not last.

* * *

In the spring of 1875 President Grant issued his next challenge to Crook: he was to deal with the Sioux and other Plains tribes who had massacred Fetterman and forced the closure of the Bozeman Trail and its protecting forts some years earlier. Always sensitive to the Indians' grievances, Crook began by devoting his efforts to expelling the whites who had gone into the Black Hills searching for gold. This was sacred territory for the Native Americans that had been ceded to them by treaty. Thus Crook tried to keep the peace; but the following year the Indians, feeling a strength that came with cross-tribal unity, moved freely, and with violence, beyond their reservation limits. A renewed war was soon under way.

The plan of battle against the Sioux-Cheyenne alliance, which could field some five thousand warriors overall, was designed by Sheridan as a three-pronged assault, not unlike General Jeffrey Amherst's ranger-led campaign against Montreal in 1760. From the north, Colonel John Gibbon led a force from Fort Shaw in Montana. Custer, nominally under the control of Brigadier General Alfred Terry, rode at the Indians from the east, starting at Fort Lincoln in North Dakota. Crook advanced from the south, beginning in Cheyenne, Wyoming. It was a conception of Napoleonic sweep; but the Indians held what the great strategist Baron Jomini called the "interior position." That is, they could mass against one or another of these columns, defeat it in detail, then move on to the next. Frederick the Great of Prussia had done this brilliantly in the eighteenth century. Now Sitting Bull and Crazy Horse would do the same.

They struck first against Crook's column of about a thousand—mostly bluecoat troopers but with a few hundred Crow and Shoshone fighters alongside them, as the Gray Fox now always sought tribal allies. In the fight at Rosebud Creek, Crook's Indian allies saved him from disaster when the Sioux and Cheyenne struck swiftly and in mass. It was something they almost never did, and they caught Crook by surprise. As one historian has described the Indian fighters, "they pressed the battle with a ferocity that astonished and disconcerted the soldiers and tested the skill of their officers."[10] Crook held on, and at the end of the day the Indians rode off; but the bluecoat advance from the south had been halted. Crook had to take his wounded to hospital and needed reinforcements before resuming his advance.

This strategic victory allowed Crazy Horse and Sitting Bull to turn next to Custer, whose impetuosity soon got him into terrible trouble. This time, unlike during the Civil War, Crook could not come to his rescue. On June 25, 1876, Custer and five troops of the famous Seventh Cavalry—more than two hundred men—were wiped out at the Little Bighorn. The Sioux and Cheyenne next turned to deal with Gibbon's column. This time they used more irregular tactics in thwarting his advance through Yellowstone country. By September Gibbon was withdrawing to wait for reinforcements and the renewal of Crook's offensive.

Crazy Horse and Sitting Bull now seemed to believe that the war was over, or at least that they had once again earned some years' respite from white encroachment. Crook and Colonel Nelson A. Miles, another enterprising Indian fighter, soon showed them the errors of their thinking. Together these officers crafted plans for a winter campaign of movement against the tribesmen, who had great difficulty fighting in winter weather. Crook hewed to his basic principle of allowing no respite to tired enemies. As the historian Russell Weigley put it, he was "always driving the Indians toward exhaustion."[11]

Miles demonstrated that he was every bit Crook's equal in this kind of fighting.[12] Indeed, an increasingly bitter rivalry between the two would soon surface. Sitting Bull saw no recourse but to escape into Canada, from which he would return to surrender. Crazy Horse, responding to an appeal from Crook, surrendered in the spring of 1877. There was talk that he would join Crook in fighting Chief Joseph of the Nez Perce, but this never came to be. Crazy Horse rode off his reservation one day, then died in a scuffle—perhaps bayoneted by a bluecoat—when he returned of his own accord.

In the campaign against the Nez Perce that followed over the summer and fall of 1877, Crook played no real part. He had been detailed off to Chicago to try to quell labor unrest there. But the press, unhappy with the slow pursuit of Chief Joseph, whom they labeled the Indian Napoleon, clamored for Crook to replace Oliver O. Howard, who showed little of Crook's penchant for hot pursuit.[13] In the end, Joseph eluded Howard but was trapped by Miles. Crook thought his Indian-fighting days were over. They were not.

*   *   *

Almost as soon as Crook left Arizona, the private contractors who took over management of the Indian reservations began to undermine the peace with corrupt practices. They would receive funds from Washington to cover the costs of running the reservations but would shortchange the Indians with inadequate food and other services, then pocket the rest of the government money. This scheme prompted rebellious behavior on the part of the Native Americans. It took years to blossom into a fully renewed insurgency, but it came nonetheless.

Geronimo was the key Apache leader in this last great rising of his people. In the late 1870s he had run off the reservation to engage in raiding—to provide for his people—and then come back. But in September 1881 Geronimo killed the chief of the reservation police and defeated a detachment from the Sixth Cavalry. He remained on the warpath thereafter, guiding a series of raids in which he was joined by a new generation of talented lieutenants, including an exceptionally gifted one named Chato.

For more than a year, into the autumn of 1882, the Apaches held the nearly uncontested initiative. They struck outlying settlements and wagon trains at will, then retreated into northern Mexico, enjoying a haven in the Sierra Madre Mountains. But Crook had returned to Arizona in September of that year, and things were soon to change. After his customary period of study and contemplation, he acted in a way that was both familiar and new: he recruited friendly Apaches to fight Geronimo, but he refrained from creating a large number of small flying columns. Instead there would be just one, and it would go deep into Mexico after the Indians, a move enabled by a "hot pursuit" treaty between the United States and Mexico that had just been signed to make such actions legal.[14]

After careful preparation, much of it consisting of finding mules of the highest quality, Crook crossed into Mexico in pursuit of his foes on May 1, 1883. His force consisted of only 250 fighters—200 of them friendly Apaches—less than half the size of Geronimo's warrior band. It was a daring move that put Crook's theories about the power of keeping on the move and the value of native allies to the ultimate test. And he passed it, for just a few weeks into this small offensive, Crook and his men came upon Geronimo's main camp—an event somewhat like the French finding Abd el-Kader's *smala*—and overran it in a short battle.

Geronimo was not there at the time of the raid, but others in the band who were nearby began to come in and surrender to Crook, whose feat and personal bravery had greatly impressed them. In the days after the battle, more than two hundred Apaches surrendered to him. Still he remained at the camp, waiting for Geronimo. When the great Apache chief arrived, Crook went out alone to meet him and his remaining warriors. This act of bravery was also respected, and in the coming days Crook and Geronimo negotiated a peace. Most of the Apaches would return to the reservation with Crook, but Geronimo and some other warriors would come in later so that they could first round up their cattle and bring the herd back with them to feed their people.[15]

Upon his return Crook, whom the press had given up for dead, was praised for his success but castigated for having trusted Geronimo to turn himself in. Retractions were necessary when the great Indian leader returned to the reservation, driving his cattle before him. And for the next two years there were no Apache attacks on troops or settlers in Arizona or New Mexico. It seemed that peace had come.

It was interrupted in the spring of 1885 when Geronimo, fearing arrest for past misdeeds, left the reservation once more.[16] His concern was unfounded, but it set off one last round of raiding. Crook viewed Geronimo's action as breaking his word of honor, and took steps to secure his territory but refrained from a new manhunt. His superiors were enraged by Crook's seeming nonchalance in the face of the renewed threat. General Sheridan now came to recommend abrogation of the treaty and removal of all Apaches to Florida. Crook, feeling that his promise to the Apaches was being broken, asked to be relieved.

His replacement was his old rival Nelson Miles, whose first act was to disband the Apache scouts. They had done much to bring peace and security to the territory but were now to be transported with the rest of the Apaches. Miles's next move was to pull together a force of some five thousand troopers to protect settlements and ride about in flying columns in search of Geronimo. His concept of operations failed completely against his enemy's ability to raid in Arizona and then return to the mountains of northern Mexico. It became clear that Miles would not succeed unless he adopted Crook's method of going into the Sierra Madre in pursuit.

Eventually Miles ordered one of his subordinates to do just this. Geronimo was found and surrendered for the last time in September 1886, based on the assurance that he would not be punished further. But he and his people *were* punished. They were separated and transported east. Crook, now a much-honored major general with his headquarters in Chicago, fought for their release unsuccessfully for the rest of his life, which was all too short. He died of a heart attack in 1890 at the age of sixty-one. In the same year the official census declared there was no longer a "contiguous frontier."

10

VELDT RIDER: CHRISTIAAN DE WET

Bundesarchiv Bild

At the same time the Indian tribes of the American West were mounting their fierce resistance to the onrush of settlement and development, a number of South African tribes were doing the same, most notably the Bantus and the Zulus. Like the Indians, they too had sterling military qualities, particularly the Zulus. But there was one big difference between the situations: in South Africa one of the "tribes," having settled there more than two hundred years earlier, was white.

In 1652, the start of an era in which the Netherlands would hold its own in a series of naval wars with Britain, the Dutch East India Company established a way station at the southern tip of Africa. The settlement grew and expanded over the years, with the original Dutch settlers joined by French and German Protestants. Together they came to call themselves Afrikaners (People of Africa) and developed a variant of the Dutch language, Afrikaans, that all spoke. They drove the Hottentot tribe from the growing and grazing lands that they coveted, and prospered uninterrupted until the early nineteenth century.

At this point Napoleon Bonaparte brought Britain into their lives, seemingly to stay. For when the Netherlands came under the control of the French Empire in 1806—Bonaparte's brother Louis was made king of Holland—the Royal Navy went off to protect the Cape colony in the name of the deposed Dutch monarch. Somehow South Africa was never returned, being formally annexed by Britain in 1814, perhaps a partial reward for its long struggle against Napoleon.

Tensions soon rose between the British and the Afrikaners, also called Boers from their word for farmer.[1] The principal problem was that the British were opposed to the Boers' enslavement and poor treatment of indigenous African tribes. Bridling at what they considered a most undue intrusion into their way of life, several thousand Boers set off on a "great trek" north from the Cape across the prairies (the *Veldt*, or field). During the period 1835–1837, they established a multitude of small, free republics where they could do as they wished—whereas their Boer brothers who remained in the Cape had to toe the British line.

Despite the distance the Boers covered in the great trek, British attempts to reassert control never ended. One of the Boer republics, Natalia, was snapped up by the British in 1843 and renamed Natal. But in the 1850s the empire did recognize the two most viable republics, the Transvaal and the Orange Free State. Both were landlocked but prosperous and quite independent-minded. Yet in the face of growing Zulu power and aggressiveness, the Boers were again drawn closer to the British, and the Transvaal was annexed in 1877. The Zulu threat abated after the War of 1879, but early British military reverses in that conflict—particularly the massacre of about a thousand Redcoats at Isandlwana—encouraged the Boers, all fine horsemen and great shots, to think that winning their freedom back might not be so difficult.

This assumption turned out to be correct, as the Transvaal was able to regain its independence in 1881 after the Boers inflicted a most severe defeat on a much larger British field army at a place called Majuba. The British tried to form up and fight using massed rifle volleys while the Boers fired independently and with great accuracy from behind cover, moving in stealthily for their final charge. One of the young Boer fighters was a farmer in his late twenties, Christiaan de Wet, upon whom this battle left a lasting impression about British susceptibility to bush-fighting tactics. When war came again, his would be one of the principal voices arguing against fighting toe-to-toe with the British in favor of a more irregular approach, and he would become the preeminent Boer guerrilla fighter.

From the Battle of Majuba forward, Anglo-Boer relations were never truly repaired. Indeed, they worsened, as in 1884 the British only grudgingly and with loudly voiced dissatisfaction gave up their efforts to ensure better Boer treatment of the Bantu. Then in 1887 gold was discovered in the Transvaal—the largest gold strike in history, and to this day the world's most important source of the precious metal. Soon all manner of *uitlanders* were coming into the Transvaal to seek their fortunes. It was like the Black Hills gold rush in Sioux country a decade earlier in North America, and it caused just as much resentment.

One way the Boers tried to cope with the influx, most of which was British, was to impose strict controls on the interlopers. Among their many constraints, outlanders were even denied the right to vote. These efforts only deepened the hard feelings of the immigrants, who by this point, as Winston Churchill noted, "equaled the native Boers in numbers . . . [and] contributed all but one-twentieth of the country's taxation."[2] But the Boers' efforts to enjoy the commercial gains from immigrant investment and labor while mitigating the potential political and social consequences only made the explosion greater when it finally came.

Tension continued to mount steadily over the next few years, much of it fomented by Cecil Rhodes, who had made a great fortune in diamonds at nearby Kimberley and who wanted in on the gold as well. He became prime minister of the Cape Colony in 1890 and maneuvered continually from this position toward the goal of outright annexation of the Transvaal. He even conspired to stage a private military invasion in the belief that conquest of the Boers would be welcomed by Queen Victoria—much as

Giuseppe Garibaldi's unsanctioned landing in Sicily in 1860 came to be embraced by Victor Emmanuel. The attack was to be led by a friend of Rhodes, one Leander Jameson, a medical man who had drifted into more mercenary activities. At the last moment Rhodes balked. Jameson, who seemingly missed the signal to stand down, went ahead. But he was no Garibaldi, and the invasion of the Transvaal proved an utter disaster.

The so-called Jameson Raid in 1895 brought the lingering crisis to a new level of intensity and gave it a greater international quality. In support of the Boers, Kaiser Wilhelm of Germany publicly congratulated them on defeating the invasion and sent a cruiser from his rapidly growing navy to Delagoa Bay as a signal of his dissatisfaction with Britain's aggressive behavior. On the other side, Jameson became something of a folk hero to jingoistic pub and saloon patrons in Britain and America—and Mark Twain traveled to the Transvaal to meet with some of the jailed raiders.

Over the next few years some negotiations occurred, but the chasm between the two sides was far greater than even the most skillful diplomacy could have hoped to bridge. For at heart the British goal was reannexation while the Boers' very firm intent was to maintain their independence. Thus the period 1895–1898 was one of continuing drift toward conflict. By 1899 the days of peace were running out. The Boers were acquiring excellent German Mauser rifles, accurate at ranges over a mile, while the British were sending troops, amassing a force of more than twenty thousand by September of that year.

Curiously the British made a decision to use no soldiers of color, even though their Indian Army had extensive and recent experience in both conventional and irregular warfare, much of it against Afghan tribes. As L. S. Amery, general editor of the seven-volume *Times History of the War in South Africa*, wrote: "It was held inadvisable to make use of any but white soldiers in a war fought between white men in a country where the black man presents so difficult a problem."[3] The Boers felt the same way, and of course few native Africans were likely to side with them. All that now remained was to see which side would start this whites-only war on the "dark continent."

The wait ended in October 1899 when the Boers took the offensive with more than forty thousand riders, their numbers a tribute to a conscription system that called upon all males between sixteen and sixty to serve in small *Kommando* units, usually with 100 to 150 riders in each. Moving swiftly, they struck against scattered British forces, about half their size in the aggregate, driving toward Ladysmith in Natal to the east, Kimberley to the west, and Mafeking in the north. They did not ride south into the Cape colony, reckoning they would rather see the British struggle to come north over great distances. It was eight hundred miles from Capetown to Pretoria, and the lack of roads would tether the British to easily disrupted rail lines.

After their first rush forward in the opening months of the war, the Boers—too few to take cities by storm and lacking the heavy artillery needed to batter them into submission—were slowed by the need to besiege their three main objectives. Yet when the first British relief forces under the unimaginative Sir Redvers Buller came along, simultaneously but separately, to lift these sieges, the Boers dealt roughly with them. The series of reverses, occurring from December 10 to 17, 1899, came to be known in Britain as "Black Week."

Just a short while earlier, de Wet had played an important role in a great victory in Natal, cleverly outmaneuvering a British force five times the size of his *Kommando* at Nicholson's Nek. There, striking at them much as Forrest would have, de Wet took a thousand prisoners, the largest surrender of British troops in a century. It was a reverse that affected British morale as badly as any of the defeats in December.[4]

In the wake of his victory, de Wet was promoted to general in December 1899 and spent Black Week making his way from the Natal front to help out General Piet Cronje in the Orange Free State. Cronje was facing off against a fresh and much larger British force under a new and much better British commander, Field Marshal Lord Frederick Roberts, an old India hand now at the head of a concentration of more than seventy-five thousand troops. Cronje hoped to confront this new threat directly while de Wet sought to disrupt Roberts's lines of communication and supply. In the early days of 1900, both approaches were pursued.

Cronje kept most of his forces together—more than four thousand men—preparing for a defensive battle against the more numerous invaders. With a few small *Kommandos*, de Wet rode about raiding here and there, diverting perhaps a third of the British main force. But this still left nearly fifty thousand troops coming down upon Cronje. When de Wet warned him of this, suggesting a timely retreat, his superior dressed him down in front of others, pointing toward the British and asking "Are you afraid of things like that?"[5] Cronje's stubbornness led to his whole force being trapped at Paardeberg.

De Wet cobbled together a relief column of some thousand riders from a number of *Kommandos* and attacked a vulnerable point in the British cordon, opening a narrow escape route. He held it against all British counterattacks for almost three days. But Cronje, still hoping for a head-on firefight, reluctant to leave his guns and supplies in a headlong retreat, and perhaps even in shock over what was happening, refused to move. De Wet finally had to retire, and Cronje and his whole force surrendered on February 27, 1900, the nineteenth anniversary of the victory at Majuba in the first war with the British.

Now the Boers had suffered their own crushing equivalent of Black Week, and Roberts was swift to seize the moment and press the offensive. But Cronje's capture led to de Wet being given overall command in the Free State, and now he intended to make mobile hit-and-run raiding the core of his concept of operations. In the events that followed, de Wet would cause endless trouble for the British advance, delaying a huge force with a relative handful of riders. Much like Nathan Bedford Forrest in the American Civil War, de Wet focused on attacking communications and transportation infrastructure. Like Forrest too, de Wet was indefatigable, almost always at the forefront of the fight. One firsthand British observer of the war, Arthur Conan Doyle, the creator of Sherlock Holmes, whose account of the Boer War was a massive best-seller in Britain, summed up how de Wet was viewed by the enemy: he was known simply as "the great de Wet."[6] And Conan Doyle made this assessment even before witnessing any of de Wet's more remarkable accomplishments during the war's later phases.

*   *   *

After the crushing defeat at Paardeberg, the Boers tottered on the brink of capitulation. Roberts certainly thought the war was won, and on March 15, 1900, he offered amnesty to all Boer fighters willing to return to their farms. Quite a few took him up on this offer. But many Boers remained in the field, fighting in small rearguard actions here and there. De Wet, however, sought ways to take the strategic offensive once again. But instead of fighting the British straight up, as the Boers had chosen to do at the outset of the war, he realized that, as Thomas Pakenham has observed, "the overwhelming numerical superiority of the British now demanded new strategy from the Boers. Indeed, the commando system was best suited not to large-scale, set-piece battles, but to smaller-scale, guerrilla strikes."[7]

De Wet now proceeded to unfold this new strategy in a series of sharp actions that disrupted the British advance. First, at a place called Sanna's Post, de Wet ambushed a column of several thousand cavalry and mounted infantry, attacking them on one flank to drive them into the rest of his small force, which he had positioned to lie in wait along their anticipated line of retreat. The result: British losses of nearly two hundred killed and wounded, and more than four hundred prisoners taken. De Wet lost three

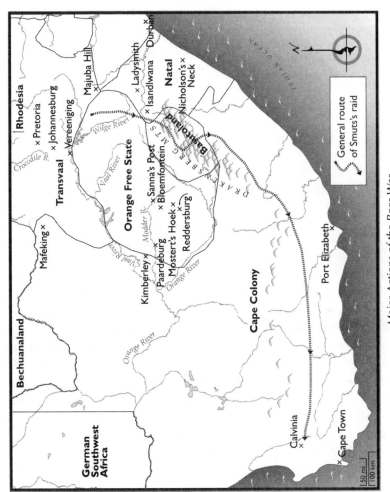

Major Actions of the Boer War

killed and five wounded. The British could not believe that a poorly edu-cated farmer-turned-soldier of middle years was capable of such sophistica-tion, and they soon spread the false rumor that Captain Carl Reichmann, the American military attaché in the field with de Wet as an observer, had actually conducted the battle.[8]

Just days after the action at Sanna's Post, de Wet's scouts informed him of a slow-moving column of some five hundred British infantry head-ing in the direction of Reddersburg. De Wet pounced on them swiftly, augmenting his force by re-recruiting some of the Reddersburg men who had just weeks before accepted Roberts's amnesty offer. De Wet soon had the British trapped on a ridge known as Mostert's Hoek, where his forces inflicted fifty casualties and captured all the remaining British troops. Thus a second remarkable victory was achieved in the span of one week running from late March to early April 1900.

For the Boers these victories were a tonic, shoring up both their mo-rale and their strategic position, and giving Roberts serious doubts about how and whether to resume his advance. Byron Farwell has argued that de Wet's actions were the key to sustaining the Boer effort in the aftermath of the catastrophic defeat at Paardeberg: "The war might indeed have been brought to a close as quickly as Roberts anticipated had it not been for one of the most remarkable men to emerge from the Boer ranks, a leader who did truly become a legendary figure in his own time: Christiaan de Wet."[9]

But, as so often happens in war, the crucial moment, the inflec-tion point, is missed or misinterpreted—and the great victory or string of victories is not properly exploited. This was to be de Wet's fate. Briefly, the situation now afforded him the opportunity to employ the regained initiative to launch a deep-striking raid into the Cape Colony. This move would completely cripple the logistical supports of the British advance, al-lowing the Boer sieges of Kimberley, Mafeking, and Ladysmith to come to successful conclusions. A deep raid by de Wet would also incite many of the descendants of those Boers who had refrained from making the Great Trek and stayed under British rule to rise up against the empire. Instead de Wet spent more than two weeks trying to wipe out a force of Boer Cape colonists who had decided to join up and fight on the British side.

These "turncoat" units that de Wet tracked down were Brabant's Horse and the Cape Mounted Rifles. He thought of them this way: "They were Afrikaners, and as Afrikaners, although neither Free-Staters nor Transvaalers, they ought, in our opinion, to have been ashamed to fight against us."[10] They were indeed Boers, these two thousand men of the Cape who cast their lot with the British, and they fought hard and well.

Although surrounded, they held off de Wet, who broke his own new rules about avoiding pitched battles. Out of hatred of these pro-British Boers, he kept calling in more reinforcements, eventually amassing about six thousand riders over the two weeks of the fighting. Still the Capemen held out; and when a British relief force arrived, de Wet barely made good his escape.

Thus the opportunity to take the war south was missed. De Wet would try to invade the Cape late in 1900, and again early in 1901, and would be driven off both times, as by now the British expeditionary forces were numerous enough to provide area coverage that made such deep strikes impractical. One of de Wet's young colleagues, Jan Smuts, eventually mounted a major raid that wound up in the more poorly protected, more sparsely populated western reaches of the Cape colony, where he operated until the end of the war. But by the time of Smuts's initiative, the main Boer field armies had long been defeated, the British logistical infrastructure was well secured, and the Cape Boers were largely cowed into quiescence. "Too late" is one of war's most tragic refrains.

The strategic initiative was now back in Roberts's hands, shored up by the more than doubling of his overall forces during 1900 to over two hundred thousand men. He made good use of his material advantages, advancing on more than one axis and benefiting from the willingness of the Boers to continue fighting him in mostly conventional ways. Soon the city sieges were lifted, the relief of Mafeking in May 1900 being most dramatic as its garrison commander, Robert Baden-Powell—later to be the founder of the international Scouting movement—had held out heroically against the Boers for 217 days.

With the sieges lifted, all that remained was for Roberts to make his way into the Boer heartland and capture the three main cities of Bloemfontein, Johannesburg, and Pretoria. He was smart enough to know that he had to keep moving fast to avoid another "Boer revival" during a pause. So he drove his subordinate commanders and his field forces to the point of exhaustion. His risk in doing so was mitigated by what Winston Churchill—who was covering the war as a journalist—described in his articles home as the "feeble resistance" of the Boers still trying to block Roberts's advance.[11]

De Wet's raiders, however, operating far behind the lines of advance, comprised an element of the Boer resistance that was hardly feeble. He and his troopers continued to strike at will against the railroads as well as to swoop down on small garrisons and detachments on the move. In all, the actions of his handful of *Kommandos* diverted roughly half of Roberts's forces. Indeed, Roberts was so nettled by de Wet's stinging blows that he began to organize formal "de Wet hunts." The first employed almost fifty thousand troops in search-and-cordon operations—and was a complete failure. The second used fewer troops and began to rely more heavily upon several flying columns, the idea being to flush out de Wet, much as more than half a century earlier Bugeaud had used a similar technique to try to catch Abd el-Kader. This didn't work either.

Still, the fall of Pretoria in June 1900 and the mopping up of other Boer main forces convinced Roberts—and Queen Victoria—that the British had won the war. Late in the year Roberts sailed for home, arriving in Britain on January 2, 1901, to a massive public welcome. He was then taken to see the queen, who made him an earl and a Knight of the Garter. On the basis of his triumph he was named Britain's military commander-in-chief, replacing Garnet Wolseley, who was made the scapegoat for the string of early British disasters suffered at the hands of the Boers.

A few weeks later Queen Victoria died, bringing an end to a reign that had lasted more than sixty-three years and given its name to an era. With her also would die British Victorian notions of war as following set rules and conventions, as a noble undertaking guided by insights drawn from the Enlightenment. Christiaan de Wet and some of his more stalwart countrymen were about to herald the emergence of an age of full-blown guerrilla warfare; and the often savage British response to the challenge from these Boer holdouts soon wiped away any remaining Victorian notions about the basic forms and niceties of conflict. Total war was at hand.

*   *   *

There was much consternation in the Boer camps after the fall of Pretoria. One of de Wet's great compatriots, Koos De la Rey, tried to take the city back, massing some six thousand troops for the counterattack. But this was just the sort of fighting the British excelled at, and De la Rey was easily driven off. Many other Boers had surrendered—roughly fifteen thousand were now in captivity—and more were coming in every day to accept the British terms of surrender. Among them was de Wet's brother Piet, whose capitulation Christiaan deemed so odious that he never spoke to him again.[12]

For Christiaan de Wet, the simple, pious farmer and father of sixteen children, there could be no question about whether to fight on. The Boer struggle for freedom was, to his mind, an unquestionably just cause; the only issue now was whether to adjust strategy once more. Given that the British were swarming throughout their country, and that the numbers of Boer fighters had been sharply reduced, largely by captures and surrenders that had taken twenty thousand riders out of their saddles,[13] de Wet felt compelled to make yet another strategic shift.

At a remote farm where he was able to rest from pursuers and gather some key colleagues, de Wet outlined an ambitious plan for the next phase of the war. While steeped in the doctrine of hit-and-run raiding, de Wet's strategy also called for a major organizational change: the *Kommandos* were to break into even smaller units than their usual 100 to 150 riders, and were to be widely dispersed. Their goal was to cause the greatest discomfiture for the British. De Wet summed up the plan this way:

> We were of the opinion that we should be able to do better work if we divided the *Kommandos* into small parties. We could not risk any great battles, and, if we divided our forces, the English would have to divide their forces too.[14]

Over the next year and more, his strategy would not only do "better work"; it would give the British fits and drive them to practices that would come to be reviled around the world.

The principal target of this global opprobrium was to be General Horatio Herbert Kitchener, who devised new methods for fighting the Boers that went well beyond the dispatch of flying columns. Kitchener, who had defeated Mahdist forces at the Battle of Omdurman in the Sudan just two years earlier, was given virtually free reign to do what was necessary to end a war that his government had believed was already over. His plan for South Africa was to control the countryside with a network of garrisoned blockhouses and barbed-wire enclosures. Hunter-killer patrols were then to drive the Boers into these fixed, fortified positions. Regarding the insurgents' ability to hide among the people, Kitchener's solution was to drain the *Veldt* of all sympathetic civilians, denying the Boers any sources of shelter and supply. In practice this meant herding tens of thousands of women and children into what Kitchener called "concentration camps," and seizing or burning crops and farms.

Disease soon spread through the camps, causing thousands of deaths and kindling an antiwar rage among the world's nascent civil society organizations. The best known protester was Emily Hobhouse of Britain, a leader of the South African Women and Children's Distress Fund and of the "Ladies Committee" that brought British and world attention not only to the squalid conditions of the camps but to the atrocities committed by imperial troops against Boer civilians.[15] She interviewed many women in the camps, recording their eyewitness accounts of murder and rape. These revelations led to a firestorm of public criticism, increasing pressure on the government to rein in Kitchener. But the fact that his methods seemed to be working against the guerrillas made Whitehall slow to act. Indeed, the concentration camps would continue in existence for a year after the war's end in 1902.

How well did this brutal approach work? Not nearly well enough. Many small Boer bands were caught by Kitchener's methods, as his forces had now been doubled to more than four hundred thousand, and were able to cover or search most of the *Veldt*. But a few thousand Boers soldiered on, inflicting stinging blows and evading British pursuit. In tactical engagements they continued to hold the advantage in mobility, being all mounted, as well as in marksmanship at ranges up to and beyond a mile. The smokeless powder they used made it hard for the British to track them, even when they were enclosed in set traps.

De Wet discovered that, even when caught in a British "drive," he and his men could still select which part of the line of blockhouses they would hit in their breakout attempt. Thus he was able to achieve local superiority long enough to escape, sometimes even to wait for pursuers to come to the breach he had made, ambushing them upon their arrival. On other occasions de Wet's forces would break into many small groups and travel separately to a new rally point. The Boers' supple organizational structure made all this possible. Indeed, it was this fluidity that most impressed the great American strategist and apostle of sea power, Alfred Thayer Mahan, who observed from the very outset of the war: "Every Boer organization seems susceptible of immediate dissolution into its component units, each of independent vitality, and of subsequent reunion in some assigned place."[16]

Throughout 1901 de Wet was regularly able to elude his pursuers via this method of breaking down and later recombining his forces. Soon it became clear to him, as he noted in his memoir, that the British "had lost all faith in their blockhouses."[17] But Kitchener was a resourceful man with huge numbers of troops at his command, so instead of continuing in his attempts to drive the Boers into the fixed, immobile lines of blockhouses, he increased the size of his flying columns, put them on each compass point of massive squares he had drawn on his map, and ordered them all to move inward. Given that his walls were now moving, and "thicker," Kitchener had posed a problem very nearly beyond de Wet's ability to cope.

Perhaps the most dangerous of this new kind of British drive came in February 1902—still summertime in the southern hemisphere—when Kitchener amassed more than fifty thousand troops for another "de Wet hunt." This time it seemed that none of the Boers would get away; but de

Wet created his own series of flying columns bent on escape, staggering the timing of their movements so that British reinforcements would leap to join their compatriots who had made first contact, creating gaps other Boers could ride through.

In this manner de Wet and many of his remaining two thousand riders escaped the greatest of Kitchener's traps—although one of his breakout groups was sacrificed and four hundred men were captured. Needless to say, this radical escape plan made it impossible for the Boers to bring their cattle along with them. So de Wet remained free to fight, but he and his men were terribly worn, hungry, and increasingly dispirited. Their only hope was that the British were just as war weary, that public opposition to the war had grown to a critical level, and that a negotiated peace was still possible. It was, despite all the bitterness on both sides.

In a development similar to the end of the French war against Abd el-Kader, mutual agreement was finally reached. It came in May 1902, and the terms, beyond calling for Boer recognition of British sovereignty, were surprisingly lenient—perhaps because of how hard and closely fought this war had been. Indeed, the Treaty of Vereeniging even called for the immediate payment of millions of pounds in compensation for the suffering of the Afrikaners, in and outside the camps. The agreement also held out the hope of self-governance and, later, independence.

It was a treaty good enough to bring even diehards like de Wet on board. He signed as president of the Free State and in a few years would actually join the government as minister of agriculture. Other fighters were also determined to remake their land under the rubric of British rule, Jan Smuts among them. But when World War I broke out in 1914, and imperial troops headed off to Europe, some old Boers, de Wet among them—though he was almost sixty now—decided this was the moment to strike again for their freedom. Their rebellion lasted about three months, put down by some of their old comrades-in-arms who saw only treachery in the uprising. One of these new loyalists to the empire was Jan Smuts, who would even hold a seat in the British War Cabinet. He would also play a role in the campaign against the Germans in East Africa, the subject of the next chapter.

De Wet was captured by a pro-British Boer, tried and convicted for armed insurrection, and sentenced to six years in prison. He was out in a year. He was worn out too, spending his last years quietly, dying in 1922 at the age of sixty-seven. But the remarkably effective fight he masterminded against a vastly superior foe—so redolent of the operations of Denis Davydov, Abd el-Kader, and Nathan Bedford Forrest—still resonates loudly among all those today who think about or are called upon to fight in irregular wars.

11

BUSH FIGHTER:
PAUL VON LETTOW-VORBECK

British Army File photo

Germany was a latecomer to the infamous "scramble for Africa," gaining its colonies there only during the decade before the Anglo-Boer War. Perhaps this was due to German unification having occurred so recently, in the immediate wake of the Franco-Prussian War (1870–1871), or possibly because the press of Continental power politics had so captured the German mind for several centuries. Maybe the Reich looked outward now because its young Kaiser Wilhelm II had become enthralled with Alfred Thayer Mahan's ideas about sea power and the need for far-flung ports and coaling stations. Whatever the reasons for coming late to colonialism, Germany quickly showed a real appetite for it. Wherever they settled—and there were four holdings in Africa from which to choose: Togo, Cameroon, South-West Africa and East Africa—German colonists brought a passion for order. But they also proved just as prone to exploit and brutalize the native populations as any of the other imperial European powers.

Misrule led to bloody, militarily vexing insurgencies in three of their four colonies in the years before World War I, giving the Germans "plenty of scope for humiliation," as the historian Thomas Pakenham wrote.[1] The natives fought guerrilla-style against German forces whose outlook was overwhelmingly conventional; and few of these troops actually had combat experience, given that the last war their country waged was in Europe more than thirty years earlier, against the French.

The most serious uprising took place in South-West Africa (Namibia today) in 1904–1905, when two tribes rebelled, one after the other. The Herero acted first, having become fed up with German expropriation of their cattle and exploitation of their women. After them came the Nama, whose motivations were more mystically inclined, having to do with a self-appointed "sacred mission" to rid Africa of the troublesome whites. Each tribe resorted to guerrilla tactics, the Nama proving far more adept. They fielded no more than a few hundred fighters, but nonetheless kept a German force of more than fifteen thousand troops hopping all over the Kalahari Desert for many months.

The insurgency in South-West Africa was largely over by the end of 1905, concluded more by German doggedness than military skill. But a few of the Kaiser's officers learned a great deal from this campaign. One of them was Paul von Lettow-Vorbeck, a career soldier who had fought as part of the international force that relieved the siege of the European legations in Peking during the Boxer Rebellion of 1900 in China. He had thrown himself into counterinsurgent operations in the Kalahari with a passion, being often at the leading edge of the action. This sort of initiative led to his suffering serious wounds to the chest and left eye. He was taken for treatment to South Africa, where he spent time visiting with many former Boer fighters during his convalescence.

Meanwhile another rebellion arose, this time in German East Africa (Tanzania today) by the Maji Maji. But this one was swiftly put down, by just a few hundred troops and at a fraction of the cost of the campaign in the South-West colony. By the end of this revolt, the German home government was beginning to realize that colonial misrule and corruption were serious problems, and that reform measures were necessary. Soon East Africa became a colony where progressive measures were pioneered, and with some success. Unlike the heavy jungles of Togo and Cameroon, or the aridity of the South-West colony, East Africa's harsher environs were offset by mountains, lakes, and a modicum of reasonably arable land. Its native population of six million began to come into some kind of existential understanding with the six thousand German settlers.

Thus the last years of peace before the Great War broke out were prosperous, peaceful ones for German East Africa. And even as the storm clouds gathered over Europe, there was hope that any major conflict could be contained there and not spread to the colonies. The basis for this hope was the Congo Act of 1885. It arose from the proceedings of German chancellor Otto von Bismarck's Berlin Conference, in which all the colonial powers agreed to refrain from bringing war to central Africa in the event of an outbreak of conflict in Europe. Somehow, it was hoped, mother countries could go to war while their colonies in the Congo River basin would remain neutral. It was not to be. In the circumlocution of one member of the House of Lords at the time, it was held that "the Berlin Act remains in force, except insofar as it has been abrogated."[2]

On some level the German central government understood that this attitude would prevail, and realized that any war with Britain on the opposing side would result in their overseas colonies being isolated from the fatherland and conquered one by one. It was also accepted that the massive German naval buildup during the prewar years—aimed at countering the Royal Navy in the North Sea—would prove virtually useless for purposes of breaking the British maritime stranglehold on the colonies. While some effort was made to create small but swift and powerful naval task forces to mount far-ranging attacks, complemented by a handful of lone-wolf raiding vessels, this form of *Kreuzerkrieg* (cruiser warfare) could at best be used simply to distract the British and perhaps delay or disrupt their offensive moves.

When war did come, most German raiders were quickly dealt with, their positions betrayed by radio reports sent by the ships they were attacking. And the great cruiser squadron commanded by the Graf von Spee, after winning an engagement at Coronel, was destroyed soon after in a sea fight off the Falkland Islands.[3] Not much help from the sea would come to the German colonies.

All that was left, then, for German strategic planners was to try to beef up their colonial armies. In Africa these were comprised mostly of native troops, with a small leavening of German officers. The forces were quite small, usually just a few thousand troops, far less than the size of the expeditionary force the Germans had sent to the South-West colony in 1904–1905. In East Africa, for example, the entire defense force at the outbreak of war in 1914 consisted of a little over 2,500 native Askaris and about 250 Germans. In all, this amounted to roughly a brigade-strength *Schutztruppe* that was assigned the task of defending a territory the size of Germany and France combined.

Given the need to concentrate manpower in Europe, where German war plans contemplated having to fight both in the east and the west (the famous Schlieffen Plan was designed to knock out France quickly, then to focus on Russia), hardly a man could be spared for the colonies. But in the case of German East Africa, one man was indeed sent: von Lettow. After his experience in South-West Africa, he had held a staff position back in Germany. Then, from 1909 to 1913, he commanded a detachment of marines, the closest thing the Germans had at the time to troops ready to fight in irregular settings.

Just four months before the outbreak of war in Europe in August 1914, von Lettow—a minor nobleman, he signed his letters only as "Lettow" when corresponding with his equals and betters—was sent to East Africa with orders to prepare the colony for effective defense against a likely British invasion. He was the right man to dispatch, being the German army's most experienced colonial warfare officer. From the day he arrived he began to think about creative ways in which he could use his tiny force to tie up huge enemy concentrations, thus helping to relieve pressure on his comrades who would be fighting on the main battlefields in Europe.

Over the course of the next four years this middle-aged man (he was forty-four at the start of the war) would conduct a vigorous, vexing, and highly effective campaign against overwhelming material odds in one of the world's most extreme climates and over some of its roughest terrain. He would be wounded in combat, suffer multiple bouts of malaria, and would even have to expend precious energy in an extended bureaucratic contretemps with the German colonial governor, Heinrich Schnee, who kept hoping that the Congo Act—which the British chose to subvert from the very outset of the war—might somehow be revived to restore peace.

In the face of all these obstacles and challenges, von Lettow rose up and mastered them—but not simply by reverting to hit-and-run guerrilla tactics from the beginning. No, his particular brilliance was in seeing how irregular concepts of operations could be used to engage the main conventional forces of the enemy. It is this innovation that should most interest us, and which most befuddled his British foes.

*   *   *

From the opening days of the war, the British viewed German East Africa as ripe for plucking. It was surrounded by colonies of the Allied powers: Britain's East Africa (mostly today's Kenya), Rhodesia, and Nyasaland; the Belgian Congo; and, from 1916 when Portugal decided to join the war against Germany, Mozambique. The Royal Navy's command of the sea

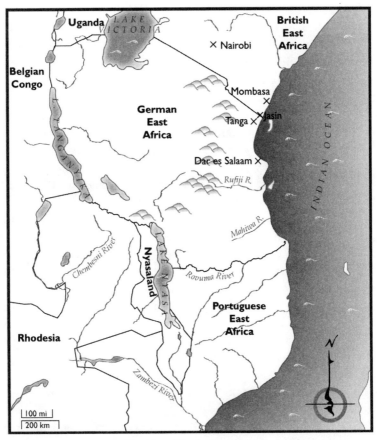

The Great War in East Africa

completed the envelopment of the seemingly helpless German colony. Thus there were many avenues of approach by land and along the coast, and only a relative handful of defenders, most of them native tribesmen armed with weapons dating from the Franco-Prussian War. However good an officer von Lettow might be, he had only a few months to work his small *Schutztruppe* into shape before war came in August 1914.

Von Lettow realized that there was simply no way to mount a conventional defense of the colony by concentrating his force in one place and trying to use his "interior position" to strike at one or another of the invaders as they came. This approach would have been classically German, echoing the strategy employed by Frederick the Great in the Seven Years' War (1756–1763) when he struck in turn from his central position against invading French, Austrian, and Russian armies. Von Lettow knew that this method would not work. The distances involved were too great, and his forces were far too few.

So instead of massing the *Schutztruppe* centrally, he broke his small army into many smaller detachments, usually of just 100 to 150 Askaris and a few German officers in each, then dispersed them around the frontiers of the colony. The idea was that each small detachment could fight an initial holding action when it came under attack; other nearby companies of the *Schutztruppe* would then come in support as needed. They would be like the antibodies of the human immune system. The whole concept of operations was made possible by von Lettow's faith in the fighting qualities of the native African troops, whose language he spoke—he was fluent in English too—and whose culture he respected, right down to allowing their families to accompany them in the field.

Aside from deploying to defend the borders, von Lettow also placed garrisons in the main coastal cities of Tanga and Dar es Salaam in the event of an amphibious invasion. Tanga was in the north, quite near the border with British East Africa, and it was here that the British chose to strike first, taking maximum advantage of their sea power. Early in November 1914 they sent an expedition of some eight thousand troops, along with a naval task force, against about two hundred German and Askari defenders. The first wave of roughly two thousand was decimated by a spirited resistance that reflected another of von Lettow's innovations: the idea of breaking his small companies into even smaller combat teams, built around individual machine-gun and sniper nests that fired for a while, then moved to new locations.

The successful initial holding action gave von Lettow time to come to the scene himself and bring additional troops, quickly raising the number of defenders to more than a thousand. The British still felt they had the edge and brought the rest of their force ashore. But when they advanced en masse against the very skillfully positioned fire teams of the defenders, they were once again beaten back. At the cost of a handful of casualties, von Lettow's forces inflicted heavy losses on the invaders: more than eight hundred dead and about five hundred wounded. The British knew they were beaten and decided to pull back to their ships and sail away.

At this point von Lettow's chivalrous side manifested itself clearly. He agreed to a truce to provide time to bury the dead and send the wounded back with the British, and even hosted a dinner for his foes before they departed. He may have been a fierce fighter with a keen, cold strategic mind, but he was also a gentleman. While the end of the Victorian Era may have seen the British immediately begin setting up concentration camps in South Africa, von Lettow was determined to wage the ideal of a "war without hate" in East Africa.

Much has been made of von Lettow's sterling character by historians and biographers, all of whom concur about his personal warmth, sense of honor, and unrelenting willpower. Among the more revealing insights into the man are reflections by the Danish writer Isak Dinesen (the *nom de plume* of Karen Blixen), who in 1914 had traveled on the same steamer to Africa with him. She was so taken with von Lettow that she wrote to her mother about him at the time, "He has been such a friend to me." Years later Dinesen wrote of von Lettow, "He belongs to the olden days, and I have never met another German who has given me so strong an impression of what Imperial Germany was and stood for."[4]

One of the attendees at the "farewell dinner" in Tanga was a bright British intelligence officer, Richard Meinertzhagen, who would also become a great admirer of von Lettow—and who was to be one of T. E. Lawrence's main "handlers" in the Arab revolt a few years later. As it turned out, Meinertzhagen would draw on lessons from von Lettow's concept of operations when working with Lawrence in the campaign against the Ottoman Turks. It is also important to observe that the British acceptance of von Lettow's truce-and-dinner offer spoke well of their higher intentions about fighting justly.

This sense of fair play extended even to occasions later in the campaign when von Lettow, out of almost all but the briefest contact with Germany by radio—his main stations having been captured or destroyed—was approached by the British who would then inform him of such things as his receipt of the *Pour le Mérite* and his promotion to major general. This said, the British did not hesitate to use a faked radio message that caused

Zeppelin L59, coming with supplies from Germany, to turn home without fulfilling its mission.

After the disaster at Tanga, the Royal Navy tried a descent upon Dar es Salaam, subjecting the city to a sharp bombardment. But the defenders returned a fierce and accurate fire, inflicting damage on a number of British vessels. Realizing that the city would be a tough target to capture from the sea, the attackers gave up and sailed off. In the wake of this failure, the British next tried a straightforward overland invasion from the north, briefly occupying the town of Jasin. But here von Lettow's concept worked yet again, his small teams driving the British out of the town in bitter house-to-house fighting.

Not content with remaining on the defensive, von Lettow seized the initiative in 1915, mounting a swarm of raids on the British East African railroad line that ran for some four hundred miles between the port of Mombasa and Nairobi. The attacks were near constant, as von Lettow had subdivided his forces even further, all the way down to units of six to eight fighters. They were able to travel fast and light, and made maximum use of explosives to disrupt the line. There were so many of these little units that the British came to think that the German force in East Africa was far greater in size than it actually was. Indeed, this perception was so strong that the British military commander-in-chief, Kitchener—whom we first met in the Boer War—simply ordered his troops in Africa to stand on the defensive and try to hold on to what they already had.

But German actions continued to mount, reaching troubling levels later in 1915. The small-unit raiders went farther and deeper, creating increasingly annoying disruptions. Von Lettow was so greatly infected with the spirit of these raids that he went on one himself—with but one other German, a few Askaris, and native porters, no more than ten men in all. They were successful in causing some disruption; but the typical British reaction—to throw out counter patrols in pursuit—very nearly led to von Lettow's capture. His raiding concept was sound, but the risks for every team remained high at all times.

Nonetheless von Lettow's raiding campaign was having the desired effect: he had convinced British intelligence, Meinertzhagen in particular, that his forces posed a real threat to British East Africa. Soon Kitchener decided that more troops were needed in this theater and that the German threat must be dealt with decisively. While von Lettow was thus sparking a reaction that brought down a vastly superior force upon his head, this was indeed his strategic purpose. He thought the best way he could serve the overall German war effort was by causing the enemy to send large numbers of forces to deal with him rather than deploying them to the Western Front in Europe. In what came next, he certainly got his wish.

* * *

If von Lettow had pretty much held the initiative throughout 1915, it soon grew clear that things were about to change in the New Year. Not only were tens of thousands of fresh imperial troops coming into the theater of operations; they were placed under a skillful, energetic new commander: the Boer-hero-turned-British-loyalist, Jan Smuts. Large numbers of the fresh troops coming in were Boers too, freed up by their recent conquest of German South-West Africa, where the German commander Colonel Victor Franke had neither acquitted himself well nor held out very long.[5] So von Lettow had indeed achieved the large diversionary effect he wanted by causing such a ruckus in East Africa; but the British response soon placed him and his troops in the gravest peril. He had to respond to the new threat swiftly, and nimbly.

The most obvious new requirement was an immediate shift to the strategic defensive, given the number and quality of enemy troops massing for a multipronged invasion of German East Africa. Von Lettow could no longer send out most of his forces in small squads; still, he did not concentrate them in a single mass either. Instead he went back to his initial concept of fielding companies of some one hundred to two hundred fighters and dispersing them all around the edges of the colony. Most were deployed in the north, where the main threat was; but enough were sent to the east to deal with the Belgians, and to the south to keep the Portuguese from driving up from Mozambique.

The basic concept of operations in each area was to fight holding actions as long as practicable, inflicting maximum losses on the enemy, then to retreat before being outflanked. It was a strategy guaranteed to slow the enemy advance and, in some instances, such as against the Portuguese in the south, it stopped them in their tracks. But the Boers came on in much greater numbers and confirmed their reputation as excellent fighters. So in the north von Lettow's campaign began to unfold as a long series of holding actions and well-timed retreats.

Again and again Smuts would throw out a column of riders to try to encircle *Schutztruppe* companies, but his flankers were always slowed enough in the dense scrub-and-bush country to allow the defenders time to pull back to their next position. So it went, week after week, month after month. The British and Boers suffered heavy casualties in their frontal assaults against Askaris and Germans armed to the teeth with machine guns—two blockade runners had successfully brought them guns and am-munition from the fatherland—and the cavalry never seemed to be able to come to grips with the enemy.

Yet von Lettow was being steadily pushed south as Smuts kept driv-ing even during the rainy season. The pestilential climate grew even worse, with mosquitoes bringing malaria and tsetse flies carrying sleeping sickness. These were, in Byron Farwell's words, "the true enemy."[6] The British suf-fered the worst from the insect-borne diseases, as their tropical uniforms consisted of short pants and sleeves that left a lot of skin for the bugs to attack. The Askaris and Germans wore long pants, jodhpurs, and long-sleeved tunics, leaving only their hands and faces easily accessible. Even so, the Germans suffered too. Von Lettow himself experienced no fewer than four major malaria attacks during the war in East Africa.

As the campaign unfolded during 1916, Smuts drove relentlessly southward and von Lettow resisted, falling back slowly, inflicting as much damage as he could, and delaying the seemingly inevitable loss of the col-ony for as long as possible. Aside from being harried by Smuts, von Lettow was increasingly harassed by his colonial governor, Schnee, who preferred to surrender and put what he called "an honorable end" to everyone's suf-fering. Von Lettow would have none of this, happy in the knowledge that his few thousand fighters had by now stayed in the field for two years and caused well over a hundred thousand Allied troops, over a million horses, and enormous amounts of war matériel to be diverted from serving the Allied cause in Europe.

The only real doubter about the need to expend huge resources going after von Lettow was Kitchener. But in June 1916, while en route to Russia on a diplomatic mission, he went down with nearly all hands—about 650 sailors—when the cruiser *HMS Hampshire* was sunk by a German mine off the Orkney Islands. It seems that after Kitchener's passing the British efforts to finish off von Lettow intensified. And the steady gain of territory, von Lettow's abandonment of cities like Dar es Salaam, and his apparent inabil-ity to resume the offensive all bespoke an apparently great British success that was finally coming to fruition.[7]

At the end of the year Smuts was called to Britain to serve on the Imperial War Council. He placed his cavalry commander, Major General Jacobus van Deventer, in charge, confident that the campaign against von Lettow was all but over. Van Deventer pursued Smuts's tactics: frontal assaults buttressed by flanking movements. Fresh forces were coming in—more Africans now, the better-acclimated Nigerians and the King's African Rifles—and the British were becoming more bush-wise. They even took

to launching small-unit raids at night on the villages that provided a substantial portion of von Lettow's grain supplies. These night raids hurt his
operations as much as any of the larger British field maneuvers ever had.[8]

The Allied forces also enjoyed some technological advantages, fielding as they did the first of the new hand grenades, "Mills Bombs," and the
Stokes-Brandt trench mortar, the latter being the deadliest weapon in all
of World War I. The Germans obtained only a few of these, and only by
capturing them on their occasional offensive forays. Their few field guns,
salvaged from the raider *Koenigsberg* that had been trapped in the Rufiji
River delta, were worn and almost out of ammunition. At the tactical level
the only German edge was in machine guns, and the British stubbornness
in continuing the practice of making frontal assaults played right into the
hands of the *Schutztruppe*'s sole area of superiority.

Throughout the remainder of 1917 the British continued to drive
von Lettow southward, hemming him in on all sides. In October van Deventer thought the campaign could be brought to an end with one more
major push by an advanced flying column of some six thousand troops at
the Mahiwa River. Most of von Lettow's remaining forces—about fifteen
hundred troops, the vast majority of them Askaris—were there; and this
time, instead of a brief defense and a further retreat, von Lettow chose to
stand his ground and fight.

The resulting battle was exceptionally bloody for the British, with
about one-third of their force killed or wounded in several days of fighting.
Von Lettow made several deft counterattacks, but in the end he credited
his victory to the stubborn British adherence to the same balky tactics they
had employed on the Western Front in Europe. As von Lettow saw it, the
British lost this battle because they still "did not hesitate to try for success,
not by skillful handling . . . but rather by repeated frontal assaults."[9] In comparison to the enemy's two thousand plus casualties, his own losses were
about one hundred killed and four hundred wounded. But proportionally it
meant that his losses were about one-third of his force, the same percentage
of casualties suffered by the British. So he continued to retreat southward,
right to the border with Portuguese Mozambique.

Even though von Lettow had landed a sharp blow against his forces,
van Deventer, overseeing more than a hundred thousand pursuing troops,
felt he had von Lettow cornered at last. But the great German bush fighter
had one more trump card to play: in the wake of the Mahiwa battle, he
intended to mount a major strategic offensive. Despite the weariness of his
greatly reduced force and the overwhelming odds posed by the huge numbers of troops coming at him from every side but the sea—where the Royal

Navy was waiting to bombard him if he dared venture near the coast—von Lettow conceived the notion of a most irregular offensive. In November 1917 it began with his crossing south into Mozambique—moving *away* from the enemy's main forces. But he did not stay away.

*   *   *

Von Lettow's offensive was launched when he crossed the Rovuma River that marked the border between German East Africa and Portugal's Mozambique colony with the small number of fighters he still had left. At Ngomano they came upon a detachment of about fifteen hundred Portuguese troops, stationed there at British urging to act as a blocking force against his movements. Instead of bypassing them in the bush, von Lettow decided to attack in the hope he would gain supplies and enough ammunition to restock his force. He was right, as the British had been landing huge amounts of arms to strengthen the Portuguese. But what the British could not give them was the ability to fight off von Lettow's *Schutztruppe* which, in his words, was so tired, hungry, and irritated by the long pursuit that, at this point they acted toward the enemy with "absolute callousness."[10] This phrasing was somewhat euphemistic, as what really happened at Ngomano came closer to a massacre. Von Lettow restored order only with great difficulty. The situation was not dissimilar to the one Nathan Bedford Forrest faced at Fort Pillow during the American Civil War.

Resupplied with arms, food, and medicine, von Lettow continued the offensive in Mozambique, where the native population hated the Portuguese and often welcomed him and his forces, reprovisioning them regularly. Thus von Lettow's Allied pursuers found themselves arriving at places he had just left—where the people were in no position to resupply them, for they had already given all they could to the Germans. So it went throughout much of 1918. Eventually the noose began to tighten on the *Schutztruppe* once more, and this was the moment von Lettow chose to shift his offensive back northward into German East Africa. From there he planned also to menace northern Rhodesia and Nyasaland. Once again, just as the British thought the campaign was ending, von Lettow brought it back to life.

Von Lettow kept up the pressure right until the end of the war in November 1918. When the British finally convinced him that the peace had really come, it turned out that the force to which he "surrendered" was near-starving, so he shared with them supplies he had just plundered from a British depot. At that moment, roughly 150,000 Allied troops were chasing him, supported by hundreds of thousands more porters, as most of the campaign was fought far from roads and railheads.

Overall von Lettow's campaign had cost the Allies combat casualties well above twenty thousand, and more than a hundred thousand of their porters died out of the million that had been mustered to the cause. Thus, in addition to the great diversion of military forces, the campaign against von Lettow had caused a massive manpower shortage in several of the colonies, all of whose economic output suffered dramatically from this loss. As Edward Paice has observed, as early as August 1917 "the Acting governor of British East Africa had to inform van Deventer that the country's manpower resources were exhausted."[11]

Not all this exhaustion came from chasing the *Schutztruppe*, as there was also a lively war for quite some time on Lake Tanganyika, where the Germans enjoyed the initial advantage. To offset this, the British went to staggering lengths to fabricate vessels appropriate for lake fighting, then to haul them up over mountains and through jungles, building some two hundred bridges along the way.[12] The labor required to do all this was staggering—far greater than the struggles of Humphrey Bogart and Katharine Hepburn in the film version of C. S. Forester's novel about this aspect of the war, *The African Queen*.

Beyond the material drain he imposed on the Allies, perhaps von Lettow's greatest service was in shoring up morale in Germany, where he was a popular hero to such a degree as would not be seen again until Field Marshal Erwin Rommel emerged during World War II. Like von Lettow, Rommel too had an appeal that crossed the lines of war. Both men were much admired by their enemies.

Upon his return to Germany early in 1919, von Lettow was placed in command of the *Freikorps* militia that was used to suppress the Spartacist revolt, a Communist-inspired uprising. In this he succeeded admirably; but what followed in 1920 were less felicitous developments. Von Lettow became involved with a plot to install a military regime in Germany, the so-called Kapp *putsch*, named after the radical journalist who fomented this attempt to overthrow the Weimar Republic. The *putsch* failed, due in large part to the unwillingness of many in the *Freikorps* to support it and the willingness of vast numbers of ordinary Germans to risk their lives protesting it.

In the wake of the Kapp episode, von Lettow, now fifty, retired from the army. He went on to serve briefly in the legislature but soon retired from public life to spend more time with his family. After the war he had married the woman to whom he had been engaged in August 1914, and who had waited four years for his return. Now he devoted himself to raising his two sons and his daughter. When the Nazis came to power—his old nemesis, Governor Schnee, was a rabid fascist—von Lettow was invited to become the German ambassador to Britain. He declined the offer and was soon under Nazi surveillance. Nothing came of it, as he was still far too respected a figure to mistreat.

Von Lettow's sons went on to serve their country during World War II. Both were killed. His daughter survived. He lived on as well, into his nineties, along the way developing a friendship with Smuts and rekindling his acquaintanceship with Isak Dinesen. He never forgot his remarkable campaign in East Africa, nor his beloved Askaris, devoting much time and effort to seeing that they received proper pensions. Upon von Lettow's death in 1964, the Bundestag determined to pay the IOUs he had given his Askaris nearly half a century earlier. They sent a banker to find and pay the survivors. As Byron Farwell recounts: "The canny banker, an old soldier himself, hit upon an infallible identification. He gave each applicant a broom and put him through the manual of arms. No Askari ever forgot the German words of command or the drill."[13] Perhaps this was the greatest tribute of all.

12

EMIR DYNAMITE:
T. E. LAWRENCE

© Bettmann/Corbis

The idea of sending off a handful of one's own soldiers to train, guide, and sometimes lead far off but friendly forces into battle is both relatively new and quite old. This advisory concept lies at the heart of the U.S. Army Special Forces, which were created in the early 1950s to guide guerrilla groups fighting behind the lines in the wake of an envisioned Soviet invasion of Western Europe. That war never came, but the Green Berets were soon employed in leading Montagnard, Meo, and Hmong tribesmen in tip-and-run fighting against the Vietcong and the North Vietnamese Army. More recently Special Forces have played pivotal roles in the terror war, notably in working with Afghan and Iraqi tribes in the fight against al Qaeda and its affiliates. But the roots of this particular approach to military affairs go far back, at least as far as the Peloponnesian War (431–404 B.C.E.), when the Spartans sent an adviser named Gylippus to Sicily to help the Syracusans defeat a large Athenian expeditionary force. His success in turning that campaign around spoke—and still speaks—to the powerful possibility of achieving major results with a minimal investment in resources and manpower.

Yet for all the obvious value of seeking this sort of military "leverage," there have been few notable instances of the practice in conflicts during the more than two millennia that have passed between the fight against the Athenians and the campaigns against al Qaeda. In his biography of Nicias, the general whom Gylippus defeated, Plutarch noted that the Spartan adviser "showed what it is to be a man of experience; for with the same arms, the same horses, and on the same spot of ground, only employing them otherwise [than the Syracusans had], he overcame the Athenians."[1] Similarly, in the fall of 2001 commanders of just eleven U.S. Special Forces "A-teams" led the very same Northern Alliance fighters who had recently lost 95 percent of Afghan territory to the Taliban and al Qaeda to a resounding victory over them.[2] But where are the military advisers between Gylippus and the Special Forces groups?

For many long centuries there were precious few. The phenomenon of military advisory begins to reemerge from its dormancy only after the Enlightenment. A case can be made that the Frenchmen who goaded some of the Native American tribes to mount terror raids on English settlements in the seventeenth and eighteenth centuries—and who sometimes accompanied them—were acting as advisers. But the fact is that the Indians had little need of advice from the French on waging wilderness warfare. What they received was therefore not military but rather hortatory in nature.

Denis Davydov, who suggested mounting a behind-the-lines campaign of deep strikes against Napoleon's supply lines in Russia, looks a bit more like an adviser in that he offered guidance to villagers looking to resist the French. But after Davydov another gap opens up, as it is a full century from his field operations to those of Paul von Lettow-Vorbeck who, with a very small number of Germans, led a force of Africans in a protracted guerrilla war against the British.

Interestingly, another adviser-driven irregular campaign was going on at the same time as von Lettow's: the Arab Revolt against the repressive rule of the Ottoman Turks. But where the great German guerrilla fighter's goal was to defend one of his kaiser's best overseas colonies, the Allied strategic aim in southwest Asia was to foment a rebellion among the Arabs that would help dismantle the Ottoman Empire. In pursuit of this desired end, the British fielded conventional armies that operated out of Egypt and Mesopotamia; but they also supported the rising of the Arab tribes in their own right, which the French did as well. Thus a kind of "third front" opened up against the Turks.

It was a much needed one, as Turkish forces—themselves the beneficiaries of a German advisory mission as well as much German war matériel—fought like lions. First, at Gallipoli, they defeated an allied amphibious invasion, the brainchild of Winston Churchill, in furious fighting that lasted from April 1915 to January 1916. Next the Turks completely stymied the advance of British forces coming out of Egypt. Then in Mesopotamia, where the British were trying to advance to the northwest, the Turks trapped and captured an expedition of about ten thousand British troops at Kut—just four months after Gallipoli.

Only the Arabs under Sherif Husein seemed to be getting any traction against the Turks in the summer of 1916, capturing Mecca from them and later, with help from the Royal Navy, the ports of Jeddah and Yenbo. But in October the Arabs suffered a bloody repulse in their attempt to liberate Medina, and it seemed that the Turks were preparing to resume the offensive in this theater.

At this point, late in 1916, a young British intelligence officer, Thomas Edward Lawrence—just recently turned twenty-eight, but with solid Arabic language skills and much experience with Middle Eastern archaeological digs—devised a concept of operations that, in his view, offered great promise. His basic idea was to wage irregular warfare, avoiding pitched battles with the Turks and striking at their many vulnerable points along the eight hundred mile long railroad line between Medina and Damascus.

Lawrence's proximate military goal was to mount continual raids that would make it difficult—but not so difficult as to prompt a retreat—for the Turks to supply their large force in Medina. He believed that the Arab advantage in camel-based mobility would force the Turks to disperse ever more forces along the extensive railroad line, creating a whole range of easy targets for the tribesmen. And, given the vast distances involved, he knew there would never be enough enemy troops to constrain Arab movements and protect all that needed protecting. The Arab army would be "a thing intangible, invulnerable, without front or back, drifting about like a gas."[3]

The Arabs' ease of movement aside, there was also the matter of munitions favorable to irregular fighting becoming more available, in particular Alfred Nobel's dynamite. Much more stable—thus more usable in the field—than nitroglycerin, this high explosive posed the prospect that even quite small raiding teams could possess great destructive power. One of the first things Lawrence learned to do, on his journey from intelligence analyst to military adviser, was to blow things up. He proved an especially apt pupil, so much so that during the course of the campaign he would personally dynamite more than twenty trains. The Arabs came to call him "Emir Dynamite."[4]

Lawrence's fundamentally nonlinear view of the Arabian theater of operations was not limited simply to making raids on the railroad. He understood that it would also be possible to mount the occasional *coup de main* against large, even well-defended, targets. This first of these was the port of Aqaba, where, after a grueling ride, he and an Arab raiding force struck from out of the desert in July 1917. The nearly twelve hundred Turks who had been holding on there against pressure from the Royal Navy were taken by surprise, over a quarter of them killed and the rest captured. Of Lawrence's force only two were lost—two dead for twelve hundred of the enemy taken out of the fight—a most remarkable result.

This victory increased the Arabs' faith in Lawrence and deepened their loyalty to him immeasurably; but it also raised his stock among his own people. This was particularly true of Sir Reginald Wingate, the chief British official, or *Sirdar*, in Egypt who had succeeded Lord Kitchener in this post when the latter went off to fight the Boers. Wingate had initially been leery of Lawrence and sought to limit his activities simply to auditing the use of supplies and munitions given to the Arabs. But in the wake of the spectacular capture of Aqaba, Wingate too became a believer, even recommending Lawrence for the Victoria Cross.[5]

After the fall of Aqaba the Arab insurgents were well supplied from the sea by the British. This major new base of operations, now protected by the Royal Navy, became a launching point for a multitude of raids over the course of the following months. Not all of these actions were conducted by camel, as it turned out that armored cars had great mobility over much of the terrain. Lawrence participated in many of these raids; but even as he provided the technical know-how for demolitions—and he was not the only British soldier doing so at the time—his thoughts turned more and more to the possible political aims of the campaign.

For Lawrence, the only truly acceptable outcome of the Arab Revolt was the creation of a free Arab state, stretching from the Gulf of Aden to Damascus, and perhaps even beyond. The declared British position at the time certainly affirmed this idea of self-rule. A message from Britain's foreign secretary, Sir Edward Grey, was being air-dropped in leaflets among the Arabs, promising in return for their rising up against the Turks that their success would result in a peace treaty ensuring "independence of all foreign control . . . [and that] the lands of Arabia will, please God, return along the paths of freedom to their ancient prosperity."[6] But some influential members of the British government opposed this idea and began quietly to undermine it.

Lawrence soon came to believe that Prince Feisal, one of the sons of Husein whose fighters he was advising, had all the qualities necessary to govern wisely. But as the campaign continued to unfold, Lawrence would find, first, that his commanding general, Edmund Allenby, was primarily concerned with using these irregular forces as a means to improve his conventional operations. Later Lawrence would learn that high-level British policymakers had little intention of actually handing over former Turkish territories to the Arabs. The French also opposed Arab independence, intending to stake claims to the areas—largely in modern Syria—where Frankish crusaders had built castles to protect their crumbling kingdoms more than seven hundred years earlier. Ironically, many of these ruined forts had been objects of close study by Lawrence before the war, during his periods of archaeological fieldwork.

Before his ultimate triumph and disillusionment, Lawrence had much more campaigning ahead of him. Allenby's calls for support had to be heeded, the fractious tribes had to be kept together, and very large numbers of Turkish troops—well in excess of a hundred thousand in his area of operations alone—had to be defeated. Lawrence had the means for doing so in the swift-moving tribesmen. And his beloved high explosives, complemented with machine guns, mortars, and a good number of armored cars, made the insurgents and the small Anglo-French contingent fighting at their side somewhat better armed than their foes.

Yet the reliability of tribal sheikhs was often questionable, and Lawrence found that he had to be his own principal provider of intelligence. This required skillful, covert infiltrations of a number of Turkish-held cities, with Lawrence sometimes taking advantage of his small stature—he was only five feet five inches tall—to veil himself and pretend to be a woman. At other times, in places where Caucasian Turks were more commonly found, he went about more openly. It was on one of these latter-type scouting expeditions, where he was a bit too out in the open, that Lawrence was briefly captured, and suffered one of his greatest personal reverses in the campaign. But before this he was to experience other frustrations, particularly in the in 1917 expedition known as the "raid upon the bridges."

*   *   *

Throughout the revolt in the desert, Lawrence's long reconnaissance missions often found him accompanied by just a few trusted tribesmen. Sometimes these patrols would extend for a thousand miles round-trip. Almost always he would return with useful information to guide the next actions

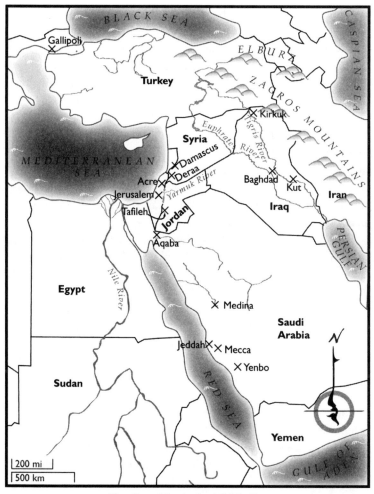

The Great War in the Middle East

of the Arabs. Sometimes this scouting would take place even while the raiding force was heading toward its intended target, with Lawrence and a few others from time to time moving out ahead. In short, information gathering was an essential task in advance of all missions, and it was one that Lawrence, as a well-trained intelligence officer, took most seriously. But sometimes he fell prey to treachery.

One of the more troubling incidents that bedeviled him occurred in the fall of 1917, when he wished to employ his Arab forces in a raid on railway bridges in the Yarmuk Valley and use this success to spark a rising of the tribes living in that area. Among the locals were Algerian descendants of those who had gone into exile with Abd el-Kader over half a century earlier. The grandson and namesake of the great Algerian insurgent rode into Lawrence's camp one day just before the raiders set out on this mission, promising "Aurens Bey" their support.

But the Algerian arrived under a cloud of suspicion, as the French intelligence service saw him as likely being an agent of the Turks, an assessment they shared with Lawrence. If this latter-day Abd el-Kader were not a spy, however, his great name could prove useful in recruiting more fighters to the cause. Feisal gave Lawrence this frank measure of the man: "I know he is mad. I think he is honest. Guard your heads and use him."[7] Lawrence decided to take him along with the raiding party.

In the mission that followed, everything that could go wrong did. The tribesmen whom the raiders met up with distrusted Abd el-Kader and refrained from joining up. Warning shots were fired at Lawrence and his men by potential recruits. Finally, one day Abd el-Kader simply disappeared. His leave-taking, whether out of resentment, guilt, or fear, meant that the local Algerians could not be brought into the operation. Still, Allenby was readying for a major push with his conventional forces—one that would end with the capture of Jerusalem—and Lawrence felt the need to mount a supporting diversion. So the raiders continued on, finally selecting a bridge to be blown up. Now the greater part of the explosives they had brought along were somehow dropped over a cliff by a fearful tribesman during a "friendly fire" exchange among nervous troops, and the bridge action was called off.

Trying to salvage something for all their efforts the raiders used what explosives they had left to derail a train and then attack it. Unfortunately they chose a train filled with hundreds of Turkish troops destined for the defense of Jerusalem against Allenby's offensive. Once their train was derailed, the troops came rushing out after Lawrence and his sixty Arabs, many of whom were killed and even more wounded, with barely forty making good their escape. The summing up of the whole enterprise was, in Lawrence's words, "past tears."[8]

If the Yarmuk raid had been a complete failure—perhaps because of the treachery of an infiltrator—what came next for Lawrence was still worse. Just over a week later, on a reconnaissance of Deraa with a lone companion, he was detained by the Turks. They seemed to think he was a deserter from their own army, and Lawrence himself thought he had somehow been betrayed to them by Abd el-Kader. In the event, he kept cover by speaking only Arabic, even under duress, and explained away his light skin by saying he was a Circassian, a member of a tribe from the northwest Caucasus Mountains.

This cover story seemed to work, but by now Lawrence had caught the eye of the local Turkish commander, who fancied him. As Lawrence tells the story, a kind of clumsy wrestling match ensued in which he held his own. At this point the frustrated Turk passed him off to his guards, urging them to teach some manners to the Circassian. They took Lawrence out and beat, whipped, and raped him, leaving him in a shed from which he escaped the next day. He eventually made it back to his comrades and resumed the insurgency with a new grimness. The massacres he oversaw, participated in, or allowed all occurred after this incident.

Some historians and biographers have questioned whether the incident at Deraa ever occurred, given the lack of witnesses to corroborate Lawrence's account. Whatever the ultimate truth, "Emir Dynamite" was a changed man afterward. Something terrible had happened to him, all in the course of the risky existence he led as adviser, intelligence gatherer, and tactical field commander in very close actions. Lawrence was wounded nine times during the Arab Revolt, several of the injuries being quite serious. Yet nothing seems to have scarred him more than the psychological damage done during his brief detention at Deraa.

Some have seen in this episode the origins of the near-madness and depression that plagued Lawrence in the early 1920s. Others have seen it as a prism through which to examine his sexuality, which to this day seems to remain beyond our ability to categorize definitively.[9] But the unassailable truth worth holding on to is that Lawrence threw himself body and soul into this campaign, leading from the front in battle and going far behind the lines to gather the information needed for each next move. His memoir, *Seven Pillars of Wisdom*, is subtitled *A Triumph*. This is certainly accurate in military terms. But the price exacted upon Lawrence the man suggests that there was, at a personal level, just as much a sense of tragedy.

* * *

Tragedy would come at the political level too. That same November, as Lawrence was suffering in the Yarmuk Valley and at Deraa, British foreign secretary Arthur Balfour declared "His Majesty's Government view with favor the establishment in Palestine of a national home for the Jewish people." This policy ran the risk of alienating Britain's Arab allies—a point that did not escape Turkish attention, as they began to woo the Arabs back—and would prove to be one of the root causes of the nearly century-long dispute over Israel that still bedevils us. In the short run, however, Sir Reginald Wingate was successful with a powerful palliative measure: increasing financial subsidies to the Arabs, who remained allied to Britain. The Arab Revolt thus shored up, Lawrence found himself in a position to engineer some remarkable field operations during the final phase of the war in 1918, when he was called upon to play a key role in the overall military campaign.

At this moment in the war, the operational challenge for General Allenby remained a daunting one, as the Turks continued to fight hard on his relatively narrow front against them in Palestine. After his liberation of Jerusalem at the close of 1917, Allenby was caught in a lull in the pace of the campaign that stretched into the early months of 1918. But events in Europe were now conspiring to complicate efforts against the Turks. First, Russia was knocked out of the war. This development was followed by the redeployment of German troops to the Western Front, where they launched a massive offensive in March. The situation for the Allies appeared gloomy, and in the Middle East the fear was that these developments would both revive Turkish fortunes and fan the flames of a different sort of Arab revolt: one aimed against continued British rule in Egypt and elsewhere.

Jan Smuts, the Boer insurgent who had become a British loyalist, and now sat on the Imperial War Cabinet, arrived to visit with Allenby. Smuts, who would become prime minister of the Union of South Africa the following year, impressed upon Allenby the need to mount a large-scale offensive no later than early May. But because of the pressure the Germans were putting on the Western Front with their Ludendorff offensive, some crack British troops would be taken from Allenby to shore up the situation there. Duly chastened by the seemingly contradictory demand to take the offensive with fewer seasoned troops, Allenby hatched a plan that relied heavily on deception—and would need considerable assistance from Lawrence.

In the preceding year's campaign, even when Allenby had an advantage in numbers, he was quite open to the idea of using deception. In the operations that culminated in the capture of Jerusalem he had feinted a drive along the coast but actually mounted a "right hook" well inland. This move was supported by a stratagem that employed a staff officer to drop his haversack, containing false indications of an intended British move, after being "surprised" by a Turkish scouting patrol and apparently wounded while escaping. The operation went as planned, and the Turks ended up concentrating far too much force along the coast, allowing Allenby to advance inland.[10]

This particular idea was dreamed up and carried out by Richard Meinertzhagen, who had smeared the haversack with his own fresh blood at the moment he sighted the Turkish patrol that he hoped would "ambush" him. He was the same intelligence officer who had crossed swords with von Lettow in East Africa earlier in the war. Now he was operating in the Middle East, often interacting with Lawrence and the others involved in guiding the Arab Revolt. The best description of Meinertzhagen ever given was provided by Lawrence, who summed him up insightfully as "a student of migrating birds drifted into soldiering, whose hot immoral hatred of the enemy expressed itself as readily in trickery as in violence."[11]

But Allenby could hardly resort to the "haversack trick" in the hope of deceiving the Turks again. And the plan for this campaign was to reverse the course of the last, as Allenby intended to drive up the coast rather than make another inland flanking movement. So the challenge lay in how to give the impression that he was mounting another right hook while really intending to strike straight at the wing of the Turkish army nearest the coast. To trick the enemy into believing he was going inland again, Allenby pulled out all the stops, relying heavily on the Arabs to mount an offensive from deep in the desert that would convince the Turks they were the advance force preparing the way for British regulars.

Allenby charged Lawrence with the task of raising his level of activity so as to divert large numbers of Turkish troops eastward. Allenby's goal was for two-thirds of the enemy army to be shifted from the spot along the coast where he intended to strike. In the event, Arab raids achieved almost exactly this degree of enemy redeployment. Their ability to do so was partly the result of growing Turkish (and German) respect for the Arab irregulars as fighters, an assessment that grew out of the pitched battle at Tafileh early in 1918.

This was a fight that was forced upon Lawrence, who was loath to slip away ahead of the Turkish troops advancing to recapture Tafileh, a town he had only recently liberated. Had he left the locals to their fate, they would likely have been massacred for joining the Arab cause—and other villagers farther north would have been increasingly reluctant to embrace the revolt. So Lawrence stood and fought, skillfully deploying his troops in holding and flanking actions against a much larger force. In this one conventional battle, Lawrence demonstrated a grasp of tactics that went beyond guerrilla warfare and demolitions. He showed how his small units, properly employed, could take on traditional massed forces with real hope of winning. In the end, the Turks were driven off with heavy losses. The great British strategist B. H. Liddell Hart called the battle "a gem."[12]

The effort to divert Turkish forces kept the Arabs and Lawrence in near-constant action up and down the railroad line, often mounting strikes at some distance from it. The Turks were frustrated by their inability to come to grips with the raiders, and their anger led to the commission of atrocities in various villages. Lawrence, his post-Deraa persona now on full display, allowed retaliatory slaughters of the Turks by his own troops as well. It was an exceptionally ugly moment in the campaign. But the end result, the redeployment of Turkish forces away from the British target area, was achieved.

Beyond helping to foster a favorable dispersion of Turkish troops, Lawrence was also charged with mounting deeper attacks against other key rail and communications infrastructures—much as Nathan Bedford Forrest did in his deep strikes during the Civil War—so as to reduce the enemy's ability to respond effectively to Allenby's offensive. Yet one more task Lawrence was assigned was to encourage the Arabs living in Syria along the way to Damascus either to join the cause or at least to welcome the Allies. In these undertakings too, Lawrence was eminently successful. The Chicago journalist Lowell Thomas, who would do so much to burnish the Lawrence legend, described the outcome of the campaign that ensued: "Lawrence and Allenby lost only four hundred and fifty men, although they completely annihilated the Turkish army, captured over one hundred thousand Turks, advanced more than three hundred miles in less than a month, and broke the backbone of the Turkish Empire."[13]

Lawrence and his irregulars arrived in Damascus, the culminating point of the 1918 campaign, on October 1, just before Allenby and the main force got there. The Turks soon sued for peace, and the Great War itself ended in an Allied victory a month later.

Interestingly, Lawrence's decision to leave the Turkish stronghold in Medina to wither was well borne out. At the war's end its large garrison was still in place under the command of Fakhreddin "Fakhri" Pasha, a skillful commander who had repelled several ill-advised assaults by some of Lawrence's more conventional-minded colleagues. But, as Lawrence had believed from the outset, this strongpoint required care and feeding that opened the Turks to a host of pinprick attacks all along its lengthy, tortuous line of supply. As Liddell Hart noted of Lawrence's overarching concept of operations, it was aimed at an enemy "as dependent as any Western state on the lifeline of modern civilization—the railway."[14]

Liddell Hart firmly believed that Lawrence should be ranked among the "great captains" of all military history, not merely as a master of irregular warfare. The basis for this judgment was in part a reflection of Liddell Hart's own preference for taking an "indirect approach" to defeating enemy forces in any kind of war, conventional or irregular. But there was something more to his view. Liddell Hart believed that Lawrence had fixed upon an essential truth of modern military affairs: advanced technology both empowers and imperils. Yes, there are always attractive new capabilities that come with advanced systems. But there are likely to be even more new ways in which to exploit the dependencies that come with the latest technologies, posing the prospect that modern militaries may be more easily, and fatally, disrupted.

In Liddell Hart's view, Lawrence had unearthed a great new truth in strategy that would soon compel military thinking: "the old concentration of force is likely to be replaced by an intangibly ubiquitous distribution of force—pressing everywhere yet assailable nowhere." And he contended that Lawrence's campaign was not a model to be used only by scattered guerrilla forces. As he put it: "What the Arabs did yesterday, the Air Forces may do tomorrow. And in the same way—yet more swiftly. Mobile land forces such as tanks and motor guerrillas may share in the process."[15]

In short, the underlying meaning of Lawrence's military career suggests that the true impact of technological change in the modern era will be to enliven and expand irregular approaches to warfare far more than it will reenergize or improve upon traditional, conventional concepts of operations.

* * *

Whatever his far-reaching effects on military affairs, Lawrence's great political project on behalf of the Arabs came largely to naught. Although some historians have downplayed his role in Arab affairs at this time—like George Antonius in his classic *The Arab Awakening*—Lawrence was indeed present at the Versailles peace talks, translating for Feisal and debating with Woodrow Wilson and Georges Clemençeau. But he failed to overcome the powerful pull of the secret Sykes-Picot Agreement between France and Britain. Negotiated earlier in the war, it gave France sway over most northern Arab territories and left the British the area south of a diagonal running from Acre in today's Lebanon to Kirkuk in Iraq.

Lawrence was terribly disheartened by this carving-up of his imagined new caliphate; but he did not lose hope. A few years later, while serving as an aide to Winston Churchill—who, in yet another of his famous comebacks, was now Britain's colonial secretary—Lawrence helped put Feisal on the throne of Iraq and did the same for his brother, Prince Abdullah, in Jordan. Iraq was to prove unstable from early on, devolving firmly into dictatorship by 1958, the throes of its turbulent politics eventually ensnaring the United States. Jordan, however, has remained a relatively stable state and, increasingly, a voice of peace and reason. Abdullah I was assassinated in 1951 in Jerusalem, but his great-grandson and namesake, son of the revered King Hussein, still sits on the Jordanian throne. Lawrence would be pleased.

After his time with Churchill, Lawrence sought to escape into anonymity. This was difficult, given that Lowell Thomas had done so much with his lectures—which Lawrence frequently attended—to turn him into a "brand." And Lawrence himself had nurtured the brand in the first place, the distinctive white robe he wore becoming the latter-day counterpart of Garibaldi's red shirt. His autobiographical account, *Seven Pillars of Wisdom*, and its more reader-friendly abridgement, *Revolt in the Desert*, fed the legend further. Despite efforts of both Lawrence and Thomas to acknowledge others' contributions in the Allied advisory mission to the Arabs, revisionist histories of the revolt would later argue that Lawrence had not done all he said he had, or that he had downplayed the role of the Arabs.[16] The current historical verdict, best expressed by Jeremy Wilson, is that "*Seven Pillars* is remarkably accurate on questions of fact."[17]

Lawrence appears to have decided that his only chance of regaining a "normal" life after the war was to give up his own identity. Surrendering his lieutenant-colonelcy, he enlisted in the Royal Air Force under an assumed name—John Hume Ross—was discovered, and then left the service only to reenlist in the Tank Corps. Now, as T. E. Shaw, he became fascinated by the future prospects for mobile armored warfare using his raiding ideas. As his biographer Robert Graves noted, during the Arab Revolt Lawrence "had fought some fifty armored-car actions, enough to evolve a whole scheme and system of battle for them."[18]

But army rigidity did not appeal to him, so T. E. Shaw became an airman again. These were his happiest years. He served as an aircraftsman and was the best mechanic wherever he was based. Others knew who he was but allowed him to live as he wished. He received little treatment that could be called favoritism, being sent off to the wilds of Waziristan in the late 1920s. There the British, in an eerie foreshadowing of U.S. drone strikes eighty years later, tried to use airpower to quell hostile Pashtun tribesmen. Then, upon his return to Britain, he became involved with the RAF's speedboat detachment, whose mission was to rescue downed pilots and crew who had ditched or parachuted into the English Channel. Lawrence loved flight, speed, and all the advances in technology that were coming so swiftly during these years.

His style of life has remained a historical and psychological puzzle. Some argue that his taking a pseudonym and assuming a humble position might have something to do with feelings of inferiority that grew from his illegitimate birth. His father, Thomas Chapman, had a wife and four daughters at the time he ran off with the girls' nanny. He had five sons with her, T. E. being the second. There is no consensus as to why he chose "Lawrence" as his new surname, but T. E.'s resort to aliases does echo his father's choice of a new life with a new name.

Other views about his return to service in the "other ranks" suggest that he needed a steady income and a social support structure. But he was a famous figure, not only for his war exploits but as a growing literary lion who consorted with the likes of George Bernard Shaw, Robert Graves, and E. M. Forster, and who could easily have earned a fine living as a writer. As to his views on the social benefits of life in the armed services, one need only glance at *The Mint*, his scathing critique of how soldiers were stamped out, to see that Lawrence loathed regimentation and spit-and-polish.

In my view, his return to military life as, basically, a mechanic, can be satisfactorily explained by his desire for settings in which he could tinker with tanks, planes, and speedboats and develop a deep understanding of their workings and potential. For Lawrence was, at heart, a technologist. He may have ridden camels into battle in the desert, but he fought in just as many armored-car actions. During the revolt he became an absolute technical expert at demolition, "Emir Dynamite." He hungered to develop a deep knowledge of technological advances, I am convinced, because he had so much to say about how the kind of irregular war he fought might be waged in almost every future conflict.

If there was a first among equals in his love of technological tools, it was certainly aircraft. Lawrence had often been flown around during the revolt—not all his reconnaissance was done on a camel's back—and sometimes the pilots let him take the controls. He was a great enthusiast about the potential of attack aircraft in irregular wars, given their ability to strike swiftly over great distances. As he once told Liddell Hart, "I'm a tremendous supporter of air."[19]

Lawrence did not live to explore fully the potential of airpower. He fell victim to a motorcycle crash in May 1935 when he had to swerve too sharply to avoid hitting two boys on bicycles. He was forty-six. Churchill walked behind his casket at the funeral, later commenting to the *Times* of London that Lawrence was "one of the greatest beings of our time."[20] Lawrence's untimely death kept him from being a part of the airpower-driven future of military affairs; but another great master of irregular warfare, the subject of the next chapter, was soon to take up this cause.

13

LONG RANGER:
ORDE WINGATE

By dint of his deeds, but especially by the eloquent words he later used to describe and draw lessons from the Arab Revolt—notably his brilliant summary of the state of guerrilla doctrine in the fourteenth edition of the *Encyclopedia Britannica*—T. E. Lawrence greatly refreshed what Walter Laqueur called an "arid" era in irregular warfare.[1] In the years after World War I, insurgency seemed to revive, while modern terrorism appeared seriously for the first time. The Russian civil war, fought mostly between 1918 and 1920, was replete with both hit-and-run raiding tactics and cold-blooded acts of terror, including regicide. Similarly bitter irregular violence was the norm in Ireland, where insurgents shifted from the failed approach of the 1916 mass rising to embrace more guerrilla-like action in pursuit of independence. In Mexico, Pancho Villa effectively began his insurgency against repressive rule—and even ran rings around American forces chasing him—but he ended badly after reverting to conventional tactics.

Some of the most illuminating examples of insurgency and terror tactics during this period came from the Muslim world, sparked both by admiration for the success of Lawrence's methods in the Arab Revolt and resentment of the European powers' continuing colonial meddling throughout so much of the Maghreb and the Middle East. In northwest Africa, for example, the guerrilla campaign of Abd el Krim in Morocco, a land then divided between Spain and France, even featured a small insurgent air force, perhaps an homage to Lawrence's enthusiastic views about the value of airpower to irregulars. But after years of reverses, the two colonial powers finally realized the need to act together, and Abd el Krim's revolt was put down decisively.

Sudan was another troubled place, plagued as it was by *habashi* slave raiders who preyed upon remote villages, a practice that had gone on for centuries and still occurs there. The British, who had controlled the country after Kitchener's defeat of the Dervishes at Omdurman in 1898, at first tried the usual limited range of conventional methods, including garrisoned outposts, patrols, and the development of native forces. None worked well until a young army lieutenant by the name of Orde Wingate was posted there in 1928. (Shown on the previous page—Wingate at a briefing, wearing his trademark pith helmet.)

Twenty-five at the time, Wingate had become interested in Middle Eastern affairs and studied Arabic at the urging of his father's cousin, Sir Reginald Wingate, who had worked with Lawrence, one of the young officer's heroes at the time.[2] Wingate was even distantly related to Lawrence on his mother's side, and the families occasionally socialized. Upon his arrival in Sudan, Orde Wingate began to think deeply about the slave raiding problem and soon began experimenting with methods for dealing with it that were radically different from what had been tried before. He raised some eyebrows, but the young lieutenant was given permission for these ventures, and he seized the opportunity.

Two things distinguished Orde Wingate's approach to dealing with the *habashis*: his determination to take the offensive against them and his willingness to lead small teams of Sudanese on long treks to set ambushes for them. The results of this seemingly simple shift were to prove remarkable. Wingate's basic pattern of action began when warning came from a border village that a raiding party was en route. He would set out immediately on a course aimed at intercepting the raiders in the remotest places rather than at watering holes, villages, or other likely sites. Many decades before global positioning systems, Wingate had an uncanny ability to reckon his exact location in the wilderness. And his ambushes were meticulously and ruthlessly carried out. His concept of operations soon forged a kind of deterrence of the raiders, and their activities waned.

Wingate spent five years in Sudan, developing his field craft and honing his larger ideas about what he would eventually call "long range penetration." His notions about the power of even small units when used to launch deep strikes against one's adversaries, while related to the actions of Denis Davydov, Nathan Bedford Forrest, and even T. E. Lawrence, went much further, for he demonstrated that these methods could also be employed against slippery irregular forces, not only conventional formations.

After leaving Sudan in 1933, Wingate had a tour of duty in Britain, during which time he married. In 1936 he was sent overseas again. This time Wingate, whose language skills included Hebrew and Arabic, found himself posted to Palestine as an intelligence officer. It was a difficult time there, as Jewish settlement had been rising in recent years, igniting tensions with the Arabs who increasingly felt betrayed by broken British promises of self-rule. The numbers of Jews arriving partly reflected Zionist enthusiasm and hope for an independent homeland; but immigration was also being fed by a growing stream of refugees coming out of Germany after Hitler's takeover in 1933. It was not long before violence broke out between Jews and Arabs.

As in Sudan, Wingate, now a captain, came into a situation where the problem was raiders, but this time they were killing to intimidate settlers, not attacking in search of slaves. The Arabs were determined not to become a minority in what they saw as their own land, one that had been promised to them. Also as in Sudan, the British response had been a primarily defensive one. Their forces patrolled Palestine's borders apparently endlessly, and though they allowed Jewish settlers to defend their settlements, they permitted no more than that.

Little progress was made against the Arab insurgents, even though gifted soldiers like Bernard Montgomery—at this point a lower-ranking general but destined to become Britain's premier field commander during World War II—were sent to grapple with the nettlesome problem. Another troubling factor in play at the time was that the basic sentiments among the British were overwhelmingly pro-Arab, and anti-Semitism ran high throughout the ranks. The desire to pursue operations against the Arab insurgents was low.

From the moment he came to Palestine, Wingate proved to be an exception to prevailing British practices and attitudes. He quickly saw that his ideas about offensive long-range operations could be applied as effectively in Palestine as they had been in Sudan. He would visit with Jewish settlers, talking up the possibilities of forming strike forces to cripple the Arab terrorists. For Wingate, "terrorism" was the right way to describe the Arab actions, given the raids on settlements in which innocent women and children were being killed. But he was also motivated by his own deep Christian belief, nurtured by his parents and the tenets of the Plymouth Brethren faith to which he adhered devoutly, that the Jews were destined to return to Israel. He intended to act in accord with God's will.

Technically Wingate was posted as the intelligence officer in Nazareth. But he was seldom there, preferring instead to make the rounds of settlements, trying to persuade leaders of the Jewish self-defense force, the *Haganah*, that their basic strategy was far too passive. It took some time, but Wingate finally convinced the Jews of his sincerity. Yet as their faith in him deepened, his own superiors grew more hostile to the obviously pro-Zionist activities of this junior intelligence officer. Thus Wingate found himself in a kind of race against time in which he strove to make headway with the Jews before he was removed from the field.

Wingate greatly aided his cause, even as he alienated his peers, by violating the chain of command and sending a memorandum directly to the general officer in charge, Archibald Wavell, which called for intensive study of the "incidence, type and numerical strength of the marauders, particularly whence they came and what frontier points they used."[3] Wavell was impressed by this message and called Wingate in for a meeting on the subject. He quickly concluded that his subordinate was on to something and authorized him to pursue his investigation. Wavell and others thought Wingate would do this by examining incident files. Instead he took to the field.

What followed was a series of meetings with Jewish settlers, and even with the secretive leadership of the *Haganah*. Wingate assured them that with a small number of elite troops he could seize the initiative and hold it against the Arabs. He used his favorite example, that of the biblical Gideon, who chose just three hundred from among thousands to conduct his remarkable, stealthy military operations. With a similar-sized force, Wingate argued, he could achieve similarly great results. The *Haganah*, persuaded that they could trust the man they now spoke of in code as *hayedid*, the "friend," accepted Wingate's proposal.

After a period of training in his offensive concepts as well as in his more general "Soldiers' Ten Commandments"—which in some ways echoed Robert Rogers's rules for rangers—Wingate was ready to begin his counterinsurgency operations with these newly formed Special Night Squads (SNS). They were comprised mostly of settlers, with a leavening of British noncommissioned officers and other ranks. As in Sudan, Wingate relied heavily upon an information system to provide early warning, but to this he added a proactive tactic of firing on Arab villages his force might come upon in the night, to gauge the reaction. If there was heavy return fire, he knew there was something to investigate.

The campaign that unfolded turned the tables on the Arab insurgents. No longer could they count on having the initiative to select their targets and strike first. The Jews showed up everywhere the raiders intended to attack. Increasingly the SNS also found its way to the villages from which insurgent actions were staged. Even when the Arabs tried to create their own surveillance system, watching for trucks that carried the SNS, Wingate foiled them by training his men to slip off the backs of the trucks one by one at dusk, undetected, rallying at a prearranged point from which they proceeded on foot. This was easy to do because the SNS was an extremely light force, armed only with rifles, grenades, and long poles, which were used to hold torches at a small distance from their exact locations in the bush, allowing teams to signal each other without becoming easy sniper targets.[4]

Wingate's force was lacking in numbers—fewer than a hundred *Haganah* fighters served with him, formed into nine teams and filled out with a handful of Jewish police.[5] But they made up for their small size and lack of firepower with total relentlessness. In battle they took to the attack, no matter the size of the opposing force, their British commander always in the thick of the fight. He was there too when prisoners were being questioned, on at least one occasion ordering the execution of a captive so as to encourage the others to speak.[6] His greatest success came at a place called Dabburiyah, near the Sea of Galilee, where a major insurgent group that had been attacking both Jewish settlers and the British oil pipeline was destroyed, very nearly to the last man. Wingate was wounded in three places during the action, but kept on fighting and leading, afterward earning both the Distinguished Service Order and promotion to major.

For all this success—by 1939 insurgent attacks dropped off sharply—Wingate's superiors also became aware of and hotly opposed to what they considered his extreme methods. A further cause of opposition to Wingate, aside from general British antipathy to the unorthodoxy and brutality of such practices and disdain for the Jews, was that many of his colleagues simply disliked him as an individual. He was arrogant and brusque far beyond his rank. He was also deliberately slovenly, often going about unshaven in a field-stained uniform and wearing a battered pith helmet. It was a kind of "anti-brand," quite different from T. E. Lawrence's skillfully crafted image in flowing white robes. But this "look" showed everybody, from those in headquarters to the *kibbutzniks*, that he was a fighter.

Wingate might have survived all this opposition but for increasing evidence that he was sharing sensitive information with Jewish leaders. This and the loss of his "top cover," General Wavell, who moved on to a higher command, brought about the end of Wingate's time in Palestine. He was sent home in 1939, his file reflecting explicitly that he should never be allowed to return there. Still, he had achieved much during his stay. As the historian Lewis Gann noted, Wingate proved in Palestine "that the counter-guerrilla, as mobile, resolute, and ubiquitous as his opponent, is worth more than the orthodox soldier when it comes to conducting anti-partisan operations."[7] This was surely so. But Wingate's proof of concept came at a great cost to his career. He returned home under a cloud, and prospects for further advancement seemed poor. It was the coming of World War II and the continuing support he enjoyed from General Wavell that ensured he would have new opportunities to develop his ideas further in the field.

*   *   *

Major Orde Wingate spent the opening days of World War II alternating between appeals for an amended performance evaluation and requests for a larger role for Jewish military units in the defense of the Middle East. He failed in both these pursuits. By the spring of 1940 he was slated to command an antiaircraft unit that was to deploy to Amsterdam. But the Low Countries and France fell before he could get there. That autumn, when it became clear that a German seaborne invasion of England was not in the offing—Hitler instead trying, with no success, to bomb the British into submission—Wingate was sent off to Cairo along with many other soldiers to fight the Italians. His protector, General Wavell, who was now commander-in-chief of Allied forces throughout the Middle East, had asked for him specifically.

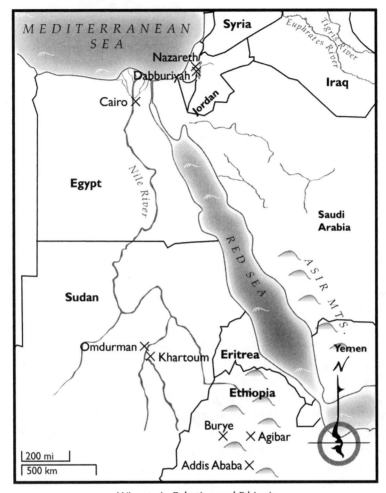

Wingate in Palestine and Ethiopia

In the days after Wingate's arrival, Wavell was putting the finishing touches on his plan for an offensive against the Italians, who had advanced from Libya into western Egypt. The attack was to open soon, but Wavell saw no part in it for Wingate. Instead he wanted the man he considered one of Britain's most innovative soldiers to lead an irregular campaign in support of operations to throw the Italians out of Abyssinia (modern Ethiopia), which they had invaded in 1935. At the time of the Italian incursion, the world had stood by shamefully and done nothing. Now the situation was about to change dramatically.

Haile Selassie, the "Lion of Judah" who had been driven into exile by Benito Mussolini's forces, was ready to lead his people to freedom.

Attempting to cobble together a force in Sudan, he received support from Wavell and Field Marshal Jan Smuts, the old Boer insurgent turned British loyalist. These two came to Khartoum to try to jump-start offensive preparations, but the lesser ranking British generals in this theater felt they simply had too few troops to go after the Italians.

At this point Wingate showed up in Sudan. His formal title, given by Wavell, was chief officer for rebel activities, and he got right to work. He soon managed to alienate the commanding generals of the conventional forces, but he also charmed Haile Selassie. He built from scratch what he called the Gideon Force, and by January 1941, when Wavell's brilliant North African offensive was nearing its high tide, Wingate and Haile Selassie set forth with a few thousand men, and far more camels, to liberate Ethiopia. At the same time far larger numbers—tens of thousands—of British, Indian, and South African conventional forces were slowly beginning to move against the Italians, coming at them from north and south. The Italians skillfully defended against these thrusts, giving ground only grudgingly. On the other hand, Wingate's small force, driving from the west toward Addis Ababa, was to pose problems that the Italians could never figure out how to counter.

In a series of actions the Gideon Force continually outmaneuvered the Italians, always taking the tactical offensive against them, even when greatly outnumbered. This was a further development, on a somewhat larger scale, of the methods Wingate had begun using in Palestine. He repeatedly divided his units so that they could strike the enemy from several directions simultaneously, most notably in a series of actions running from Burye to Mankusa in late February and early March. By April, having suffered minimal losses, Wingate's troops had inflicted four thousand casualties on the enemy and captured fifteen thousand men and millions of rounds of ammunition.[8] All this was accomplished with virtually no air support, due in part to the fact that as Wingate's fortunes waxed, Wavell's were waning in the face of an offensive mounted out of Libya by an energetic German general sent there to retrieve the situation, Erwin Rommel.

Wingate seemed incapable of viewing the larger reasons for the paucity of his support, believing instead that others were intriguing against him. To some extent this was surely true of the conventional force commanders fighting in Ethiopia, whose progress was slow and difficult and who clamored even more loudly than Wingate for more resources. He could not be content in the knowledge that his theory of long-range penetration had done well in yet another field test, that he had expanded its demonstrated range of applications by showing how, beyond countering insurgents and terrorists, his small units could befuddle and defeat a much larger conventional army. Instead of reveling in such validation, all Wingate tasted were ashes.

Perhaps the most aggravating moment came when, as he readied himself and Haile Selassie to enter Addis Ababa, orders arrived early in April telling Gideon Force to stand by while a South African division took the capital. There was apparently serious concern in London that if Haile Selassie went in first there would be riotous celebrations and a mass murder of Italian captives.[9] So Smuts's Boers went first. Haile Selassie returned to his capital three weeks later, and while he was greeted with great enthusiasm, the people remained orderly.

For Wingate there was still an endgame to play out, as some large Italian formations remained in the field. Gideon Force marched north against eight thousand enemy troops at Agibar. There Wingate divided his tiny force yet again—a key portion of it being under the command of the explorer and adventurer Wilfred Thesiger[10]—and struck at the Italians and their remaining native allies from all sides, eventually besieging them. On May 23, 1941, the entire enemy force surrendered.[11] Thesiger would go on to take some of Wingate's ideas with him to his future service in North Africa with the Long Range Desert Group, an organization inspired by concepts of the "deep strike" mantra Wingate had been intoning for years.

Wingate, who had spent every day in the field for more than four months and had fought in almost every action of his tiny force, always against superior numbers, was by now worn out and suffering from an attack of malaria. Further, he was angry and increasingly paranoid over the many slights, real and imagined, he had been made to suffer, including being given second-rate troops at the outset of the campaign and little air support during the fighting. His assessment of his operations in Abyssinia, written after he returned to Cairo in June 1941, reflected this state of mind. It was filled with ad hominem attacks on other British leaders in the field and caused an uproar, largely due to its surly, personal tone. Yet Wavell read it with concern and interest, and let Wingate know that he hoped to launch a postmortem on the campaign that would lead to future improvements.

Wavell's time in charge of this theater, however, had run out. His successes against the Italians in East and North Africa had been more than offset by bruising defeats in Greece and Crete, as well as by Rommel's startling first offensive in the western desert and Wavell's failed counterattack. Just as Wingate was being attacked by his colleagues for the tone and content of his report, his protector Wavell was replaced with the far less sympathetic

Sir Claude Auchinleck. Wingate grew depressed about the prospects for an inquiry and for his own career.

His malaria attack also worsened. On July 4, 1941, his fever was at 104 degrees when he stumbled back to his hotel room, locked the door, stuck a hunting knife into his neck, and fell to the floor. Colonel C. J. M. Thornhill, who was staying in the next room, heard the snap of the lock and the thump of the body hitting the floor through the thin wall between the rooms. After failing to break into Wingate's room, Thornhill hurried to the manager for the master key. They entered just in time to keep Wingate from bleeding to death.[12]

A psychological examination of Wingate, while he was in the hospital, concluded that his suicide attempt was brought on by a combination of depression, exhaustion, and illness. It also noted that he was likely to make a full recovery, physically and mentally. In September he sailed on a hospital ship to South Africa, Mediterranean waters being largely impassable at the time because of German and Italian control. From there he took a troopship back to Britain, arriving in November 1941. His legion of detractors thought he was finished. They were wrong.

*   *   *

Once home, Wingate's doctors were inclined to see him as unfit for service; meanwhile his superiors seemed intent on court-martialing him for self-inflicted wounds. His recovery faltered and depression returned. But a Jewish doctor with Zionist ties took an interest in the case of *Hayedid* and was able to bring in another colleague, Lord Thomas Horder, to consult. Horder had been personal physician to British monarchs and prime ministers in more than forty years of medical practice. He examined Wingate and came away convinced that he was still able to serve his country.

Thus Wingate was neither sacked nor court-martialed. But he had virtually no friends in the service, either, and prospects for a new posting appeared grim. At this point Wavell, now commander in India, reached out to him. British armies had taken terrible beatings in Malaya, Singapore, and Burma at the hands of Japanese forces that often employed infiltration methods not unlike those Wingate advocated. Perhaps Wavell wanted someone near him who thought along these lines. Or he may have acted out of compassion toward Wingate. Whatever his motives, in April 1942 Wavell arranged for Wingate to serve with him once more.

At the moment an invasion of India appeared imminent. The seemingly unbeatable Japanese forces would likely be assisted in such an attack by a rising of Indian nationalists' intent on overthrowing British rule. Aside from plan-

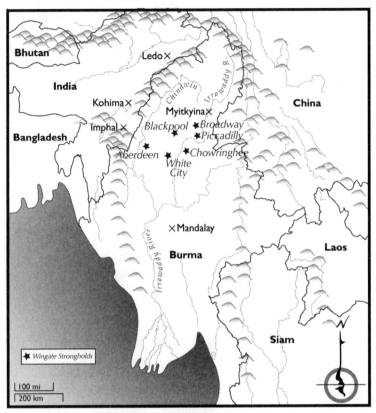

The China-Burma-India Theater

ning to exploit a popular rebellion, the Japanese were also developing a regular force of disaffected Indians, recruited from among prisoners taken in earlier campaigns. They were to fight under the command of Chandra Bose, a sharp critic of Mahatma Gandhi's nonviolent pursuit of independence, who had gone over to the other side. When the Japanese finally launched an invasion in 1944, Bose was part of it, at the head of about 150,000 Indians.

But in mid-1942 Wavell was in dire need of ideas for disrupting Japanese invasion plans. He could not count on reinforcements because in North Africa Auchinleck was being driven back to the gates of Cairo by Rommel. Wavell needed something else that would allow him to defend India actively but with limited resources. He needed the very sort of capabilities that Wingate held out the promise of providing.

Not one to miss such a seemingly miraculous opportunity for self-redemption, or to aid the one British military leader sympathetic to his ideas, Wingate quickly set to work bringing all his knowledge of long-range penetration and irregular warfare to bear on the problem of operating in Japanese-occupied Burma. He refused to believe that the enemy had an unbeatable edge in jungle warfare and began crafting the concept of operations that would, early the following year, lead to the first of two "Chindit" expeditions ("Chindit" comes from Wingate's corruption of the Burmese *Chinthé*, for "lion.").

After many months of planning and training, in February 1943 Wingate led some three thousand troops, a single brigade, into Burma on foot, their gear carried by a thousand mules. Over the next few months they raided Japanese outposts, disrupted their rail lines, and attacked other logistical sites. The Chindits were resupplied from the air and, lacking artillery of their own, relied on the occasional air strike to support their ground operations. By May, when they were being closely pressed from all sides by Japanese columns intent on their destruction, Wingate ordered dispersal into smaller teams with better chances of eluding pursuit. The retreat of the Chindits, like their raid itself, was replete with bitter, small-scale firefights.

About two-thirds of Wingate's men made it back safely. Of the thousand who didn't, half fell in the fighting, the rest were taken prisoner. Many conventional officers saw this as too high a price to pay for too little strategic gain—they noted that the Chindits had caused little lasting disruption to the Japanese buildup for an offensive into India.[13] But Wingate and his supporters saw something else: solid proof of the value of his concept. As Leonard Mosley put it, regarding the first Chindit operation: "Wingate and his three thousand troops lived in and off Japanese territory, and demonstrated the capacity of British troops not only to withstand the sweaty terrors of the jungle but their ability to outwit the enemy at the game of jungle warfare."[14]

Beyond the evidence that long-range penetration worked, and could be improved upon, this first expedition's psychological effects proved to be profound. After an endless string of defeats and retreats, the British were back on the offensive in Asia. When word began to spread, Wingate was dubbed the "Clive of Burma," an allusion to the great eighteenth-century hero who had won India for the empire in the first place. Winston Churchill, Britain's prime minister since the spring of 1940, asked that Wingate be sent to see him when he came to Britain. Wingate arrived at Downing Street in August, and his brief scheduled meeting with the prime minister turned into a lively discussion over dinner. Churchill recalled, "I felt myself in the presence of a man of the highest quality."[15]

On impulse Churchill decided to bring Wingate along to the Quebec Conference with Franklin Roosevelt for which he was leaving the following morning. As they crossed the Atlantic on the *Queen Mary* in August 1943, Wingate was given the opportunity to brief the British chiefs of staff who were traveling with Churchill. The chiefs took time from planning sessions for the upcoming Normandy invasion to hear him out. They were impressed. At Quebec he made less of an impression on President Roosevelt, who found him a bit odd. But General H. H. "Hap" Arnold, commander of the U.S. Army Air Forces, was deeply drawn to Wingate's concept of long-range penetration operations and became intent on providing the next expedition—for all this high-level attention meant there *would* be one—with better air support.

The meeting between Arnold and Wingate sparked development of the American "air commandos" who would, some months later, take most of the Chindits far behind Japanese lines on gliders and in transports. In this second expedition, U.S. airmen supplied the Chindits' remote "strongholds" completely from the air, provided close support by attacking enemy formations on the ground, and evacuated the wounded. This last function was of crucial importance to the troops themselves, as on the first raid into Burma the wounded had had to be left to die or be captured. Thus Churchill's spur-of-the-moment decision to take Wingate to Quebec set in train a series of events that led to greatly increased capacities for the Chindits—and prefigured ideas about air- and heliborne operations. Decades later they would come to be called "vertical envelopment."

For the second Chindit operation Wingate, now a major general, was given command of three brigades, a division-sized force. In March 1944 two of the brigades were inserted by air into remote places, some more than two hundred miles behind enemy lines. They became strongholds from which the Chindits mounted their raids. The third brigade made the trek overland and started out a month earlier. There were also American troops, Merrill's Marauders, to a degree configured like the Chindit forces, who joined the campaign. The Japanese now had a lot to worry about in their rear areas. Raiders popped up seemingly everywhere, destroying bridges and rail junctions, ambushing troops on the march, even attacking fixed positions.

Wingate lived to see little of this. As general-in-charge he hopped about from one stronghold to another by air, going to and from India as well. On March 24, 1944, the Mitchell B-25 in which he was traveling went down in a storm. None survived. The crash was so violent that it was near impossible to sort out the remains; all that was recognizable was Wingate's battered pith helmet, still intact.

What of the campaign after Wingate's death? Perhaps this phase offered the surest proof that his ideas about deep penetration and the role of airpower in irregular warfare were valid: those who carried on after him performed outstandingly. No historians seriously question their tactical skills. They spent months far behind the lines, not just surviving but also doing considerable damage to the Japanese, who had finally launched their long-awaited invasion of India just as the second Chindit operation was getting under way. Even though U.S. General Joseph Stilwell continually sought to integrate the raiding forces more closely into his own offensive campaign plans, aimed largely at the capture of Myitkyina (pronounced *mich-in-uh*), they were also able perform their more disruptive tasks, helping to defeat the Japanese invasion of India.

The Chindits were disbanded in 1945, apparently a sign that this kind of irregular operation was not to be nurtured. In the West after the war a long debate ensued between Chindit supporters and those who argued that the strategic impact of their operations was slight and that the resources devoted to them could have been put to much better uses.[16] While helicopters would come to the fore, unsuccessfully, in American counterinsurgency operations in Vietnam two decades later, there were—and remain—few signs that the legacy of the Chindits is substantial.

Thus the world still awaits its next Wingate, a commander willing to work with a small force and mount sustained deep strikes. It is a form of action seen among several of the earlier masters profiled in this book, notably Rogers, Davydov, Forrest, and Crook. But this mode of operations has fallen into disuse. Perhaps the dark American experience in Vietnam sapped the ardor of those who would otherwise wish to explore the edge that airpower gives irregular forces in mobility and lethality. Even when a revival of Wingate's techniques has occurred—as in the U.S. Special Forces campaign in Afghanistan in the fall of 2001—it has quickly given way to larger, more conventional, and more problematic, operations.

The greatest damage to the cause of long-range penetration may have been done by the historical controversy itself. Soldiers usually do not like to embrace an approach that is controversial, for this implies risk and a willingness to stand against much criticism. Yet war is the riskiest of all human activities, and the need to fight with an edge should impel thoughtful soldiers to seek out advanced, even if perilous, concepts of operations.

When it comes to Wingate's great Chindit experiment with long-range penetration, the historical debate should be re-enlivened by focusing less on the criticism of his colleagues and more on the opinions of his enemies in the field. Here one finds a tremendous respect for Wingate's operations. More than thirty Japanese unit commanders who fought in Burma, when interviewed after the war, said that "the raiding force [Chindits] greatly affected Army operations and eventually led to the total abandonment of Northern Burma."[17]

It is just as important to consider the views of Wingate's Israeli friends, for long-range penetration grew from roots planted in Palestine. Wingate's willingness to strike deep, to seize the offensive always, notwithstanding the numerical odds, these became and remain the core practices of the Israeli Defense Forces. Moshe Dayan, who served with Wingate in a Special Night Squad and later became one of Israel's most accomplished soldiers, confirmed his profound influence: "Every leader of the Israeli Army, even today, is a disciple of Wingate. He gave us our technique, he was the inspiration of our tactics, he was our *dynamic*."[18]

There can be no higher praise for a soldier than to have such a great impact, on friend and foe alike.

14

UNDERSEA WOLF:
CHARLES LOCKWOOD

If long-range penetration played a key role in driving Japanese forces out of the jungles of Burma, this concept of operations was to have an even greater impact at sea in the wide-ranging naval war sparked by the Japanese Navy's surprise attack on Pearl Harbor on December 7, 1941. Just as Orde Wingate's deep-striking Chindit irregulars had allowed the British to take offensive action early on against a militarily superior foe, American submarines would mount widespread, insurgent-type strikes—daring incursions that routinely lasted six to eight weeks—at a time when much of the U.S. Navy battleship fleet had been sunk and the Japanese had a better than two-to-one advantage in aircraft carriers. The time would come when American mass production would restore, then at last overturn the material balance in conventional naval power; until then, and even afterward, submarines served as the principal striking force against the far-flung Japanese maritime empire.

This would continue to be the case even in the wake of the great American victory at Midway in June 1942. Despite the loss of four carriers to one U.S. carrier in that battle, the Japanese retained their large advantage in conventional sea power. As Ronald Spector has put it: "The Japanese still had sufficient forces after Midway to again take the initiative for another try at the U.S. fleet."[1] In the six-month struggle for Guadalcanal, which commenced not long after Midway, American naval losses exceeded those of the Japanese—though the favorable "exchange ratio" (of losses inflicted to losses suffered) enjoyed by the Imperial Navy cost it more dearly, at least in a proportional sense, due to the growth of the American fleets.[2] The point is that undersea warfare remained at the forefront of U.S. naval strategy at this juncture in the war and continued to be the leading edge of the Pacific campaign even during the island-hopping invasions to come. Resources devoted to this theater of operations were always being constrained by the Allied priority of going after "Germany first."

That American naval leaders would embrace this form of irregular warfare at sea was hardly a foregone conclusion. Submarines were seen as something close to illegal weapons, given the German record of unrestricted U-boat attacks during World War I, at a time when there was not yet a highly reliable technology for detecting a submerged boat. The millions of tons of losses inflicted by U-boats on merchant shipping in the 1914–1918 war at sea dwarfed the results achieved by German surface raiders, most of whose depredations were swiftly curtailed. Despite the speed and fighting power of these swift surface vessels, their positions were usually pinpointed by radio reports, and they were quickly hunted down. Thus these heirs apparent to the classical form of the *guerre de course*, or "war of the chase," that had been waged by most leading states since the "sea dogs" of Sir Francis Drake's day in the sixteenth century, gave way to stealthy, deadly submarines. The grave new threat they posed was so apparent that all maritime powers sought to outlaw or sharply curtail their use.

The submarine clearly overturned the rules governing traditional naval warfare. Yet despite this heightened general sense of awareness, and the more specific aim of preventing the Germans from ever building their U-boats again, submarines continued to thrive as a weapons system. Even the great Washington Naval Conference of 1921–1922 concluded with a treaty that affected only surface vessels; no agreement could be reached on prohibiting the production and use of submarines, and all the major naval powers continued to build them even though they feared them.

Germany too threw off its shackles after some years of constraint imposed by the Treaty of Versailles, mounting a new U-boat offensive at the outset of World War II. The highly pernicious effects of this campaign in the early going only redoubled American opposition to unrestricted submarine warfare in the two years of peace that remained to the United States before Pearl Harbor. Beyond diplomatic protests against the U-boat campaign, American naval forces began to wage an undeclared war at sea during this period, with convoy escort vessels often involved in edgy incidents with German submarines.

American strategists were also hindered in seriously considering a submarine-led commerce raiding campaign by the navy's prevailing view that this was an inferior operational approach. Submarines, it was asserted, could only raid and run, not maintain open sea lanes for extended periods. This view was very much in line with the analysis of the great American apostle of sea power, Alfred Thayer Mahan, whose classic formulation was that commerce raiding, though beguiling to strategists, had never been decisive in a major conflict and was among the worst of war's "specious attractions."[3]

These diplomatic and operational objections notwithstanding, the dire circumstances accompanying the late U.S. entry into the war at the close of 1941, the savaging of the Pacific Fleet in the surprise attack on Pearl Harbor, and other sharp losses that came in the following weeks and months swiftly muffled ethical inhibitions or latent strategic snobbery toward commerce raiding. Thus a submarine campaign intended to be as ruthless as the one being conducted on the other side of the world by the Germans was commenced, placing the U.S. Navy in the peculiar position of simultaneously attacking via this mode of operations in the Pacific while defending against it in the Atlantic.

The American decision to resort to irregular warfare at sea should not be seen as driven simply by exigent circumstances, however. There was actually considerable historical precedent for operating in this fashion. The embryonic U.S. Navy during the Revolutionary War (1776–1783) was basically a small raiding force whose exemplar was John Paul Jones. The overwhelming British advantage in ships of the line during the War of 1812 guaranteed that the lighter American fleet of frigates would focus on hit-and-run operations too. And when the first round of naval arms control was played out in the Paris Conference of 1856, where the leading powers of the day sought to outlaw privateering, it was the United States that came to the vigorous defense of using "sea dogs for hire." The U.S. secretary of state in attendance at the conference, William Marcy, argued that giving up the *guerre de course* would create conditions where "dominion over the seas will be surrendered to those powers which have the means of keeping up large navies."[4] Americans, who had written the right to authorize commerce raiding into their Constitution,[5] were not about to allow an international ban on the practice.

No doubt there were regrets in Washington just a few years later when, during the Civil War (1861–1865), Confederate naval units and privateers engaged largely in commerce raiding, inflicting a great deal of damage to Union shipping.[6] While it was not enough to have a truly decisive effect on the outcome of the war—perhaps because the Confederates had only one short-range submarine, the *Hunley*, which was lost on its first operation—rebel sea raiders did enough damage to leave a "strategic memory" in place attesting to the efficacy of this form of warfare. In the dark days after Pearl Harbor, it was this and earlier manifestations of the American tradition of sea raiding that helped inspire a new generation of sailors to strike back in this fashion.

The early going for submarine operations against the Japanese Imperial Navy was hardly smooth. America's Asiatic Fleet, based in the Philippines, had twenty-nine submarines capable of long-range operations, but they proved incapable of harassing the ships supporting the many amphibious landings the Japanese made there. In December 1941 these submarines mounted more than forty attacks on Japanese ships, expending nearly one hundred torpedoes, but sunk only three small merchant ships.[7]

The problems were twofold: faulty technology and inadequate human resources. The Americans' Mark-14 torpedo tended to run at too great a depth, often passing far below its targets' hulls. When it did hit, the torpedo's detonator regularly malfunctioned.[8] Added to this was the "skipper problem": few submarine captains had trained for long-range patrols, and all believed—perhaps a bit too conveniently—that their boats were more vulnerable to depth charges and other enemy countermeasures than they actually were. This serious misperception led Asiatic Fleet commander Admiral Thomas Hart, who fled Manila Bay in a submarine, to urge great caution upon his submarine captains.[9] His wrongheaded guidance came at a time when the more aggressive use of submarines, including reset depth levels for their torpedoes, might well have significantly hampered the Japanese invasion of the Philippines.

In the event, the Japanese naval and amphibious *blitzkrieg* rolled on mostly unimpeded for many months after Pearl Harbor throughout the southwestern Pacific. Despite American willingness to wage unrestricted submarine warfare, the results achieved against the Japanese continued to be quite poor until both the technological and human capital problems were addressed. In the course of resolving these difficulties, Charles A. Lockwood came on the scene, helping bring solutions in both areas. From early 1943 until the end of the war in 1945, he commanded all submarines in the vast Pacific theater of operations. More than any other man, Lockwood turned the American submarine force into a deadly weapon, one that would eventually account for just under a third of all Japanese warships sunk, including eight aircraft carriers, a battleship, and eleven cruisers. His submarines would also sink about two-thirds of the Japanese merchant fleet, about five million tons.[10]

*   *   *

Charles Lockwood grew up in Missouri at the turn of the twentieth century, near the Mississippi River that, as a boy, he dreamed of sailing down to the Gulf of Mexico. His imagination was also fired by stories of American naval successes in the war of 1898 against Spain, which featured great fleet actions off Cuba and in the more distant Philippines. He was bright enough to earn admission to the U.S. Naval Academy, but his grades there held steady in the lower half of his class. He graduated in 1912 without particular distinction and served on two battleships over the next two years. But in 1914, newly transferred to the Asiatic Station, Lockwood was given command of a small submarine, *A-2*. He was soon enthralled with the emerging technologies that were, even then, making undersea warfare into what he thought would become the leading edge in naval affairs.

Because the United States entered World War I late—in 1917, after American anger had been sufficiently stoked by U-boat attacks, and the German naval and merchant fleets had long been bottled up—the Americans engaged in virtually no submarine action. Only a single enemy vessel was sunk by U.S. submarines before the armistice in 1918. But Lockwood drew the interesting postwar duty of commanding the *UC-97*, a surrendered German U-boat given to the Americans to study. He sailed it west across the Atlantic, then through the Great Lakes, learning much along the way and developing a deep respect for German design and engineering skills

Lockwood next returned to Asia, where he served on the China Station's Yangtze River Patrol, made famous by Richard McKenna's classic novel *The Sand Pebbles*. He commanded two small gunboats during this time and operated at a great distance and with little oversight from senior officers. Day to day he found himself dealing with pirates, warlords, and missionary relief societies. These experiences, which placed such a premium on the personal judgment and initiative of the commanding officer, would serve him well two decades later as he built up—or, more accurately, rebuilt—a new corps of submarine skippers who would spend most of their time far off on patrols, under little direct control.

After his tour as a gunboat captain, Lockwood returned to the growing submarine service. He pioneered the idea of "division attack" by several boats operating in what his German counterpart, Karl Doenitz—also a junior submarine officer during World War I, but who had gained more combat experience—would come to call "wolf packs." This idea of attacking in numbers was thought to be the antidote to the convoy system, which had dealt the U-boats a serious blow in World War I by using small antisubmarine warships to shepherd clusters of merchant vessels.

Lockwood also got into a major dispute with Thomas Hart, who would see his Asiatic Fleet destroyed at the outset of the Pacific War, over whether the American submarine fleet should be comprised of short-range and defensive or long-range boats capable of taking the war to the enemy's distant pressure points. Lockwood favored long-range submarines and, through doggedness and an unbreakable faith that he was right, eventually prevailed. But when war came it was Admiral Hart who was in charge of the more than two dozen submarines operating in the teeth of the Japanese invasion.

Now a captain, Lockwood found himself on the other side of the world, serving as the American naval attaché in London. He lived there during the Nazi blitz, regularly bringing Washington's top secret cables to Winston Churchill, now Britain's prime minister. In this post Lockwood learned a great deal about the German submarine campaign, a naval offensive that came perilously close to defeating Britain in the early dark days of the war. "The U-boat attack," Churchill observed, "was our worst evil."[11]

For three months after Pearl Harbor, Lockwood continued to request sea duty. In March 1942, perhaps the darkest moment in the war against Japan, he was given command of submarines in the southwest Pacific and promoted to rear admiral. Arriving in Perth in Western Australia, he began immediately to shore up the morale of the battered submariners. The care he showed for his captains and crews was to become one of his trademarks, a brand nicely described in his nickname, "Uncle Charlie." Like his German counterpart Doenitz, Lockwood made sure to see off his boats in person and to greet them upon their return. He also ensured that they were well supplied with good food for their long-range missions that sometimes lasted up to eight weeks.

Beyond being good human relations policy, his close ties to the boat crews allowed Lockwood to debrief them quickly and skillfully. What he found was deeply disturbing. Based on debriefings, he became convinced that the Mark-14 torpedo tended to run much deeper than its setting, causing many "misses." The Bureau of Ordnance would not accept his conclusion initially, so Lockwood used the stopgap measure of having his skippers reset the torpedoes to run at much shallower depths in the hope that this overcorrection would enable them to hit more targets. While this did result in an uptick in sinkings, new reports came in of "duds," torpedoes that struck as intended but did not detonate.

Eventually the navy would address both the depth and detonator problems, but it took another year to do so, well into 1943. Thus the early submarine campaign was greatly hobbled by technical deficiencies. Lockwood found he had a "skipper problem" too, and had to sack many of his too-cautious captains in favor of bolder ones. The problem stayed with him when he took command of all submarines in the Pacific theater in February 1943, after his predecessor died in a plane crash. Before all his personnel moves were complete, about a third of the submarine skippers in the Pacific had been sacked. Lockwood may have been Uncle Charlie, but he was one tough uncle.

With better captains manning his boats, and the torpedo problem finally being fixed, Lockwood was poised to launch a major offensive against the Japanese. Interestingly, he chose not to emulate Doenitz's wolf-pack operations. Instead U.S. attack submarines were sent out mostly as "lone wolves," their skippers generally maintaining radio silence and conducting their operations according to the dictates of their own judgment in the patrol areas designated for them. Late in the war Lockwood did send a small wolf pack to the Sea of Japan—nine boats, a fraction of the dozens that Doenitz often brought together in convoy battles. There it operated successfully; but this case was an exception in a campaign largely dominated by single raiders.[12]

Lockwood chose the lone-wolf approach out of concern that coordination of the wolf packs by means of back-and-forth radio communications ran the risk of enemy decryption and direction-finding technologies, the two elements that did so much to defeat Doenitz's U-boats.[13] Lockwood also had the advantage of intelligence gleaned by American cryptanalysts who had broken the Imperial Navy's codes (the famous "Magic" operations) often giving him advance knowledge of enemy sailings. This allowed him to economize on his use of force, sending just one or a few boats—but to more areas, where the code-breakers assured him the inviting targets would be. Just as this "Magic" decryption capability had proved of immense value in the Midway campaign, it was to play a significant role in submarine operations throughout the war.[14]

Aside from ramping up the campaign against Japanese commerce, Lockwood's submarines performed a range of other tasks during the Pacific War. They provided aid to guerrilla operators, usually in the form of arms and equipment but sometimes they rescued insurgents being harassed by the Japanese, taking the fighters and even their families onboard. Submarines also played a crucial role in providing photo intelligence of islands that were to be invaded. Their stealth allowed them to approach close enough to take extremely useful pictures.

Later, when the air war against the Japanese was in full swing, submarine pickets would stand by at sea to rescue downed pilots. By this means hundreds of fliers' lives were saved, including that of the young pilot who would become the forty-first president of the United States, George H. W. Bush. In short, Lockwood found himself overseeing a wide range of operations in support of the larger sea war being masterminded by his immediate superior, Admiral Chester Nimitz. But he never allowed these diverse tasks to keep him from his core mission: to sink Japanese naval and merchant vessels. Once he had the right personnel in place, and the torpedo detonator problem fixed, he unleashed the full ferocity of his campaign.

* * *

Over the last two years of the war in the Pacific, Lockwood, now a vice admiral, demonstrated great virtuosity in the use of his finely honed instrument. He commanded a force of submarines capable of operating throughout a naval battlespace that, despite Japanese reverses, encompassed an area measuring more than two thousand miles from north to south, and nearly that distance from east to west. When it was observed, early in 1944, that Japanese oil tanker capacity had increased by three hundred thousand tons since Pearl Harbor, Lockwood focused his efforts on these ships. The result

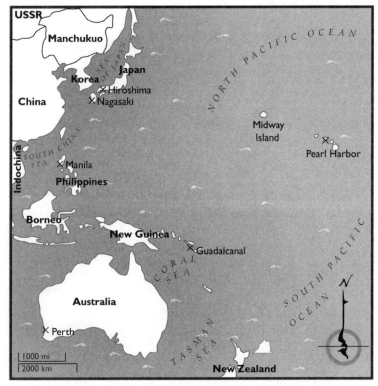

Area of Submarine Operations in the Pacific War

was massive tanker sinkings throughout the year, the high point being in October 1944 when a third of the 320,901 tons of Japanese merchant ships sunk were tankers.[15] During this period the American submarine force also began to target Japanese escort vessels, exacting a terrible toll among them as well.

By November 1944, with the sea virtually drained of enemy merchant ships and escort vessels declining sharply in numbers, Lockwood shifted target emphasis once again, this time to Japan's troop transports and larger warships. In this month alone, just a handful of American submarines accounted for two transports filled with troops, thousands of whom died, the battleship *Kongo*, and the fifty-nine-thousand-ton aircraft carrier *Shinano*. The Japanese submarine fleet, which had focused almost exclusively on targeting Allied warships, never came close to achieving results like these. By war's end Japan had lost just under seven hundred warships of all sizes, more than two hundred of them sunk by submarines.

This success may suggest that American submariners in the Pacific enjoyed one field day after another against indifferent opposition. The truth
is that these remarkable results were achieved against a first-rate Japanese
navy that fought bitterly to the end. There were many hard-fought actions
between subs and Japanese escort vessels, including dramatic surface battles
at night (the American vessels mounted three-inch deck guns) and long
cat-and-mouse hunts with many hours of depth charging as skippers dove
and turned their boats in feverish evasive maneuvers.

The key point to remember here is that in the vast majority of these
actions, the submarines were on their own—seventy crewmen and seven
officers, fighting outnumbered and without hope of timely reinforcement
or air support. Nonetheless they always strove to take the offensive, like
Orde Wingate's Chindits and Special Night Squads. Or, going back further, like so many other great irregular forces, from Rogers's rangers to
Forrest's rebels, and on to de Wet's *Kommandos*. The tactical essence of irregular warfare is the offensive, conducted with ferocity and pursued unless
the enemy's sheer numbers compel an end to the action—until the next
attack is launched.

One of the engagements that Lockwood considered particularly exemplary of the gallantry of his captains and crews began just after midnight
on October 23, 1944, in waters off China's southeastern coast. Commander
Richard O'Kane, skipper of the *Tang*, had come upon a large convoy of
Japanese ships headed for the great Leyte campaign in the Philippines then
getting underway. *Tang*, completely alone, drove into the middle of the
convoy on the surface, attacking and sinking two tankers and a freighter,
then narrowly missed being rammed by a transport, which hit another ship
instead. By now Japanese escorts were closing in, so *Tang* broke contact
until the next day. Resuming its attack after dark, *Tang* next took out
another tanker, a transport, and a destroyer. Twisting and turning his boat
in evasive surface maneuvers, O'Kane was able to line up one more target
with his last two torpedoes. He fired; one ran straight and hit its target, but
the other malfunctioned—Lockwood had fixed the depth and detonator
problems, but guidance often remained an issue—and it circled back and
hit *Tang*, sinking it.

O'Kane and a few sailors were blown off the conning tower into the
sea when the hit occurred. They met up with the five crew members who
had managed to escape from inside the boat. Everyone else died. These
nine were captured by the Japanese and imprisoned until the end of the
war. O'Kane lived to be awarded the Congressional Medal of Honor by
President Truman. Lockwood was standing at his side at the ceremony. As

to the *Tang*, in its eight months of war it accounted for twenty-four enemy ships sunk, almost a hundred thousand tons.[16]

Not every skipper performed at O'Kane's high level of efficiency, but many came close. Lockwood had gone out of his way to select the kind of men who would thrive on independent action and who were relentless in their pursuit of the offensive against the Japanese. In this he succeeded beyond all expectations, as the relative handful of sailors under his command—2 percent of all navy personnel—accounted for more than half of Japanese naval losses.[17] In merchant tonnage Japan fell from six million at the start of the war to less than two million by its end, net of new production and captured vessels. Most of the ships that remained were "small wooden vessels" that plied the waters of the Inland Sea.[18] This result reflects the kind of high return on investment that can come with a skillful irregular approach to battle. But it came at great cost. Nearly a quarter of the submariners who fought on the more than two hundred boats that served in the Pacific War died on the four dozen that were sunk in the fighting. Forty of their skippers were among the dead. The submariners in all oceans, some twenty thousand men in all, suffered the highest casualty rate of any branch of the U.S. armed forces in World War II.

As this bitter war neared its close in August 1945, President Harry S Truman, who had assumed office after Franklin Roosevelt's death in April that year, resolved to use atomic weapons against Japanese cities to compel a rapid surrender and avoid the need for an invasion. Aside from the ethical nuances of this decision, another option was available: to compel surrender by means of tightening the submarine blockade. This was certainly the preferred view of Admiral Nimitz, Lockwood's immediate superior. General of the Army Douglas MacArthur also opposed nuclear attack.

But perhaps the military voice closest to Truman, his chief of staff Fleet Admiral William Leahy, was the most articulate in emphasizing the impact of the irregular naval campaign. Leahy told Truman that Japan was "already defeated and ready to surrender because of the sea blockade."[19] Despite this, and in the face of opposition among senior military leaders, Truman went ahead with the nuclear attacks on Hiroshima and Nagasaki, and the war ended in August. Whether the sea blockade would have compelled surrender—which I believe—remains a lively subject of academic discussion.

For Lockwood, the end of the war allowed time for introspection about the future of naval warfare. Based on his experiences, and his deep knowledge of how close the German U-boats came to winning the Battle of the Atlantic, he concluded that submarines, with all their capacity for irregular warfare, would play a dominant role in naval affairs in the years to come. He lobbied hard for the creation of a major submarine command but ran up against a naval leadership that instead sought to make the aircraft carrier the center of the postwar navy.

After Lockwood retired he continued to argue that the submarine would be the true capital ship of the future. Years before Admiral Hyman Rickover became the father of the nuclear submarine, Lockwood was writing of such vessels, which would cruise for many months submerged, their reactors seldom needing refueling, their limits driven only by food requirements and the psychology of human endurance. Of their power, Lockwood had no doubts: "This submarine could drive every surface ship from the face of the sea."[20]

While the U.S. Navy did not heed his advice, the Soviets clearly did. They refused to emphasize carriers during the Cold War (and even today) and instead built hundreds of submarines. Today China seems to be following this model, taking a distinctly irregular approach to twenty-first-century naval affairs. In the one hard-fought, major sea war between advanced countries since World War II, the duel for the Falkland/Malvinas Islands between Britain and Argentina in 1982,[21] two British submarines ultimately bottled up the entire Argentine surface fleet. Only air attacks from land bases imperiled the Royal Navy in this fight. As the military historian John Keegan observed about the Falklands conflict, in a view quite in line with Lockwood's thinking: "The era of the submarine as the predominant weapon of power at sea must therefore be recognized as having begun."[22]

Lockwood continued to write about his experiences in several best-selling books. Although he had nothing of the literary style of Lawrence, the two shared a larger vision of the power of "the few," properly employed, to bedevil "the many." Like Lawrence, Lockwood recognized the great value of stealth and the initiative it granted to small forces to strike at the enemy's crucial pressure points. He also shared Lawrence's fate as an innovator, in that he too failed to inspire major changes. When he died in 1967, the navy was still carrier-centered. It remains so today. But if Lockwood was right in his belief that the submarine was becoming the most potent naval weapon, bringing irregular warfare to the fore at sea—much as ranging and raiding tactics came to dominate in the North American wilderness in the eighteenth century—the United States and its allies have much to worry about. The first submarine captain, Jules Verne's Nemo, was a terrorist who struck at modern warships and merchant steamers with impunity. The next Nemo may be one too.

15

PARTISAN: JOSIP BROZ, "TITO"

© Bettmann/Corbis

In at least one important respect, the German armored *blitzkrieg* that over-ran France in 1940 and the Japanese carrier aircraft attack on Pearl Harbor in 1941 had quite similar effects: both were such disabling blows that they allowed the aggressors free reign for conquest, at least for a while. The fall of France permitted the Germans to move with impunity across virtually all of Europe. The crippling of the U.S. Navy opened up the Pacific and East Asia to Japanese conquest.

The British tried hard to make a conventional stand in each theater of operations. But in Africa their initial successes against the Italians were soon overturned by the arrival of Rommel's *Afrika Korps*. In Europe, Brit-ish expeditionary forces sent to the Balkans to stem the fascist tide were driven from the mainland, then from the island of Crete in a series of bruis-ing defeats. In the East the empire suffered even more humiliating losses in Singapore and Burma. Despite the deep entanglements of the Germans in Russia (from June 1941) and the Japanese in China, Britain and the United States still found it difficult to open up new fronts for massive conventional campaigns.

During these dark early years of World War II, the principal counter-moves available to the remaining forces of resistance were to a great extent irregular in nature. As noted in the preceding two chapters, the strategic situation in the Pacific placed a premium on the waging of irregular warfare against Japan with Wingate's long-range penetration groups on the Asian mainland and Lockwood's submarines at sea. In Europe, Nazi control, almost complete from the fall of France to the invasion of Normandy four years later, also required an emphasis on unconventional operations. Winston Churchill, who was still holding out against Hitler in Britain, and someone very well acquainted with irregular warfare from the time of his experiences with the Boers forty years earlier—not to mention what he had learned from his friendship with T. E. Lawrence—was determined to foster strong resistance to Nazi rule throughout the occupied countries. With a mix of local insurgents and British-led commando raids, the main goal of the Special Operations Executive he established was to "set Europe ablaze."[1]

Thus a host of British elite forces formed up, including the Spe-cial Boat Service, the Special Air Service, and the Long Range Desert Group. More than crafting such capabilities in his own military, however, Churchill—and the few others who were open to such ideas—also wanted to promote insurgencies among the occupied peoples of Europe. Some among Americans also supported this notion upon their country's entry into the war at the close of 1941. Soon small Allied "Jedburgh" teams—

named after the castle where they trained—were parachuting into occupied territory to help organize resistance and conduct sabotage.

During the years of Nazi control, armed insurgents sprang up in virtually every occupied country. Europe truly was "set ablaze," per Churchill's order. But the strategic results of this irregular campaign were mixed. The Germans responded ruthlessly to such insurgent attacks, killing large numbers in reprisal for any losses they suffered. They were also skillful at infiltrating resistance units, rolling up insurgent networks with alarming regularity. The commandos, coming ashore from small boats, and the Jedburghs, who usually parachuted in, suffered enormous casualties. German occupation, for the most part, didn't end until massive armies invaded and drove them out in bitter fighting.

Overall the sense of most leading historians is that the Special Operations Executive and the various resistance movements, even the large number of Russian partisans operating behind German lines in the East, had for the most part little strategic effect. Of the most dramatic rising, that of the Poles in August 1944, the military historian John Keegan concluded that the Germans "found the means to fight—and eventually defeat—the insurgents without drawing on their front-line strength."[2] Such was the case in virtually all the other antiguerrilla campaigns conducted by the armed forces of the Third Reich.

But there was one insurgency whose results proved an important exception to the often lackluster performance of other commandos and resistance fighters: the struggle against the Nazis in Yugoslavia led by Josip Broz, the man who came to be known to the world as "Tito." In nearly four years of continuous fighting after the German invasion in the spring of 1941—one of Hitler's drives that quickly and easily defeated the government forces arrayed against his *Wehrmacht*—Tito would demonstrate his mastery of many aspects of irregular warfare and roll back the occupation.

He succeeded in doing so, for the most part, with little material assistance from either the Russians or the Western Allies. For some time the Red Army was far too busy fighting off the Germans; later, Soviet leader Joseph Stalin saw little of value in allowing a strong indigenous movement to arise in an area where he hoped to hold postwar sway. And the British, for their part, spent the first years of the resistance in Yugoslavia supporting the more favored general of the monarchy-in-exile, one Draja Mihailovich, whose Serbian "Chetniks" spent much of their time trying to weaken or destroy Tito.

Yugoslavia was a young nation cobbled together in the wake of World War I. The Germans were well aware of the ethnic and social divisions that roiled just below its surface, and exploited them with considerable skill. They also maintained large numbers of troops in the country, adding to their forces as the European war turned against them, out of fear of an Allied landing in the Balkans. Thus as the war dragged on their relatively small occupation force increased to twenty-five divisions (eight of them Bulgarian, some Italian forces too), well over a quarter million troops. The occupiers also enjoyed local air superiority for the most part, which allowed them to bomb resistance strongholds and from time to time to mount airborne operations.

At the outset, in the summer of 1941, Tito surveyed a bleak scene, and conditions throughout most of his remarkable campaign remained daunting. He had to fight for years with little outside support, and struggled against both the highly skilled German military and the main resistance forces of Mihailovich favored by his own country's legitimate government. But Tito had advantages too. Yugoslavia's mountainous terrain made it difficult for the occupiers to operate easily with large forces, which allowed Tito to "packetize" his own units and disperse them throughout the country. This dispersal was not unlike Lockwood's choice of sending lone submarines out to a wide range of distant patrol areas, and was also similar in placing a premium on having fine local commanders who were capable of operating with minimal instruction.

Indeed, it was said that the skills of Tito's best lieutenants—Djilas, Kardelj, Popovic, and Ribar—were so consummate that all Tito had to do in a major strategy session was point to one of them, saying "*ti*" (you), then to a point on the map, saying "*to*" (that). This may or may not have been the origin of his *nom de guerre*, "Tito." More likely "Tito" was just a code name he used during his early days as a socialist/Communist agitator. It was a Croat name occasionally used at the time, rendered in English as Titus.

For all the skills of those around him, Tito was himself an accomplished soldier. Born in 1892 in a Croatian village near Zagreb, then a part of the Austro-Hungarian Empire, he was drafted into its army the year before World War I broke out. He took to soldiering naturally, very soon rising to sergeant. He was particularly adept at fencing and won a service-wide competition on the eve of war. But during the Balkan crisis that led to the wider conflict, and even after the fighting started, Tito began acting on his growing socialist sentiments, spreading antiwar propaganda among the troops. Briefly imprisoned, he was released and sent off to fight the Russians.

He distinguished himself in battle and was soon promoted to sergeant major, the youngest in the Austro-Hungarian Army. But even fine soldiers suffer misfortunes, and in 1915 Tito was wounded and captured by the Russians. After treatment in hospital, he was sent to a prisoner-of-war labor camp in Siberia and was later released by the Bolsheviks during the revolution. He joined the Reds in the Russian civil war, and made his way back to Yugoslavia at the end of the major fighting in 1920, with a teenaged wife, Polka, in tow. He found steady work as a machinist during these years but also served as a Communist organizer. His party prospered under the constitutional monarchy, becoming the third-largest faction in the Yugoslav legislature, holding nearly sixty seats.

The rise of the Communists was viewed with great concern by the government, and in 1928 a crackdown ensued in which Tito found himself once more in prison. Instead of the few months of incarceration he suffered at the hands of the Habsburgs, or his year-plus as a POW in Russia, this time he was imprisoned for five years. Upon his release he moved to Vienna, himself, as his wife had left him while he was in prison. Next he went to the Soviet Union for a year, becoming a member of the NKVD, the organization from which the KGB would emerge. He had apparently gained Stalin's favor during his stay in the USSR. For during this time of Soviet purges of all those even suspected of disloyalty, the secretary general of the Communist Party of Yugoslavia fell victim to "official murder" while in Moscow in 1937. Tito, on his return to his homeland, took his place. Although the Communists were still not a legal party, Tito, now "Comrade Walter," continued to lead and organize it, building secret cells and nodes in a network that would prove highly useful during the years of resistance to the Nazis. Indeed, after King Peter II fled during the invasion in 1941, it was the Communists who mounted the opening attacks on the Germans.

But this first uprising, characterized by mass action in several places, was easily put down—much as the French dealt with the popular insurrection against their rule in Spain in 1808, the only major difference being that the Germans had considerable help from local collaborators, including Tito's own Croats. Thus, like so many of the other masters of irregular warfare, Tito suffered a very serious reverse at the outset of a crucial campaign. He would learn from it, crafting a new concept of operations that would ultimately defeat smart, tough, and more numerous foes. And he and his colleagues would do it largely on their own.

*　*　*

By the fall of 1941 Tito had about fifteen thousand fighters under him, roughly the manpower of a reinforced infantry division, but much of his force was without weapons. Still, he commanded roughly triple the number

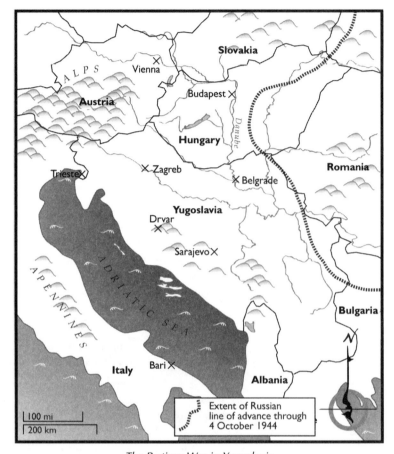

The Partisan War in Yugoslavia

of troops that Mihailovich had. Most were deployed in northern Yugoslavia, which made them particularly susceptible to an offensive by a corps (three divisions) of crack German troops who drove them out of Serbia in less than a week that November. Tito and the men who escaped the German net made their way south to Bosnia, but there was little rest to be had. A new offensive mounted by Italian troops and Croat collaborators soon drove them down to Montenegro. Here the rough terrain made it hard for enemy forces to get at them, but it was even harder for the insurgents to strike back from their remote mountain fastnesses.

This was the low point of Tito's campaign. The Germans, Italians, and their Yugoslav collaborators had proved militarily adept at fighting in rough terrain and were absolutely ruthless in their dealings with civilians who they thought might be aiding the insurgents. Atrocities swiftly mounted, turning Yugoslavia into what Churchill sadly called "the scene of fearful events."[3] For his part, Mihailovich came to a "live and let live" accommodation with the occupiers while he served as the official leader of the resistance authorized by the government-in-exile and was receiving British aid. Indeed, his Chetniks went even farther down the path of treachery, often providing information to the Nazis about Tito's forces.

It was during this crisis that Tito devised what turned out to be the war-winning idea of mounting a wide-ranging offensive with small combat formations. In the darkest days of the fight he ordered a march north, keeping some fighters in the south and dispersing his forces widely among his trusted subordinates. All of these "columns" recruited vigorously while on the march. Soon the occupiers found that, far from having successfully pacified Yugoslavia, they now had to deal with insurgent activities erupting in several different places at the same time—a "strategic swarm," if you will. Tito's bold stroke resembled the daring offensive move made by Nathanael Greene at one of the lowest points during the American Revolution, which reenergized the guerrilla campaign in the south.

The German reply to the renewed insurgent threat was to send ever more troops, amounting to well over a hundred thousand in 1942, and more than double that number of German and other Axis-allied troops under German command by the end of 1943.[4] These antiguerrilla forces conducted large-scale counteroffensives that led to the killing or capture of thousands of Tito's fighters and came close to catching him on more than one occasion.

But such sledgehammer blows could only deal with parts of the insurgency at any one time. And when counterinsurgent forces moved to deal with a threat emanating from another area, the seemingly hacked-off limb of the resistance in the province they had just come from grew back, often stronger than before. As Walter Laqueur has described the central reason for the turnaround, "Tito had realized that the strength of the partisan movement lay in its dispersal."[5]

Coming to grips with the fact that they were dealing with a hydra-headed insurgency, the Germans began trying different methods for coping with the multitude of small enemy units striking in many places. First they attempted to rediscover Kitchener's methods from the Boer War, in particular his mix of blockhouses and rapid reaction forces. In the German case in Yugoslavia, these consisted of a network of *Stuetzpunkte* ("strong points") and a ranger-like force called the *Jagdkommando* ("hunter command"). The arrays of mini-forts were strategically placed at important junctions—roughly six miles apart—and the commandos were situated in places where they could rapidly come to the aid of a number of threatened posts.[6]

But these were mostly defense-oriented changes. The Germans knew they needed to be able to use their many small units they had created on the offensive as well, and here again they borrowed from Kitchener. Where "sweeps" had dominated the "de Wet hunts" forty years earlier, the Germans now used the same tactic of deploying hunter units to push the insurgents into a waiting line of troops, calling it a "partridge drive." Other tactics included the simpler "battue shooting," in which all the small units on the edge of the encirclement would simultaneously drive inward.

Early on the Germans learned that the insurgents could escape through gaps in the formations leading the drives and shoots, so they added another tactic in which those on the edge of an encirclement stayed in place while *Jagdkommando* teams drove wedges into the enemy positions, like putting a stick in a beehive. As the insurgents fled, they were cut down or captured by the forces still waiting in position at the perimeter.[7]

To varying degrees, all these tactics worked, though the notion of encirclement followed by select wedges driving inward may have been the most effective. But no single enveloping maneuver ever trapped more than a relatively small portion of Tito's widely dispersed forces. His way of organizing the resistance had inoculated it against such methods. His partisans suffered losses in these fights—but so did the Germans and their allies. And always some of the insurgents escaped, sharing their growing knowledge of how to outfox the hunters with others in the resistance.

By 1943 the tide began to turn against the occupiers. Not only did Tito's dispersion of forces enable him to slip the Germans' heavy punches, but his troops' presence throughout the country proved a boon to recruitment. And as his numbers rose, the Axis forces were being seriously depleted by Italy's signing of an armistice with the Allies in September. Italian troops stopped fighting the Yugoslavs, and large numbers of them went over to Tito, naming themselves the Garibaldi Division of the resistance forces.

The Germans now began making systematic use of perhaps their most powerful irregular warfare innovation: pseudo gangs. Pioneered in fighting against the Russian partisans, these were small units—platoon-sized, usually, some few dozen soldiers in each—that dressed like resistance fighters and patrolled around in efforts to locate Tito's units. When they succeeded in doing so, either they ambushed the partisans or called in regular troops and aircraft to pummel them.

The overall effectiveness of these units was enhanced by their employment of local collaborators who could speak correct dialect and help carry off the deception that these hunter-killers were just fellow fighters from another nearby unit. Their record in Russia and the Balkans—and the subsequent adoption of this technique by the British—led the irregular warfare expert Otto Heilbrunn to conclude: "If pseudo gangs can possibly be formed, they must be formed, in every anti-guerrilla war."[8]

But even the success of such skillful operations by pseudo gangs and commandos was not enough to overcome a partisan movement that was now too large to be crippled by such small-scale strikes. In the wake of the Italian collapse, Tito's partisans were further strengthened when the Big Three Allied leaders—Churchill, Roosevelt, and Stalin—meeting in Tehran from late November to early December, made a clear choice to drop their support for Mihailovich. In practical terms this meant that Tito would now begin receiving arms, equipment, and intelligence from the Allies.

In this regard Churchill followed through most consistently, guided by the insights and advice of his representative to Tito, Brigadier Fitzroy Maclean—whom, some say, was Ian Fleming's model for James Bond. But Churchill's own son Randolph parachuted in to fight with the partisans as well, and Churchill himself made sure to maintain a cordial correspondence with Tito.

Overall the British effort was exemplary if not materially decisive during the remainder of the war in Yugoslavia. Certainly it outshone the Russian contributions, as Stalin remained concentrated on defeating the main German army and was reluctant to build up local forces in areas that he intended to become Soviet spheres of influence. So, in a most ironic turn, the Communist-led partisans in Yugoslavia, headed by an NKVD operative, were largely spurned by Moscow while the Western supporters of the exiled king provided increasing amounts of material support.

Despite all these adverse developments and their own declining resources, the Germans were not finished. They fought on, partly due to Hitler's reluctance to give ground anywhere on the edges of his tottering empire, partly because Balkan bauxite, oil, and other needed resources for the war effort came from or passed through Yugoslavia. In the final phase of the war, the Germans used all their existing tactical methods, and introduced yet one more—an airborne commando strike—that very nearly gave them victory over Tito in May 1944. They also made a point of increasing their efforts to exploit ethnic tensions, fomenting the killing of Serbs by Croats and Slovenes, and vice versa. Indeed, the deep-rooted civil strife that would destroy Yugoslavia fifty years later was nurtured by the Germans in this last phase of their war against Tito.

*   *   *

By the spring of 1944 it was clear that the second front Stalin had wanted for three years would soon be opened in Western Europe. German units began to be redeployed to the west, where eventually a force of sixty divisions was amassed to oppose the Allied landing in France, more than half of them under the command of Rommel. Now Tito and his lieutenants began to feel an easing of the pressure that they had been under for years, and they were enjoying the ample supplies sent by the British and Americans. Yugoslav partisans had even linked up with elements of the British Special Boat Service that were now operating in the Adriatic Sea, which gave them a whole new capability for mischief. It appeared that a highly favorable endgame was unfolding.

But the Germans still had some important pieces of their own in play. In late May 1944 they undertook a final strike against Tito that was their most innovative of all: Operation *Roesselsprung* (Knight's Move). Unlike their earlier offensives, in this one the Germans used a very small number of elite troops, not more than a few battalions in size, that were dropped in stealthily by parachute near Tito's headquarters in Drvar. They struck like a thunderclap, though the partisans inflicted severe casualties on the Germans' first wave. A wild series of firefights ensued in which several thousand partisans were killed. Overall German losses were minimal. Tito himself was very nearly captured, barely making good his escape, as Walter Roberts has related these events, by "climbing up a dry run cut by a mountain waterfall."[9]

Shaken by these events, and still pursued by German follow-on forces, Tito agreed to be temporarily evacuated across the Adriatic to Bari in liberated Italy. He stayed only briefly before returning to direct the fight, but he accomplished much. To counter remaining German threats from the air, a Balkan Air Force was created on June 1, just a week after the near-fatal raid on Tito's headquarters. As Fitzroy Maclean notes, the BAF consisted of about five hundred combat aircraft, nearly half of them fighters, which precluded any future airborne operations by the Germans.[10] Now their "knight's moves" were over, and with them any hope for quelling the insurgency. With the simultaneous success of the Normandy invasion in the west and the great Soviet summer offensive in the east, the Germans had far more serious difficulties to deal with than those posed by Tito in the Balkans.

In the fall of 1944 Tito became a "Marshal of Yugoslavia." He continued to enjoy a cordial relationship with Churchill and increasing supplies from the Western allies. As the war neared its end, even the Russians provided assistance, slowing their drive toward Berlin and redirecting forces to a more southerly axis of advance. Stalin now wished to thwart any British or American moves to achieve and sustain influence in the Balkans, or possibly even in Central Europe.

Despite this growing attention from Britain, the United States, and the Soviet Union, Tito remained his own man, winning the war to free his country on his own terms. As Walter Laqueur has concluded: "Yugoslavia is one of the few cases in history in which a partisan movement liberated a country and seized power largely without outside help."[11] This sense of self-accomplishment would play a significant role in enabling Tito to keep Yugoslavia from becoming a Soviet satellite in the postwar years. Further, having achieved their own victory was to prove a key element in Yugoslav foreign policy in the postwar period, as Tito strove to steer a course independent of the wishes of the opposing sides in the Cold War.

Fitzroy Maclean, in his biography of Tito, called him a "heretic" for so defying Stalin and the Soviet Union. Tito's lieutenant, Milovan Djilas, saw something different: the successful insurgency had forged what he called a "new class" that would pursue communism on its own terms, free of outside controlling interests. Whatever the influence of "heresy" or social innovation, one can also see the continuing play of nationalism in Tito's policies during this period. The idea of nationhood had driven the politics of the Balkans for a long time. Indeed, it was nationalist sentiment that had much to do with the assassination of the Austrian archduke Franz Ferdinand, touching off World War I. Some thirty years later, Tito believed it his greatest mission to assert the unity and independence of a distinct, free-thinking and -acting Yugoslav nation.

He followed this course by a variety of means. First, immediately after the war ended, he demanded that all Allied military forces—American, British, and Russian—leave the country. This accomplished, Tito then called for national elections in which the people were to decide what form of government they wanted. It was a vote won overwhelmingly by the communists, which resulted in the king's abdication and Tito's becoming prime minister of the republic. Soon after, Mihailovich, now a fugitive, was captured, tried, and executed.

The matter of governance and any internal challenge to his regime settled, Tito next tried to reduce interethnic tensions by moving people about, outside their home provinces, and encouraging the intermixing of ethnic subgroups. In this manner he blended nationalist fervor with his belief in the classic Marxist formulation that class trumps ethnicity. During his lifetime, it was a formula that worked.

The early postwar years proved a heady time for Tito, who had now succeeded as both warlord and statesman. His long run of luck may have impelled him to test its limits, leading him into confrontations with both East and West. His aggressive stance toward territories on the Italian border, the city of Trieste in particular, led to a number of dangerous incidents, including the shooting down of several American transport aircraft. Eventually forced to back away there, he next supported a communist insurgency in Greece, one that Stalin had already abandoned. The Greek guerrillas were defeated, and Tito's attempt to control events in Albania also backfired. By now the Soviets were just as angry with him as were the Western allies. Tensions with Stalin grew over Tito's uncontrolled actions, so much so that several attempts were made to assassinate him. All were thwarted, and Tito sent a curt note to Stalin advising him to stop sending assassins or else he would send one of his own—and wouldn't need to send another.[12]

It is tempting to psychoanalyze Tito's behavior at this point, drawing a connection between his risk-taking as a statesman and his inveterate philandering. His first wife left him when he was in prison during the late 1920s, and after her came a long series of paramours and wives. His second wife was said to have left after coming home to find him in bed with a mistress. Other reports suggest that his serial affairs may have reflected his reactions to wives who tried to control him too closely—just as he bridled at any international attempts to constrain his rule of Yugoslavia or, for that matter, his foreign policy.

But Tito eventually settled down with one woman, Jovanka, a Serbian peasant thirty years his junior whom he married in 1952, just a year before Stalin's death. He stayed with her for more than twenty-five years. She had joined the partisans during the war and nursed Tito back to health after serious surgery. They separated shortly before his death, but he made clear to all those around him that he still loved her.[13]

This domestic stability seemed to accompany less confrontational foreign policies. Tito graciously ended his drive to control Trieste soon after his marriage to Jovanka, and went out of his way to conciliate with Moscow. He was even willing to sacrifice his friendship with Milovan Djilas—one of his most gifted lieutenants during the war and a leading Yugoslav intellectual—by disgracing him when, as his biographer Richard West noted, his anti-Soviet writings "were embarrassing Tito in his attempts to improve relations with Stalin's successors."[14]

Whether his growing reasonableness was the product of a happy home life or simply the dynamics of power politics at the time, Tito became a leading voice for a calm, steady stewardship of world affairs during the nuclear-tipped Cold War era. He helped form and lead the movement of so-called nonaligned states, establishing a particularly warm relationship with Haile Selassie, the ruler of Ethiopia who had marched with Orde Wingate to fight for his country's freedom. Tito also kept in touch and visited with Winston Churchill, whom he described as "a great man. He is, of course, our enemy and has always been the enemy of communism, but he is an enemy one must respect."[15]

At home Tito's emphasis on cultivating a broad national rather than a narrow ethnic identity held his country together and fostered prosperity under his concept of "market socialism." But the nationalities problem was never very far below the surface. Serb-Croat tensions continued to simmer, and both of these antagonists harbored grievances aimed at the Bosnian Muslims. Against these forces of discord, Tito responded with his many repeated calls for "brotherhood and unity" throughout the country.

At the time of his death in 1980 at eighty-seven, Tito's view still prevailed. Four years later, at the Winter Olympics held in Sarajevo, the world witnessed Tito's vision of Yugoslav nationhood. Yet the following decade saw Sarajevo, and much of the rest of the country, turned into a charnel house that would consume the lives of hundreds of thousands of innocents. Tito's dream was shattered.

The fall of Yugoslavia should be viewed as having occurred in spite of all that Tito did, not *because* of what he did. As Misha Glenny observed, for all his exploits as a partisan leader, perhaps Tito's greatest accomplishment was that he "succeeded in ending the mass slaughter of Croats and Serbs born of the complex conflict which developed among the ruins of monarchist Yugoslavia during the Second World War."[16] He did this by promoting a greater national identity, which he shored up during the dark war years—despite Nazi efforts to foment internecine strife—and continually reinforced during the many decades of the Cold War. That a homegrown fascist, the Serb leader Slobodan Milosevich, would one day pick up the Nazi playbook again and reawaken old hatreds does not detract from Tito's accomplishment. The dissolution of Yugoslavia merely confirmed something that Tito believed all along: the only truly mortal threat to his nation would come from within.

16

COUNTERINSURGENT: FRANK KITSON

Victor Patterson

Armed resistance to foreign occupation, so widespread during World War II, rose to an even higher level of activity in the postwar years. This was because the idea of nationhood—a key to Tito's success, which had depended on all the various Yugoslav ethnic groups flocking to his banner—came to animate "peoples' liberation movements" around the world that aimed at throwing off colonial control. The view that common people could drive out their conquerors and colonizers was as old as Clausewitz's discussion of it in his classic *On War*. And surely Abd el-Kader and Garibaldi who, knowingly or not, acted on Clausewitz's formulations were early exemplars of this ideal. The same could be said of Lawrence. But Abd el-Kader failed, and in order to win Garibaldi had to ally with the royal House of Savoy. Even Lawrence saw the Arab Revolt end in a reassertion of outside rule, for the most part, with new masters. But Tito's striking success at irregular warfare, so thoroughly consolidated in the years after the fighting ended, became the benchmark for many other aspirants.

Soon life grew hard for the world's colonial powers, as the "big war" against the fascists was followed by a spate of small conflicts aimed at the imperialists. Almost all these wars of liberation, many of them supported by the Soviet Union, were conducted using various mixes of insurgent and terrorist tactics. As Robert Taber once put it, this was an era of "the war of the flea."[1]

Possessing the world's largest empire, Britain was particularly pressured by these movements. Containing or countering them became a principal strategic goal, beginning almost immediately after the final defeat of the Axis powers. It was to prove a rearguard action at best, however, given that during the period 1947–1980, forty-nine colonial entities would break free from the British Empire.[2] But the manner in which the British met these many challenges to imperial control reflected a growing sophistication on the part of their military. Fresh from its many massive battles against the Germans and Japanese, Britain learned to wield its arms with a new suppleness.

The early going was hardly auspicious. Britain simply let India go in August 1947, with Pakistan being split off and a war between the two new nations erupting immediately. The following year Israel was granted its nationhood, in part due to world sentiment in the wake of the Holocaust favoring establishment of a home for the Jews, but in part also because the Jewish insurgents that Orde Wingate had done so much to train had worn down British will. Burma was also set free about this time; but thereafter it was determined in the high councils in London to hold on to the remainder of the empire, come what may. A series of insurgencies and terror campaigns soon erupted, putting British skill and resolve to the test.

One of the most vexing uprisings broke out in Kenya, which Britain had controlled since 1887. Tribal lands had been appropriated and settled by a few thousand white planters who employed and oversaw an indigenous population numbering in the few millions. The Kikuyu, at slightly less than two million, were the largest tribe and the one most dispossessed of its traditional territories by the colonists. They were also the most resentful and, once the dust had settled from World War II, began agitating for their freedom. At first they simply sought to follow Gandhi's model of nonviolent resistance, which had worked so well in India, but the British reaction in Kenya was to hunker down and hold out.

When, inevitably, violence occurred, notably the killing of a pro-British Kikuyu chief by Mau Mau fighters[3] in October 1952, a full-blown state of emergency was declared. But by then Kikuyu discontent was so great that it took only a short while for more than fifteen thousand fighters to take the Mau Mau oath and begin killing in the name of independence. Members of the constabulary and pro-British Kikuyu were among the principal targets at the outset of this conflict, but white farmers were also attacked. More than two dozen of them were murdered, enough to terrorize the roughly forty thousand Europeans living throughout Kenya at the time.

The most spectacular single act of terror committed by the Mau Mau was the so-called Lari Massacre in March 1953, in which another pro-British tribal chief's village was overrun and seventy men, women, and children were slaughtered. In the wake of this terrible incident, British reinforcements began to arrive, bringing troop levels to more than twenty thousand by June 1953 when General George Erskine arrived. They were soon employed, quite ineffectually, in a mixture of garrison duty and broad-based sweeps to hunt down the Mau Mau.

General Erskine was sensitive to the shortcomings of this approach and was well aware that over 90 percent of the Kikuyu supported the Mau Mau.[4] Other tribes like the Kamba and Masai were also climbing onto the insurgent bandwagon. As the historian John Newsinger wrote, "The inability of the security forces to defeat the rebels was attracting men and women from other tribal groups to the path of armed struggle."[5] In the words of Sir Michael Blundell, the leader of the European settler community in Kenya, the authorities were losing "the battle for the mind of the African everywhere."[6]

At this low point in the summer of 1953, a twenty-six-year-old British officer from the Rifle Brigade, with which he had been serving in Germany for seven years, was sent along with other reinforcements to help in the fight against the Mau Mau. Frank Kitson came from a family with a two-century-long tradition of service in the Royal Navy, which he had broken due to asthma. He joined the army instead, beginning his training in the last months of World War II. His initial instruction and his years of service as an occupier in Germany did little to prepare him for the conflict in Kenya.

Kitson, for some reason posted to Kenya as an intelligence officer, strove hard to make up for his lack of preparation with intensive reading about the history of the Kikuyu and with flights over Kenya. He also studied closely the social organization of the insurgency, especially the wide reach and considerable stealth it enjoyed because it was broken into small, widely dispersed "gangs" of fighters. Kitson began to crystallize his insights about irregular warfare, views that he would one day sum up succinctly: "The problem of defeating insurgents consists very largely of finding them."[7]

While Kitson was learning, Erskine was developing his own plan to create "safe areas" and conduct sweeps for the enemy, but neither of these remedies showed signs of doing serious harm to the insurgents. By the spring of 1954 he was frustrated enough to launch Operation Anvil, a mass detention of Africans in Nairobi, the goal being to sort out the Kikuyu from among them for resettlement. After this method was employed in the city, it was taken to other parts of the country. Ultimately more than a million Kikuyu were detained and resettled.

Much suffering accompanied this policy, which the British government strove to hide. Erskine was a friend of Winston Churchill—now nearly eighty, and prime minister yet again after a postwar hiatus—who had given him a letter authorizing him to take whatever measures he thought appropriate in Kenya. Erskine carried the Churchill letter around in his glasses case, and whenever he faced objections from his subordinates or the settlers he would, as the historian Caroline Elkins notes, "stop them in their tracks by snapping the case open and then shutting it."[8]

In the midst of Operation Anvil, Kitson was developing his own concept of counterinsurgency operations, primarily to have friendly Kikuyu go out in the field pretending to be Mau Mau. The idea was basically the same as that employed by the Germans in Russia and the Balkans during World War II: such pseudo gangs could be used to gather intelligence about the insurgents and even stage raids and ambushes against them. But for the most part it had been the Germans themselves who went about impersonating their enemies, including regular combat forces on occasion, an achievement pulled off by the famous commando Otto Skorzeny both on the Eastern Front and later during the Battle of the Bulge.[9] Kitson's particular innovation was to "turn" a small number of Mau Mau detainees, by a mixture of harsh-then-gentler treatment, convincing them to join the British cause in this covert fashion.

Kitson and his colleagues managed to recruit about fifty former insurgents to the anti–Mau Mau cause. They trained in teams of seven or eight, and were sent out initially at night under the command of British officers in blackface. Early on they were used simply to gather intelligence. Later they were employed with some regularity to mount ambushes. In both types of endeavors the Kenyan cadre performed highly effectively and showed so much initiative that they were eventually allowed to operate on their own. In his own way Kitson had rediscovered George Crook's insight that tribal peoples are hardly monolithic; they have their differences that can be exploited, and some can be trusted to undertake counterinsurgent work against their fellows. For Kitson, a key to the success of his pseudo gangs' infiltration work was that the tribespeople "were fairly gullible about accepting anyone who appeared to be a Kikuyu and a friend."[10]

Over the course of about a year of such operations, Kitson and his minions basically destroyed the Mau Mau as a fighting force. Until his pseudo gangs had been set loose, the massive sweeps and aerial bombardments that characterized the campaign had proved largely wasted efforts—as John Newsinger observed, "out of all proportion to the results obtained."[11] But Kitson's "countergang" concept, which was also adopted by the police Special Forces, became, in the view of the great historian of irregular warfare Robert Asprey, "the most successful of all methods employed."[12] These activities were coupled with conciliatory social reforms and even included the embrace of the former Mau Mau adherent and idol Jomo Kenyatta, who would become president of an independent Kenya. Ultimately the policy and tactics led to a restoration of order and a secure peace.

*   *   *

For Kitson, Kenya was just the beginning of what would turn out to be a long career in counterinsurgency. As the Mau Mau revolt was winding down he was sent off to Malaya, where yet another vicious guerrilla war had been raging for several years. Here were skillful Communist insurgents whose roots lay in resistance to Japanese occupation during World War II, much like the "Huks" who operated in the Philippines, first as partisans, later as antigovernment guerrillas. But in Malaya the insurgents enjoyed far less popular support from the indigenous population; instead they were favored by the ethnic Chinese minority that had settled there. After a brief attempt to cooperate with the British when they returned at the end of the war against Japan, the Communists mounted a bloody irregular campaign for independence.

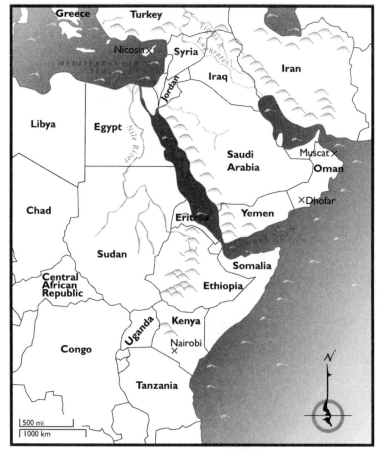

Kitson's Primary Areas of Operations

The guerrilla war in Malaya began with the assassination in June 1948 of three colonial estate managers, all of them British, by the Communists. A week after these acts, a state of emergency was declared and followed by mass detentions of suspects and military "sweeps." The dead hand of Kitchener still ruled British counterinsurgent strategy. But neither of these measures worked, for the insurgents had built among the Chinese population a robust network of cells and nodes known as the *Min Yuen*. The guerrillas were widely dispersed, as Tito's forces had been, and operated in very small units, with handfuls of individuals mounting attacks. A year on into the emergency, they were committing more than a dozen acts of murder or sabotage every day.

The British response was still more detentions, with thousands of deportations—mostly of ethnic Chinese—and liberal use of the death penalty for such offenses as possession of firearms. Security forces grew swiftly to about fifty thousand, and then doubled by 1951, stepping up the sweeps. For all these efforts, however, the operational tempo of the insurgency only accelerated, in part due to the reaction of the ethnic Chinese to the cruelty of British policy.

While the approach to counterinsurgency in Malaya was redolent of Boer War era practices, the Briggs Plan, named after the British director of operations, Sir Henry Briggs, featured the new twist of separating the ethnic groups from one another in their own "strategic hamlets" and breaking the connection between the Chinese population and the insurgents. This, combined with continuing sweeps by massive numbers of forces (relative to the few thousand guerrillas operating in Malaya), began to wear down the enemy. Throughout the mid-1950s the campaign ground on, making progress by inches.

Alongside this attritional approach, some elements of the counterinsurgent forces were trying out innovative ideas, including the notion of enlisting friendly locals to infiltrate the guerrilla ranks. The recruitment of Chinese operatives by the British "Special Branch," while not rising to the level of Kitson's pseudo gangs, began as early as 1952, more than a year before they formed up in Kenya.[13] During this same period, and not far from Malaya, the Philippine Constabulary had established its own Force X that fought the Huks, also using the pseudo-gang concept, and quite successfully.[14]

Thus when Kitson arrived in Malaya in 1957, he came with useful lessons from Kenya and joined colleagues who had already begun to experiment with the techniques that had given him so much success in the fight against the Mau Mau. In fairly short order, pseudo operations were undertaken in Malaya, and the guerrillas proved almost completely unable to cope with this new approach to fighting them. Sometimes the pseudos would meet up with guerrilla units, get the drop on them, and blast away. On other occasions they would place beacons near insurgent camps as they were allegedly passing through. These homing devices served to guide the attack aircraft that would then come through to bomb the guerrillas. Both techniques worked splendidly. By 1960 the "emergency" was over.

During the 1960s Kitson continued to master his craft. From 1962 to 1964 he commanded troops and provided advice on how to counter guerrilla forces opposed to the newly independent government of Cyprus, a decade before the Turkish military invaded and divided that island. Later

Kitson was involved in Oman, largely in an advisory capacity, as this Arab country dealt with its own internal difficulties. These took the form of hit-and-run raids mounted by separatist forces trying to break the province of Dhofar (a remote part of Oman that abuts Yemen) away from the rest of the country. Here too pseudo operations proved their worth, and the insurgents were ultimately defeated; though by the time the British Special Air Service fielded a strong pseudo force in Oman, the *firqat*, Kitson was already on to his next posting.[15] Even in his absence, these operations went exceptionally well, with the rebel forces regularly detected, tracked, and ambushed in true pseudo fashion. Success in Oman was a testament to the power of the concept.

By 1967, now in his early forties, Kitson was named to command the First Battalion of the famous Royal Green Jackets, whose reputation for marksmanship and bush fighting (their green jackets were originally used as camouflage, differentiating them from the traditional Redcoats of earlier centuries) was without peer in the British military. He was also writing about his experiences and crystallizing his thoughts and as the decade came to a close he enjoyed a fellowship at University College in Oxford during the 1969–1970 academic year. While he was there, a whole new irregular war—this time close to home, in Northern Ireland—erupted and worsened to the point that a major British military campaign was in the offing. Thus in 1970 Kitson, now a brigadier, found himself in the middle of what has come to be known as the Troubles. A terrible new challenge awaited him.

* * *

It is curious that, for all their growing expertise in irregular warfare, British military leaders—even when empowered by Kitson's pseudo operations concept—were unable to hold the tottering empire together. One insurgency after another was defeated or contained, yet one colony after another was set free. In 1963, for example, Kenya was granted independence, and that same year Malaya formed the key part of the new country of Malaysia, both of these developments occurring despite the fact that insurgents had been decisively defeated in each place. In part these outcomes were due to the unacceptable economic cost of maintaining the countries under colonial control. But they also went free because the promise of independence had been used as a means of garnering local support for the counterinsurgent campaigns waged against independence-minded insurgents.

By 1970, when Kitson was sent to confront terrorism and insurgency in Northern Ireland, a part of the United Kingdom, more than forty of the nearly fifty colonies Britain would lose after World War II were already gone. Now an irregular war was brewing at home, its goal being the union of the North with the rest of Ireland. For nearly half a century after formation of the largely Catholic Irish Free State in 1922, Northern Ireland with its Protestant majority had remained, most of the time quite peacefully, within the United Kingdom. The Catholic minority in the North had refused to provide support for the Irish Republican Army of the Free State and its earlier attempts at terror campaigns, one that began during World War II—to take advantage of Britain's diverted attention to the Nazi threat—the other in the late 1950s.

But in 1969 the powder keg exploded when the perceived oppression of Catholics reached a point of no return. The sparks that touched off the conflagration were the violent repressions of a number of peaceful civil rights marches—the Northern Irish Catholics were emulating the methods of Dr. Martin Luther King, Jr., that had gained such traction in the United States just a few years earlier. The Protestant gangs intent on attacking the marchers were not prevented from doing so by the constabulary; on the contrary, some off-duty police actually joined in these attacks. Their rationale was that the marches had been orchestrated by the IRA, not that they represented a homegrown outcry against social and economic injustice. Soon even more violence arose from this scapegoating of the "foreign agents" by the Protestant majority. As one of the great scholars of this conflict, J. Bowyer Bell observed, "For those who cannot defeat their own demons, outside agitators, illusive and invisible, are often summoned up as the cause of trouble."[16]

The initial deployments of British troops to Northern Ireland were chiefly intended to quell the violence and protect the Catholic minority. Yet these troops, and the Protestant population, quickly became the targets of an IRA-led insurgency that consisted mostly of setting off bombs—what we now call "improvised explosive devices" (IEDs) largely by members of the Provisional IRA that had split from the parent organization in 1969. The "Provos," whose fighters probably never exceeded one thousand, presided over a death toll that rose rapidly during the first years of the fighting, when Kitson was there. It went from 25 in 1970 to 174 in 1971 and 467 in 1972.[17] By the following year casualties were cut almost in half and then continued to plummet as a range of measures, including several devised and carried out by Kitson, began to take effect against this largely urban guerrilla movement. All this was achieved without ever seriously impinging on the haven the IRA enjoyed in the Irish Free State.

Just what had Kitson done to improve the situation? John Newsinger has concluded that "Kitson was responsible for developing the use of covert operations in Northern Ireland."[18] To a great extent these measures consisted of dressing up British soldiers to look and act like IRA gunmen. Here there was much less need to "turn" detainees, and no one had to go around in blackface as they did in Kenya. British battalions of six hundred to seven hundred troops commonly had as many as 20 percent of their number going about in pseudo fashion. One well informed view was that "fifty soldiers in civilian dress were more effective than four hundred in battle-dress."[19]

But some activities with which Kitson was associated went far beyond pseudo operations. For example, covert British teams that went on patrol looking like guerrillas and trying to ferret out the enemy seem sometimes to have shot first and made inquiries later, leading the historian Charles Townshend to describe their actions as "assassinations."[20] There is even some indication of these covert forces' darker deeds extending to the killing of innocent Catholics in the hope of sparking ramped-up retaliatory violence aimed at the Protestants rather than at British soldiers—an extremely unethical form of "deflection."[21] Torture charges were leveled at Kitson; but these, like the other ethically unacceptable actions of the British, remain, even in the light of history, no more than allegations.

* * *

In the midst of Kitson's stay in Northern Ireland in 1971, what would become his best-known book, *Low Intensity Operations*, appeared. Aside from its homage to the counterinsurgency techniques he had been mastering in various theaters of operations over the course of the 1960s, a curious tone of political ruthlessness is apparent in his call for the creation of a "British national security state." It implies on some level that the extreme measures employed against the IRA were consonant with strategies to ensure the survival and security of the state. Kitson himself seemed to realize, eventually, that he had gone too far with this formulation, and he backed away from it in his subsequent *Warfare as a Whole* (1987). In the years after his departure from Northern Ireland he stepped further away from his more radical concepts—at the same time he was stepping up in the military hierarchy.

His first posting after his time fighting the Troubles was as commandant of the British School of Infantry from 1972 to 1974. Kitson always placed high value on education, and he made sure that his traditional military would have an officer corps steeped in the principles of irregular warfare that had so dominated his own career. Thus were his famous formulations diffused from these pupils to the entire British military, among them his assessment that "insurgents start off with nothing but a cause and grow in strength, while the counterinsurgents start with everything but a cause and gradually decline."[22] Kitson had a great gift for clarity that sometimes echoes Edward Gibbon's pithy insights into the ancient Romans.

After holding divisional command during the late 1970s, Kitson rose to become commander-in-chief of United Kingdom land forces from 1982 to 1985, a period that included both continuing operations in Northern Ireland and a full-blown war with Argentina over the Falkland Islands. He also served as military aide-de-camp to Queen Elizabeth II. Aside from decorations for bravery in his early counterinsurgent days, he also became a knight commander of the British Empire. When Kitson retired in 1985 he had a wealth of official honors and the respect and admiration of peers in the military. How different his end was from Robert Rogers or T. E. Lawrence.

Yet there are two problems with this flattering portrait of a great irregular warrior. First, the methods he employed in the field, while highly successful in the short term, often depended on longer-term inducements—like the promise of independence—that actually undermined the empire's ability to retain colonial control. He may have helped defeat insurgents in Kenya and Malaya, but both countries went free soon after these conflicts ended. And in Northern Ireland, where independence was not a bargaining chip, the twilight struggle went on for decades after Kitson's departure. Pseudo gangs hardly put an end to the IRA's efforts. Seen in this light, Kitson's many campaigns, taken together, seem to constitute a mad Arthurian quest to shore up a tottering empire.

The second problem has to do with the legacy Kitson left in the realm of strategic thought about irregular warfare. While assessments of his innovations have almost all been glowingly positive over the years, judgments about the most successful tactics in his two famous campaigns, in Kenya and Malaya, have focused on the Kitchener-like detentions and sweeps rather than the pseudo gangs. This emphasis has resulted in the notion, still dominant today, that counterinsurgent forces must outnumber their foes by at least ten to one in order to have a good chance of defeating them. This point of view, as it relates to the lessons of Malaya, was summed up by Lucian Pye, in his day one of greatest American experts on Asian military and security affairs: "Guerrilla warfare cannot achieve victories over an enemy vastly superior by conventional military standards."[23]

Thus the lessons of Kitson's clever, deceptive irregular operations have tended to be lost, with the emphasis instead being on "surging" forces into the various theaters of irregular operations that have opened up, from Vietnam to Iraq and Afghanistan. The fallacy of Pye's conclusion was growing apparent even at the time he was writing it down in the mid-1950s, as

French counterinsurgent forces were being defeated in Vietnam, losing half the country. Soon Americans would take their place; yet their "vastly superior" air and naval forces, along with more than half a million troops, would fail to stop the insurgents from conquering the other half.

Kitson's greatest insight is that irregular warfare need not, perhaps should not, be waged by the numbers. His concepts hold out the possibility of doing more and better with less. He recognized that the fundamental challenge in confronting insurgents and terrorists was to find them. He understood that intelligence, in a looming age of irregular wars, was no longer simply a supporting arm. It had to be an integral part of what military professionals call "operational art." Kitson's insight implied the need for formations that can mount pseudo operations, soldiers capable both of finding and, on the right occasions, shooting at the enemy.

In the years after his retirement from active service, Kitson's counsel was sought by military and security officials in several countries confronting insurgent or terrorist threats. His sagacity, drawn from his many experiences in the field, continued to prove highly effective in settings where no vast superiority over the enemy existed.

Today Kitson's ideas are overlooked, for the most part, by the greater states still held in thrall to troop surges and muscle-bound notions of "overwhelming force." But they are honored by those smaller nations whose independence often came in the wake of insurgent and terrorist campaigns, the likes of which Kitson spent his most active years opposing. As we shall see over the next three chapters—which take us from Vietnam to the terror war—it is Kitson's concept of counterinsurgency, not Pye's and his successors' preferences, that hold out the better hope of prevailing in the irregular wars now underway and those to come.

17

PEOPLE'S WARRIOR:
VO NGUYEN GIAP

Perhaps the greatest single benefit to be had from waging irregular warfare is the improved prospect of victory over a materially much stronger adversary. To be sure, some of the "masters" profiled in this book have fought on the side with the big battalions, but even they had difficulties to overcome. The British in eighteenth-century North America outnumbered the French and their Native American allies by far, but they were vastly inferior in bush tactics, and at the outset Rogers's rangers were virtually on their own in confronting their foes. The Russians had far more people than France but fewer soldiers in the field than Napoleon in 1812; the defeat of the *Grande Armée* was due in large part to Denis Davydov's highly successful raids. In his campaigns against the Sioux and Apache tribes, George Crook was backed by the enormous resources of his government, yet he chose to operate in small units, his ranks often filled with "turned" enemies—somewhat akin to Frank Kitson's pseudo gang approach. As for the other masters of irregular warfare, all operated against heavy odds for part or all of their campaigns. Yet most emerged victorious, and each put up a hard fight, no matter the numbers.

Of all these remarkable results, none is more memorable than the victory of Vietnamese insurgents in thirty years of warfare, from 1945 to 1975, against two of the world's great powers: France and the United States. The newly unified nation forged by this fighting would then more than hold its own in a short, sharp conflict with the People's Republic of China, a disaffected former patron determined to punish the Vietnamese upstarts for intervening to end the genocidal (but nonetheless Communist and Beijing-friendly) Khmer Rouge regime in Cambodia. Just how all these victories were won is a remarkable tale, one best told through the story of Vo Nguyen Giap, the able soldier who served as creator and overall commander of the fighting forces of the Vietminh, the North Vietnamese army and the Vietcong.

Giap was born in 1911 into a family of modest means living in the coastal town of An Xa in the Quang Binh province of Vietnam, some sixty miles north of the old imperial capital of Hué. His intelligence was quickly discerned, his education encouraged. This was the heyday of French colonialism in Southeast Asia (or Indochina, which included Laos and Cambodia), so Giap learned to speak French in addition to his native tongue, well enough to teach it at the high school level. But he also taught history and was particularly drawn to the French Revolution and the campaigns of Napoleon. Thus began his dual interest in social reform and military affairs. For Giap, the two would always go hand in hand.

Living in Hué and continuing his education while teaching by studying law on the side, he became radicalized as the inequities of French colonial rule grew more apparent to him. By the late 1920s the energetic Giap added to his already full schedule of activities by joining a secret society, the Tan Viet (Great Vietnam), and hiring on with an anticolonial newspaper, *Tieng Dan* (The People's Voice). Both as secret operative and reporter, Giap was intent on serving the cause of Vietnamese independence. Neither the Tan Viet nor the newspaper was Communist, but the propaganda of the secret society, as the historian Cecil Currey has assessed it, "sounded very Marxist."[1] Giap soon came under government suspicion and was sent to prison for subversive activities, serving more than a year at hard labor between 1930 and 1932, the same time that Tito was in the middle years of his own sentence for revolutionary activities in Yugoslavia.

Upon his release, Giap returned to teaching, news reporting, and, undaunted, his secret activities in support of Vietnamese independence from France. Like Tito he became stealthier, and managed to avoid further incarceration, advancing to the ranks of the leading members of the indigenous resistance to continued French rule. He also got married during this period, to a dedicated revolutionary woman named Quang Thai, whom he had come to know during his time in prison. They worked closely together for their cause throughout the 1930s and had their only child, a daughter, in January 1940. She was born five months before the fall of France to a German invasion.

In the wake of the Nazi *blitzkrieg*, with the collapse of France's Third Republic clearly looming, Giap and his fellow revolutionaries reasoned the time was right for an open break with the French. One day in May 1940 Giap and Quang Thai disappeared abruptly. He went to China for advanced political and military instruction; she left the baby with relatives and stayed on the run, but still in the country, being hunted the whole time and captured a year later. She was tortured, most probably sexually abused, and beaten to death in prison.[2] Giap would not learn of this for several years, as he spent World War II in and out of China and Tonkin (the northern part of Vietnam), organizing insurgent cells into the force that would become the Vietminh.[3] It was during this time that he met and began his long, close partnership with Ho Chi Minh, the revolution-minded son of Vietnamese intellectuals who had spent long years in exile—much of it working as a sous chef in France.

During the war years the collaborationist Vichy government had reached an accommodation with the Axis powers that allowed it to remain in control of Indochina. It wielded power in a repressive manner aimed at stamping out the insurgents. Vichy also agreed to allow the Japanese to use their territory for staging operations against the British and the Nationalist

Chinese forces of Chiang Kai-shek. Thus Giap and his comrades had to elude both French and Japanese forces, in the process becoming ever more skillful at stealthy movement. It was a talent that would be put to great use in the decades to come.

Ho, seeing that Giap had a natural bent for strategic affairs, urged him to take as much Chinese military training as possible. Giap was as always an apt pupil, absorbing Mao Zedong's ideas about people's war. In his famous *Guerrilla Warfare* (1937), Mao argued for a rural hit-and-run campaign to wear down the stronger opponent, later taking the battle to the cities and mounting conventional offensives with massive forces. Giap did not wholly accept this formula, believing instead that it was possible to conduct an irregular campaign in the countryside and in the cities simultaneously. He drew this conclusion from his study of Napoleon, who made a habit of attacking several points at once, causing confusion and compelling his enemies to disperse their forces widely. Giap believed that adopting such a concept of operations against the French, or any occupying power, would be a highly practical choice for guerrilla forces.[4]

While Giap was able to move back and forth between China and Tonkin, Ho was kept in custody by Chiang Kai-shek's anti-Communist Kuomintang forces until 1943, then on "parole" in Liuchow for another year after finally, but falsely, promising that the Vietminh would join the fight against Mao. During this period Giap necessarily became the de facto political and military head of the Vietminh movement, working tirelessly to build new cells, train cadres, and manage finances. He also began to direct small-scale guerrilla operations against the forces of the Vichy French, the brutality of whose countermeasures intensified as the threat posed by Giap and his cadres grew.

Ever more aware of the rise of the Vietminh, and increasingly stung by their ambushes and acts of sabotage, the French launched a "white terror" in response. It was nothing short of criminal, with summary executions of suspects in the field and bounties paid to Vietnamese who would turn in the decapitated heads of rebels. Of due process there was no hint. But there was also some subtlety on the part of the French, who strove hard to have friendly Vietnamese infiltrate Giap's organization. Between the terror and mistrust, Vietminh morale and numbers began to sag, a decline only partially offset by an occasional retaliatory strike. The French were proving to be formidable opponents.

As the war neared its end, with the Vichy regime collapsing and the Japanese now on the defensive, Giap and his movement enjoyed a bit of a breather. American intelligence operatives now entered the picture, their warm assessments of Ho and Giap leading to airdrops of U.S. supplies to the Vietminh. An added bonus during this period was that as the Japanese withdrew, they turned over their outposts and some matériel—perhaps out of malicious pique at the French—to the Vietminh, who used this opportunity both to wipe out other insurgent factions and to declare an independent republic.

But the French were determined to reassert colonial control over Indochina. While the "white terror" was largely curtailed by the new postwar government in favor of a negotiated settlement of issues in dispute, Vietnam's freedom was not viewed in Paris as an acceptable option. Still, Ho and Giap pursued a negotiating strategy, reasoning that by this means they could at least arrange for the departure of the nearly two hundred thousand Kuomintang troops that had barged into Tonkin. In this they were successful; but by late 1946 wider-ranging talks broke down and a renewed insurgency flared up just a week before Christmas.

The fighting took on what was to become the trademark form of Giap's future offensives: simultaneous strikes on outposts throughout the country, in both urban and rural zones. These were augmented by acts of sabotage against infrastructure, particularly small bridges, so numerous in a land of marshes, mountains, and rice paddies. French conventional forces struck back with powerful daylight sweeps, retiring to their fortified encampments at night. The dynamic that emerged—and persisted right on through the American intervention—was one in which, as the noted historian of the Vietnam War Joseph Buttinger put it so clearly and concisely, "many regions controlled by the French during the day became Vietminh territory after darkness fell."[5]

Giap, who had been building his forces and honing his doctrine for employing them, and who had already been fighting the French for some years, was well prepared for the conflict that had come. In the years 1947–1949 neither side could gain a decisive advantage, but it was a period in which Giap's strength grew to such an extent that he could contemplate mixing in a more conventional offensive along with his guerrilla operations—much as Nathanael Greene did during the American Revolution. He was also inspired by Mao's just-concluded victory over Chiang and pressured by the exhortations of his Chinese military advisers to mount a major conventional offensive. Soon there was also the influential example provided by the way Communist forces were handling United Nations troops—so many of them American—in the ongoing fighting in Korea.

Like Greene against the British regulars, Giap proved as yet unable to win a pitched battle against the French. His Vietminh did manage to raid many remote outposts, generally killing or capturing their entire garrisons, with French dead and missing exceeding seven thousand in this phase of the fighting. But the Vietminh suffered heavy losses when, during 1950 and through the summer of 1951, they shifted to attacking the French in better-prepared positions, incurring some twenty thousand casualties of their own. The insurgents could not sustain such losses, given that these costly conventional attacks were now being regularly repulsed.

It was a dark, low period in Giap's life. Ho soon called a meeting of the Communist Party to discuss the situation and even advanced a motion to relieve Giap of his command. But then Ho turned matters around by arguing eloquently against his own recommendation, and the political bureau voted to keep Giap in charge of the Vietminh. Why had Ho acted in this way? Cecil Currey thinks that Ho's support for Giap never wavered, but that he had put forward this motion to "to allow discussion and criticism and to clear the air of any developing movement to unseat Giap."[6] He may also have stayed with Giap to keep Chinese influence over his insurgency at a minimum.

Ho's stratagem worked. With his bureaucratic flanks now shored up, Giap could concentrate once again on resuming the offensive against the French. But he intended to do so in a different way, rekindling his unique, skillful blending of Mao's guerrilla guidance and Napoleon's notions of swift, multiple movements to dislocate enemy forces. Still, the challenge was a stern one. The French were flush with their victories in the field and now enjoyed considerable American material support. Giap had to call on all his skill and daring in the fighting that followed.

*   *   *

After the failures of 1950–1951, Giap returned largely to hit-and-run tactics, both to keep the French off balance and to restore the morale of his own cadres. The insurgents' success in rattling their foes may be measured in the rise of French forces to roughly two hundred thousand troops by 1953, with nearly five hundred thousand friendly Vietnamese serving on their side as well. All this was happening while Giap could muster perhaps a hundred thousand fighters, including his hard-core cadres and local, village-based units. To their numerical superiority the French added increasingly active airpower and riverine "naval assault divisions." In the view of the great chronicler of this conflict, Bernard Fall, the small, heavily armed boats of the *dinassaut* were perhaps the most innovative French advance in counterinsurgent methods, as they made it possible to penetrate the jungle and mount amphibious raids deep into what had previously been Vietminh

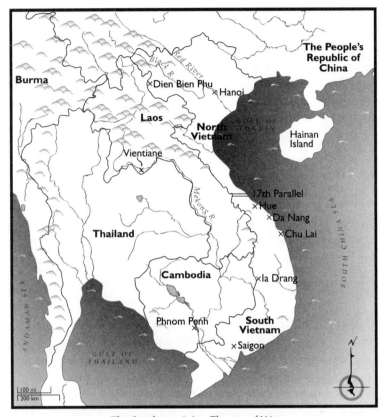

The Southeast Asian Theater of War

sanctuaries.[7] In the sharp firefights that characterized these operations, the French often came out ahead.

Despite effective counterpunches such as those landed by the *dinassaut*, when Giap made a point of shifting to the Napoleonic notion of striking at multiple targets from several directions at once, he retook the initiative. By mounting small-scale attacks throughout the country, he induced the French to disperse half their own forces and about three-fourths of the friendly Vietnamese—just under five hundred thousand troops in all, counting both French regulars and local levies—to garrison duties in cities and villages throughout the country. This considerably reduced their offensive striking power.

But Giap was not satisfied simply with blunting French prospects in this manner; he wanted to take the strategic offensive. Thus he persuaded Ho to agree to an invasion of Laos, a part of their Indochinese colonies that the French had thought was safe from insurgent threats. It was a stroke that opened up a whole new threat the French felt they had no choice but to counter, as many Laotians were sympathetic to the Communists. In November 1953 the French commander General Henri Navarre sent ten thousand troops to a Vietnamese valley town surrounded by rough country very near the Laotian border, which had long been a crossroads for trade between Burma, Siam (Thailand), and China. Its name: Dienbienphu, which in Vietnamese means "the arena of the gods."

Navarre believed that he could both cut off supplies to Vietminh forces operating in Laos and provoke the enemy into a pitched battle there. For his part, Giap believed firmly that beating the French at Dienbienphu would break their will to continue fighting, so he concentrated half his total combat forces in this area, roughly fifty thousand troops. Giap also mustered some twenty thousand bearers to keep the force supplied and haul his heavy artillery into position—echoing von Lettow's reliance on porters in German East Africa during World War I. During this time the Vietminh began to make large-scale use of bicycles, not pedaling them along trails but rather loading them with hundreds of pounds of rice or ammunition and *pushing* them. The effort was nothing short of monumental.

For their part, the French saw that the fight they had provoked was coming. They now relied on resupply and reinforcement from the air, their garrison at Dienbienphu growing to about seventeen thousand by the time the siege was in full swing. French attack aircraft inflicted regular losses on Vietminh supply convoys but could not interdict the overall flow. Bicycles easily steered around bomb craters, which on dirt roads could be quickly filled in anyway. Aerial attacks had even less effect on Vietminh artillery emplacements, skillfully sited as they were on inner slopes instead of hilltops, and well protected by antiaircraft guns supplied by Mao. This positioning brought Giap's two hundred big guns much closer to their targets and allowed them to be aimed over open sights.

The senior French artillery officer at Dienbienphu, Colonel Charles Piroth, had vowed that the Vietminh could never move heavy artillery into the hills above them. But when the enemy barrage opened up on the evening of March 12, 1954, and was swiftly accompanied by massive infantry assaults that caused at least a thousand casualties by midnight, Piroth pulled the pin on a grenade and blew himself up. The rest of the French fought on skillfully, holding off the attackers and in some places throwing them back in hand-to-hand fighting. After three weeks of conventional-looking frontal assaults, the Vietminh had lost ten thousand men, about 20 percent of their total combat force. Yet the French garrison held. It was a moment that kindled memories of the disastrous, failed Vietminh offensives of 1951 and, in the words of the historian Michael Maclear's understatement, "caused General Giap to pause."[8]

Giap knew that he must change his approach if the French were to be defeated in this Southeast Asian Verdun. His solution was to call off all massed frontal assaults in favor of a far more irregular approach: the Vietminh would "dig their way" to victory. Over the next weeks his troops dug more than one hundred miles of trenches, coming at the French simultaneously from every point of the compass. When they came close to the defenders' positions, they mounted raids, mostly at night. One by one the French strong points were lost to this "creeping swarm." In Giap's own words, the battle had become a straightforward matter of "gnawing away at the enemy piecemeal."[9]

By late April 1954 it was clear that the fall of Dienbienphu was only a matter of time—a very short time. French leaders in Paris strove desperately to persuade the United States to intervene with aerial bombing before all was lost. President Eisenhower considered joining the fight in this manner and even contemplated the use of tactical nuclear warheads, under the code name Operation Vulture. But he was strongly opposed in Congress by a key Democratic leader there, Senator Lyndon Johnson. Ironically, it was Johnson as president who took the United States to war in Vietnam a decade later.[10]

Britain's prime minister Winston Churchill, when consulted by Eisenhower, argued strongly against trying to solve the Vietnam problem with heavy bombing. Churchill had been around irregular operations since the Boer War more than half a century earlier, and was himself overseeing counterinsurgencies in Malaya and Kenya at the time. He preferred more subtle military approaches and greater reliance on the Vietnam peace negotiations about to get under way in Geneva. Of the great British leader's abhorrence to the idea of aerial bombing in this case—perhaps even with atomic weapons, the French journalist and historian Jean Lacouture noted: "Churchill, who was a fighting man, thought it impossible, extremely dangerous."[11]

The French surrendered at Dienbienphu on May 7, 1954, their remaining eight thousand soldiers marching off into captivity. Giap's forces had suffered casualties in excess of twenty thousand killed and wounded, more than double the French losses. Far from being the "arena of the gods," Dienbienphu had become, in the words of Bernard Fall, "hell in a very small place."[12]

The day after the French surrender, peace talks opened in Geneva. When they concluded some ten weeks later, Vietnam had been divided in half at the Seventeenth Parallel. Ho, Giap, and their comrades would rule in the north, the seemingly Western-friendly former emperor Bao Dai in the south, until national elections took place no later than July 1956. In the event, the United States came to strongly oppose holding any such elections—for it was clear that Ho would win them—and tensions slowly grew, along with the sporadic but sometimes spectacular violence that led to the resumption of all-out war.

During the decade of relative calm between the end of his fight against the French and the start of the war with the Americans. Giap was busy expanding the North Vietnamese army to 350,000 troops, and building local militias that came to total more than 200,000 members. His second wife, Ha, made a special point of encouraging him to slow his pace, to take real vacations from time to time. She succeeded in cultivating Giap's inner warmth, so much so that another general, Nguyen Chi Thanh, once said to her: "Giap still has the attitudes of a bourgeois because of you."[13] Perhaps this was so. But given his skillful, sustained preparations for war—this time against the United States with its incomparable airpower—it is hard to see any sort of bourgeois softness in him. In the years of conflict that all too soon came again, his American opponents would come to see only the flash of his steel.

* * *

Given that the American Cold War strategy of containing the spread of communism enjoyed wide bipartisan support, it is hardly surprising that Lyndon Johnson decided to intervene to stop Ho and Giap from taking over South Vietnam. The only real question was *how* to do it. President John F. Kennedy had emphasized the use of Special Forces to help train the Vietnamese to defend themselves. Even after Kennedy's assassination and Johnson's ascension to the presidency, military thinking about intervention was still small in scale. The violence rising in the South was insurgent and terrorist in nature, and was fomented for the most part by the armed wing of the People's Revolutionary Party, the National Liberation Front—or, as its fighters came to be known, the Vietcong.

Giap, the hero of the war against the French, now found himself fighting on two fronts: one against the American-supported regime in the South and one against his internal rivals. Chief among the latter was General Nguyen Chi Thanh. In 1960 he seems to have succeeded in convincing Ho to replace Giap as commander of insurgent operations in the South. As always, however, Ho may well have been playing a deeper game. By taking Giap out of the picture, at least temporarily, he was better able to portray the Vietcong to the world as an independent group of freedom fighters—though, as Cecil Currey notes, Hanoi "controlled the NLF lock, stock, and barrel."[14]

The campaign in the South unfolded much as the insurgency against the French had. Cadres were cultivated and local fighting units formed up, and acts of violence against remote government outposts were skillfully blended with occasional attacks in cities. While it had by now become clear that the United States would never allow elections that might result in unifying North and South Vietnam, making war the only solution in Ho's eyes, the declining legitimacy of the government in Saigon only fueled the Communist cause.

The situation was further complicated by the erratic policies of a U.S.-favored strongman, Ngo Dinh Diem, who had rigged elections in 1955 to overthrow Bao Dai and commenced several years of his own incompetent rule. He was ousted in a military coup in November 1963 and executed. Thereafter South Vietnam was subjected to a series of unsuccessful would-be dictators. For Ho and Giap, the death of Diem and the chaos in the Saigon government prompted an escalation of their military campaign. But Giap's great rival in the North Vietnamese Army, Nguyen Chi Thanh, remained the commander in the south, and was praised by the Politburo in Hanoi for his preference for large-scale pitched battles. Giap, who had failed in using this approach against the French, strenuously opposed this policy, but was overruled.

In the fighting that followed in 1964, the insurgents were for the most part badly bloodied and beaten back by South Vietnamese forces and their American advisers. Thanh was discredited and Giap restored to command of the campaign. His view of much more irregular, protracted operations—conducted by Vietcong insurgents and North Vietnamese Army units, with some pitched battles fought under favorable circumstances—finally prevailed. Soon NVA units were marching southward to complement Vietcong operations, both types of units being supplied with matériel brought down via the Ho Chi Minh Trail, which ran along a gentle southward curve from North Vietnam through Laos and Cambodia.

It became clear to Ho and Giap that the Americans would fight determinedly to stop them. In the wake of the Tonkin Gulf incident in August 1964, when a U.S. destroyer appeared to have been attacked by North Vietnamese patrol boats, Congress authorized President Johnson to step up military action in Vietnam. As the historian John Prados describes the politics of this incident, it was a "heaven-sent opportunity" for Johnson to get exactly what he wanted—permission to go to war without a declaration of war.[15]

The small U.S. military mission in Vietnam began to grow more quickly, and by the next year major formations were deploying there. From a few thousand advisers, the "military assistance command" grew to 125,000 troops in August of 1965 and to more than half a million troops by 1968.

Giap had thought deeply about the challenge the Americans would pose, and concluded that three principal threats had to be mastered: (1) the possibility of an invasion of the North; (2) sustained aerial bombardment; and (3) the tactical mobility that U.S. forces enjoyed because of their use of helicopters. To cope with the threat of invasion, he included the North in his plan for building local militias. In the South the village-based support network would help sustain the insurgents' offensive, but in the North they would be used to help resist an invasion. Neither Giap nor Ho realized it at the time, but American leaders were loath even to contemplate an invasion of the North, fearing (unjustifiably, in this case) that the Chinese would intervene as they had when General Douglas MacArthur drove north in Korea in 1950.

To cope with sustained air attack, Giap was already confident that his "bicycle corps" of porters on the Ho Chi Minh Trail could be harassed but not defeated by such bombardment. His forces in the field, however, would need a great deal of protection against attack aircraft. Thus he oversaw a massive program of building underground facilities, covering South Vietnam with a honeycomb of subterranean barracks, supply depots, schools, and hospitals connected by tunnels. At home in the North, he and Ho began a major effort both to disperse factories and to move them underground as well. All these measures proved effective in thwarting the aims of American air-power, from the tactical to the strategic level.

The notion of "air assault," largely the brainchild of the American commander, General William Westmoreland, was likely the single most difficult challenge that Giap faced. In 1965 he saw the power of this mobile approach demonstrated on two key occasions. In August, at the Marine enclave at Chu Lai on the coast, Giap's gathering forces had been struck in the rear by a Marine battalion that had moved right behind them by helicopter. This heliborne strike force was joined by another battalion coming from the sea and by garrison troops sallying out of Chu Lai. The result: nearly a thousand Vietcong confirmed killed in the fighting over three days, with a loss of fewer than fifty Marines.

The next major engagement was against the U.S. Army's famed First Cavalry Division, now mounted in helicopters rather than on horses. In a sustained action in the central highlands, at Ia Drang in November, U.S. troopers killed more than twelve hundred enemy fighters but lost nearly three hundred of their own men. Still, these engagements seemed to bear out Westmoreland's belief that "mobility plus firepower equals attrition."[16] In the afterglow of these victories, "Westy" was named *Time* magazine's man of the year for 1965.

Chastened by these losses, Giap reverted to the same pattern he had employed against the French: small-scale actions throughout the country, in both rural and urban areas. Over the next two years this became the principal pattern of attack as Giap's forces picked their targets with great care, inflicting more and more casualties on the Americans, and beginning to erode their will to fight. Many of the American losses came from booby traps set on jungle trails, an early generation of improvised explosive devices. In the face of Giap's shift to mostly irregular tactics, Westmoreland continued to strive, increasingly in vain, to conduct the pitched battles he preferred, overriding the Marine Corps' preference for distributing their forces in small packets at the village level throughout South Vietnam.

The Marines' innovative idea was to work with the Vietnamese people in "combined action platoons" to secure them from attack, much as a later generation of American soldiers worked at the small-unit level with friendly "sons of Iraq" to improve the security situation there. In both cases the locals fought hard, side by side with the Americans, in defense of their families. This approach had become a central principle of the 1960s era counterinsurgency tactics. But this notion went against the "big unit" formula for success, leading to what Defense Secretary Robert McNamara described as "considerable disagreement between Westy and the Marines."[17] There were also a number of clever army field officers who became adept at hit-and-run, ambush-style warfare and who lobbied from below for a shift to this kind of fighting. They too failed to effect change.[18]

The stage was thus set for Giap to repeat the success he had achieved against the French. By 1968 he felt sufficiently confident to launch a sustained series of simultaneous attacks throughout South Vietnam in February and March, the so-called Tet offensive. A thousand Americans were killed and many thousands more wounded in defending against these assaults, and friendly Vietnamese forces suffered even more heavily. But the attackers were deeply damaged too, although almost certainly they did not suffer the forty thousand killed in action that official U.S. body counts announced. In any event, President Johnson declared in March 1968 that he would not seek reelection, suggesting, as the journalist Don Oberdorfer put it, that Giap may have "suffered a battlefield setback in the war zone, but still won the political victory in the United States."[19]

Indeed, Giap simply reverted to smaller-scale insurgent attacks for the next several years, waiting out the Americans. When they were gone save for a relative handful of advisers, he mounted yet another major offensive, around Easter 1972. This one was stemmed by a combination of South Vietnamese forces and American attack aircraft, but North Vietnamese elements were now in possession of several areas of the Republic of Vietnam and remained in place after the Treaty of Paris was signed in 1973. Then, in the spring of 1975, when there was no hope at all of American intervention, the South was overrun in a last, swift invasion.

Giap did not command this final campaign. He had been heavily criticized for the losses suffered in the Easter Offensive, and Ho—who had died in 1969—was no longer around to shield him with his subtle political ploys. Instead he now fell prey to maneuvering that took away his field command, leaving him with such titles as minister of defense and chairman of the military committee. From this remove he observed the final campaign against the Saigon regime, which nonetheless clearly bore his stamp. North Vietnamese regular forces worked in close conjunction with guerrillas, local militias, and other cadres, and won a complete victory.

While 1975 was a year of celebration in Hanoi, it was "Year Zero" in neighboring Cambodia where the genocidal Khmer Rouge had come to power and begun the business of the "killing fields." Although they had initially been supported by North Vietnam, their brutal excesses soon alienated Hanoi. Even so, it was not until the close of 1978 that Vietnam took military action against the Khmer Rouge, by which time more than a million innocent Cambodians had been slaughtered.

The North Vietnamese Army swiftly drove the Khmer Rouge from power in January 1979; but China, which had been friendly with the regime in Phnom Penh, bristled at the intervention. In February some three hundred thousand Chinese troops invaded at various points along the nearly five-hundred-mile-long Sino-Vietnamese border. Giap, still minister of defense, oversaw a skillful defense that featured his trademark mix of regular and irregular forces. The Chinese left with a bloody nose a month later. In this clear test of strength against the forces of Mao's people's war, Giap's own brand—a blend of Mao and Napoleon—proved superior.

For the next dozen years after the war with China, Giap served in various capacities in his government, retiring early in the 1990s. He has lived on quietly ever since; he will be one hundred in 2011. His ideas about irregular warfare live on as well, in particular his skillful combination of insurgent and traditional tactics and his penchant for striking simultaneously in several places. Few military leaders of conventional or guerrilla forces have records of accomplishment that come close to Giap's. He truly marched to the beat of a different drummer, the one that guides the master of the irregular.

18

BANDIT QUEEN: PHOOLAN DEVI

Anthony Bruno

Perhaps the earliest and most persistent form of human violence is raid-ing: sudden surprise attacks by a few fighters intent upon theft, destruc-tion, or killing to terrorize, or some combination of these. Raiding has long played a role in warfare—for example, the great Mongol invasion of central Europe in the thirteenth century began as an extended raid. But raiding has also been tied, possibly even more closely, to crime, mostly in the form of banditry. From ancient high seas pirates to "road agents" and a host of other bush and mountain pass brigands, bandits have been with us for ages. Yet there is a gray area, somewhere between war and crime, where the purposes of this practice are aimed at more than just pecuniary gain. This is the realm of "social banditry," a phenomenon characterized by the pursuit of higher goals. These might include attempts to redress injustices within a society. Robin Hood tried to do this by taking from his Norman overlords and giving to the oppressed Saxons. Another form of action comes closer to insurgency, with the violence aimed at driving out an occupier, as the Jewish zealots sought to do against the Romans at the time of Christ.

There is yet one more intriguing subset of social bandits: the avengers. Where "noble robbers" and freedom fighters have always tended to cali-brate their use of violence and retain some connection to ethical strictures about the use of force, avengers, feeling terribly wronged, strike back with-out restraint against their tormentors. As Eric Hobsbawm has suggested, the very identity of the avenger is closely tied to the ability to "prove that even the poor and weak can be terrible."[1] In some respects the rise of modern terrorism, including that conducted by al Qaeda and its affiliates, may be explained primarily in terms of the weak proving to the strong just how "terrible" they can be.

This third type of banditry, the form most distinct from crime for gain or insurgent rebellion, is the subject of this chapter, in the person of Phoolan Devi, a poor young Indian woman whose family was system-atically robbed and exploited while she herself was raped repeatedly and subjected to sustained, violent abuses of other sorts. That she became an avenging *dacoit* is no surprise.[2] That she became a folk hero and was even-tually elected to the Indian parliament, however, is a remarkable testament to her mastery of the irregular.

India, where her story unfolds, has a long history of banditry going back at least to the days of the Scythian raiders who came down from the steppes to the subcontinent in the sixth century C.E. The practice contin-ued during the era of the Moghul (i.e., Mongol) rulers a thousand years later. Given the sharp class and caste differences that evolved in Indian society, bandits tended to follow the "noble robber" pattern, these *dacoits* targeting upper-caste Brahmins in particular, and redistributing enough of their wealth among the poor so as to retain the goodwill of their low-caste fellows.

There seem to have been far fewer *dacoits* who fell into the category of insurgents, like Mexico's great bandits Emiliano Zapata and Pancho Villa—though, as John Reed once observed, Villa often crossed the line into pure criminality, for "he encountered the twentieth century with the simplicity of a savage."[3] Far from overturning the system, many *dacoits* were at least in part co-opted to help keep the social system functioning, even after the British conquest in the late eighteenth century. For example, among the larger gangs—those numbering in the several hundreds rather than the more usual few dozens of members—the nineteenth-century *dacoits* of Badhak became for a fee the protectors of river ferries in their region. In central India the Mina ensured the safe passage of the rajah's treasure convoys. The Ramosi protected villages in the vicinity of Bombay.[4] Thus a kind of political economy of banditry emerged that was characterized more by symbiosis than parasitism.

This is not to say that all was light, as there was surely a dark side to criminal gangs in India during this same period. The most notable malefactors were the Thuggee, whose principal practice was to infiltrate caravans, posing as merchants, then strike from within at the opportune moment. Strangling with a garrote was their preferred killing method. To get a number of their fighters inside the caravan, the Thugs patiently inserted new "merchants" at substantial intervals from one another, often as much as a hundred miles, to allay suspicion. Then they generally struck at predetermined ambush points where outside Thugs were lying in wait to join in the attack.[5]

A flavor of Frank Kitson's pseudo gangs may be found in these Thug practices. Eventually, however, the great British administrator in India during the early nineteenth century, William Sleeman, also employed a stratagem very much like the pseudo gang concept to recruit turned Thugs to go after their fellows—a practice that also echoes George Crook's use of friendly Apaches to track their renegade brethren. In this fashion Sleeman finally broke the Thugs.

But for all these efforts to make the roads of India safe for commerce, pilgrimage, and general travel, banditry persisted and even grew during the century between the defeat of the Thugs and the end of the British Raj. A major attempt was made to contain the threat of social banditry with the Criminal Tribes Act of 1871, the first in a series of laws that sought to identify and restrict the movements of those so labeled—or stigmatized, depending on one's point of view. Many of the tribes initially listed as "criminal" were actually being punished for having sided with the Sepoys in the rebellion of 1857 against British rule. But later versions of the law, enacted in 1911 and 1924, spread the stigma far beyond the original insurgents in expanding efforts to stamp out social banditry.

Yet the *dacoits* persisted, their actions during this period showing a mix of "noble robber" and insurgent motivations. That they remained a force even after Indian independence in 1947, after reasons for rebellion should have been obviated, suggests that economic inequity had a lot to do with the continuance of such practices. The Indian government, faced with this intractable problem, resorted to reinstating a version of the old British law, now called the Habitual Offenders Act, which was passed in 1952 and is still on the books.

In practice this law looks quite a bit like its British predecessor, and for more than half a century it has had a pernicious effect on members of over five hundred tribal groups, a total of some sixty million Indians. Their movements are monitored and constrained, and they are subject to other restrictions that make it extremely difficult for them to make their way in the world honestly, or to slip the bonds of caste and class. By some scholarly assessments, the law actually seems to have created more *dacoits* than there would otherwise have been.[6]

Into this world of the largely dispossessed, Phoolan Devi was born in August 1963. She was the daughter of a poor *dalit* (untouchable) who nonetheless had managed to acquire about an acre of land, the centerpiece being a good timber-giving *neem* tree. Uttar Pradesh, the north central Indian state where Phoolan was born, is more than a quarter million square miles in size with a population, largely poor and rural, of more than 150 million. Its terrain is sculpted in part by the Chambal and Yamuna rivers, and is dominated by a nearly six-hundred-mile-long swath of mostly rough country replete with labyrinthine gorges, mazes of ravines and small connecting rivers.

This region has perhaps been best and most simply described as "strange and tortured . . . the Indian badlands."[7] In short, it is ideal country for *dacoit* hideouts, and banditry has enjoyed a long history here. In its insurgent mode it goes back at least as far as the resistance mounted by the deposed Tomar rulers who had been driven from Delhi by the Chauhans in the twelfth century. By the sixteenth century, however, *dacoity* had become primarily criminal in purpose, being driven now by feuds between the factions of competing Rajput princes. While guerrilla resistance to

Moghul rule characterized some behavior during this period, greed came to dominate the nobler motivation. And matters stayed this way for centuries.

When Phoolan was eleven years old, so most accounts go,[8] her cousin Maiyadin came to her village and, declaring himself head of the family, had the *neem* tree chopped down for timber sale. He would also later take the opportunity to relieve Phoolan's father of his land. To both actions her father apparently submitted with only mild protest. Not so Phoolan, who despite her youth called Maiyadin out publicly for his act of thievery. Soon she found herself betrothed—also the doing, it seems, of her cousin—to a man more than three times her age who lived several hundred miles from her village. Married off to him, Phoolan now had her sexual awakening in the form of rape and a socialization to beatings and confinement.

Ever resistant, Phoolan was soon returned to her home village of Gorha ka Purwa, being deemed too young to fulfill her duties as wife. Three years later, in 1977, when she was returned to the same man, she bucked against his familiar abuse and was taken back home a second time. The terrible dishonor brought upon her family by her husband's rejection was so great that no marriage alliance was possible. Phoolan recalled it as a time when her mother "would go from village to village asking, 'Is there anyone who will marry my daughter? Even someone lame or blind?' But there was no one."[9] Now even the young men of her own village tried to prey upon her, seeking her out as an easy target for physical and sexual abuse. In the face of these ever-present threats, Phoolan became more watchful, and much tougher.

She also rekindled her anger at Maiyadin, continuing to castigate him publicly for his acts of thievery against his own extended family. Although illiterate, it was she who argued the case brought against Maiyadin in the Allahabad High Court. She lost, but her sheer audacity enraged her cousin, whose anger had been simmering ever since the failure of his earlier attempt to dispose of her in a distant marriage. Soon after the court fight, in 1979, Maiyadin arranged her arrest for stealing small items from his home. While in jail she was beaten and raped yet again, this time by the authorities. But upon her release she was still not willing to give up her fight with Maiyadin.

It seems that he now had her kidnapped by a largely higher-caste band of *dacoits*. (Such gangs exist because the attraction of easy access to wealth and emotional release through violence have an appeal that goes well beyond the poor and dispossessed.) Some dispute that she was in fact kidnapped, arguing instead that, being desperately unhappy, she simply "walked away from her life."[10] However she came to this pass, Phoolan's time among the bandits of the ravines now began.

*   *   *

At first it seemed that the old pattern of rape and beatings was to continue, this time in a more exotic setting, among harder men than any she had previously known. A local *dacoit* leader, Babu Gajar, appeared to want her for himself, at least at the outset. But after three nightmare days for Phoolan, the gang's second-in-command, Vikram Mallah, a *dalit* among higher-caste

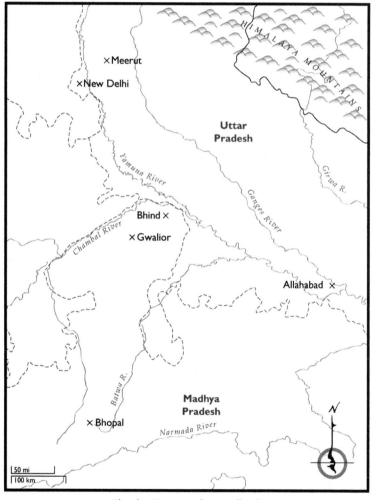

Phoolan Devi's Indian Badlands

criminals, killed Babu and took charge. He took Phoolan too, but treated her with respect, for it seems he knew of her long, determined fight against Maiyadin. Soon they were lovers, his courtship a skillful blending of small gifts and instruction in bandit fieldcraft. Phoolan proved an excellent rifle shot and quickly learned how to move with speed along the edge of rivers and streams, where traction was reasonable and no footprints were left behind for trackers.

For about a year Vikram led the gang on a series of wide-ranging exploits across Uttar and Madhya Pradesh. The favorite targets of their raids were higher-caste villages, but they also managed a few train robberies. To catch their victims by surprise and get the drop on guards, the *dacoits* often wore police uniforms for, as Richard Shears and Isobelle Gidley put it, "What villager would dare fire at an approaching group dressed as police?"[11] This ruse, while employed regularly and effectively with highly prized, official (but stolen) police uniforms, was a hard one for Phoolan to participate in, given that she was only about five feet tall, and no uniform this small could be had. Not wanting to be left out of the raids, Phoolan made the necessary alterations herself and was thus able to join in the action.

After each raid or robbery, the band easily eluded their pursuers by slipping back to the ravines. Beyond the fact that their activities were criminal, Vikram and Phoolan seemed to have much in common with Garibaldi and his wife Anita, who rode and fought side by side in campaigns conducted in both the jungles of South America and the hills of central Italy. Both couples were intensely devoted to each other, finding a strong bond of love in the midst of conflict and omnipresent danger. And where Garibaldi was separated from Anita only by her death while she was fleeing with him after the fall of the Roman republic, Phoolan was to lose Vikram to assassins' bullets.

It happened when two of the upper-caste gang members, the brothers Sri and Lala Ram, who had just returned to the ravines after serving prison time, outraged by the killing of Babu and the captaincy of a *dalit*, shot Vikram dead in Phoolan's arms. After this killing they took Phoolan to the village of Behmai where, according to all accounts, she was held captive for more than three weeks, gang-raped, and repeatedly beaten. Sri Ram perpetrated much of this abuse and orchestrated even more. In a psychological attempt to break her spirit, after repeated rapes and beatings her captors publicly humiliated Phoolan by sending her stark naked to fetch water from the well, in front of all the women and children of the village.

Some of the townsfolk, appalled by the way Phoolan was being treated, sought ways for her to escape. Apparently some of her *dalit* friends, old associates of Vikram, also hovered nearby, wanting to help her. But the catalyst for the action to free her was a kind old Brahmin priest, Santosh Pandit, who used his high caste and moral presence skillfully. One night he quietly took her from the village. Phoolan was in terrible shape at the time. As Pandit recalled, "When I brought her out of there, she looked like a bag of bones and feathers."[12] He helped her when she stumbled, but Phoolan insisted on walking out of the village for the most part on her own two feet, vowing revenge. She collapsed just outside Behmai.

After recovering from her abuse, Phoolan, still a teenager, cobbled together her own gang with the help of Man Singh, a *dacoit* who would become her new lover. Over the next year and more they mounted re-peated raids, then retreated to the ravines to elude their pursuers. When the commotion died down after each action, and the vigilance of their potential victims relaxed, they would strike once more. Raid, retreat, and raid again; this was their cycle of life—until St. Valentine's Day 1981, when Phoolan brought her gang to Behmai in search of revenge against the Ram broth-ers. They were not there; still, Phoolan was in full retributive mode: she executed twenty-two villagers.

For two years after this massacre in Behmai, Phoolan and her gang were relentlessly but unsuccessfully hunted by the authorities. Their raids continued, often accompanied by quite terrible violence. Their retreats were skillful, taking full advantage of the rabbit warren of ra-vines that made sustained, accurate pursuit so difficult. At the height of the hunt, more than two thousand police were on the trail of Phoolan and her dozen or so gang members. But they seldom got very close, as the intelligence network she had created by bribing local politicians and policeman—which had proved so useful in helping the gang select juicy targets—also served as an early warning system against the many sweeps designed to track her down.

In some respects this phase of Phoolan's life resembles the last years of Abd el-Kader's resistance to the French when, even after long years of fighting, he still was able to elude capture. Just as Abd el-Kader was eventu-ally persuaded to come in from the cold by a thoughtful Frenchman, Leon de Lamoricière, so too Phoolan was finally coaxed to surrender in February 1983, along with about a dozen of her comrades, by the police superinten-dent of Bhind, Rajendra Chaturvedi. It may have helped that Lala Ram had just sent Phoolan a note informing her that he had killed her principal tormentor, his brother Sri Ram, in a dispute over a woman.

The surrender was carefully negotiated—not to say choreographed—with Phoolan, still armed, walking out of the ravines and coming to the surrender site to perform obeisance to portraits of Mahatma Gandhi and the Hindu goddess of power, Durga. Bollywood music blasted from loudspeakers, then quieted. Finally Phoolan stepped to the podium, wearing her trademark red bandanna—a latter-day echo of Garibaldi's red shirt—and raised her .315 Mauser rifle above her head. The crowd of nearly ten thousand that had gathered roared.

Phoolan had insisted on more than just a showy surrender. She had been a skillful negotiator with the police superintendent, insisting on the return of her father's land that had been stolen by her cousin Maiyadin. In addition, she requested that her brother be given a government job, and that the family be allowed to keep her goat and cow. The demands were hardly excessive; indeed, in the public's eye they seemed far more in line with simple justice. It was a shrewd move by Phoolan, which burnished her public image. Despite her illiteracy and inexperience in such matters, she seems to have had an innate grasp of the nuances of branding. In any event, the surrender ceremony of the bandit clearly foreshadowed the rise of the politician.

She was to be a progressive legislator, not just a firebrand, following a path very much in line with Eric Hobsbawm's assertion that "social bandits are reformers, not revolutionaries."[13] But before any part of this bright future could unfold, there was prison. After the surrender ceremonies Phoolan was bundled off to jail in Gwalior, where she spent the next eleven years. She was never tried or convicted on any charges.

Her fellow gang members did agree, after some years, to be tried on a range of charges. But none of them had to do with the massacre at Behmai, as no witnesses were willing to come forward—and all the gang members were acquitted. Phoolan viewed with scorn their willingness to be tried, and remained a tiny but haughty prisoner. Finally, in 1994, as the fast-growing political muscle of the hundreds of millions of lower-caste Indians, more than three-fourths of the electorate, was finally being flexed in a significant way, Phoolan was pardoned. Instead of returning to the ravines, she decided to run for political office.

*   *   *

In 1996 the Hindu nationalist Bharatiya Janata movement swept into power, breaking the nearly half century of control that the Congress Party had exercised since Indian independence. Phoolan, now thirty-two, ran as a candidate of the Samajwadi (i.e., Socialist) Party, based in Uttar Pradesh, and proceeded to win a seat in the lower house of the Indian parliament. Among other things, public office gave her immunity from prosecution against the many charges still pending against her for the years of *dacoity*.

Phoolan had spent the time between her release and the national elections cultivating her brand as a woman who was simply seeking justice. In the process she turned herself into one of the most celebrated figures in the country. Curiously, more than a century earlier, Abd el-Kader and Garibaldi had become global celebrities, but in a burgeoning information age replete with well-tooled feminist tropes, Phoolan's fame was largely limited to India. Even there, views were mixed. Perhaps this was because of her criminal past, particularly her leading role in the Behmai massacre.

But it was not only her rap sheet that kept Phoolan's fame from spreading like Abd el-Kader's or Garibaldi's; she took some actions of her own that limited, or at least clouded, perceptions of her. At a petty level there were charges of abuse of office in the form of nepotism and cronyism, and of arrogance as seen in her use of clout to reroute trains on the already chronically cluttered Indian rail system in order to ease her own travel. Then there was her famous feud with the producers of the 1994 film *Bandit Queen*, supposedly based on her life and directed by Shakhur Kapur. Phoolan took great issue with the film's claim to be a true story and succeeded in having it banned in India—hardly the way to promote one's brand.

Her great objection to the film was that it presented her, as she told the journalist Mary Anne Weaver, "as a sniveling woman, always in tears, who never took a conscious decision in her life. I'm simply shown as being raped, over and over again." When Weaver pointed out that she had indeed been subjected to terrible sexual abuse, Phoolan replied with great force:

> You can call it rape in your fancy language. . . . Do you have any idea what it's *like* to live in a village in India? What you call rape, that kind of thing happens to poor women in the villages every day. It is assumed that the daughters of the poor are for the use of the rich. They assume that we're their property. In the villages the poor have no toilets, so we must go in the fields, and the moment we arrive, the rich lay us there; we can't cut the grass or tend our crops without being accosted by them. We are the property of the rich. . . . You will never understand what kind of humiliation that is.[14]

Her point was that sexual exploitation was a fact of life for the poor women of India, almost all of whom become similarly scarred and yet most of whom persisted, finding their way in life even in the face of this awful injustice.

Phoolan dedicated her legislative efforts to trying to end such practices through the force of law, but she had only modest success in curtailing such long-standing, culturally tolerated customs. Beyond the treatment of women, she also fought hard—again with modest results at best—to improve the lot of the poor by bringing them clean water, electricity, education, and medical care. Her appeal at the polls was also problematic: she was voted out of office in 1998, though reelected in the following year.

Thus her life continued to unfold. She had become a Buddhist "to escape the perpetual damnation of the Hindu caste system."[15] She lived in comfort in a government-supplied home and often walked to her work in parliament. She married again, though just how happily remains a subject of speculation and dispute. Nonetheless the rhythms of her life were flowing in a kind of harmony that could hardly have been expected, given her rough beginnings. On July 25, 2001, the old life seemed to reach back for her when three men approached her as she came home for lunch after a morning's legislative work. They gunned her down on her doorstep and made good their escape via a waiting car.

In the following days, responsibility for the assassination was alternately claimed and denied, but the reason for the murder seemed clear: it was vengeance for the Behmai massacre. The widows of the men killed at Behmai praised those who killed Phoolan, none of whom have ever been convicted of the crime. As for *dacoity* itself, the practice lingers on in India but in ever-diminishing proportions. Phoolan's nation has come into the twenty-first century, it seems, determined not only to make its mark internationally as a commercial and politico-military power but also to pursue many of the reforms she fought for at home.

Like Garibaldi, Phoolan was a nation builder, another example of how this process may be pursued from the bottom up. In her case, the use of social banditry in pursuit of reform ties her closely to the "healthy" mode of criminal activity that supports the rise of justice in modern states through the deeds of the leader who, in the words of Reinhard Bendix, "fuses personal courage and largesse with an implacable ruthlessness." The temptation is always there, Bendix notes, to explore the darker side of banditry, lapsing into practices like those of the Sicilian mafia that tended to shore up the power of the corrupt few and "support or extend their dominion over the population."[16] Phoolan managed to avoid being drawn to this latter realm, which was perhaps her greatest triumph.

In her last years Phoolan suffered the smears of those, including rival *dacoits*, who claimed she had become a gang leader only because of her relationship with Vikram Mallah. In the West, the equivalent criticism of a successful professional woman would be that she owed her advances to her husband, father, or other male benefactor. True, Phoolan initially learned her fieldcraft from Vikram, and her status as his consort had much to do with her ability to form and lead a new gang of her own.

But these facts do not diminish her accomplishments. Phoolan *was* a highly skilled *dacoit*. She could run all night through the maze of ravines, shoot with great accuracy, and displayed a mental toughness that was clearly forged in the crucible of her early years. While she acknowledged the importance of her connection to Vikram, she used a reference to India's famous woman prime minister, Indira Gandhi, to make the point that, however one comes to power, one must be able to exercise it skillfully. As Phoolan told Mary Anne Weaver, "Wasn't Indira Gandhi Prime Minister of India? Yes, if she had not been Nehru's daughter, she might not have been, but she lasted in office far longer than he did."[17]

Men often rise to positions of power and authority on the basis of their lineage and connections—a look at the Bush and Kennedy clans in the United States should suffice to confirm this—but ultimately they succeed or fail, make their mark or don't, on the basis of their own merits. So it will be with future generations of women leaders. So it was with Phoolan in her limited world that ranged from the ravines to the halls of government.

Whatever the limits imposed on Phoolan's scope of operations and time in the field, her mastery of the art of the irregular should be unquestioned. She proved as indomitable and as skilled in bush tactics as Robert Rogers, the great leader of rangers in the eighteenth-century North American wilderness. Her ruthlessness in rising to leadership as a bandit rivals that of Mina, the pioneering Spanish *guerrillero*. And her ability to elude her vastly more numerous pursuers, for years, compares favorably with the evasive maneuvers of the great Boer insurgent Christiaan de Wet. Phoolan even went a step beyond all of them in terms of her ability to translate her field operations into political power—not the highest office, but an actual place in government as a reformer, helping break her society's bonds of class, caste, and gender. She will likely be seen as a guiding spirit of India's social modernization, a process that will surely be the key to this remarkable country's rise to the ranks of the world's great powers.

Beyond what her story has to say about the development of Indian society, Phoolan's career may well have heralded the renaissance of social banditry as a world phenomenon. For what we call the "age of terror" is one replete with examples of insurgents and avengers. In the course of blurring the lines between crime and terrorism, these bandits are giving fresh energy to irregular warfare as well. But Phoolan was hardly the only exemplar of this emerging trend.

19

CHECHEN LION:
ASLAN MASKHADOV

http://exhibition.ipvnews.org/photo_119.php

For nearly two hundred years, Russians have been trying to gain and sustain control over Chechnya, a small land located in the Caucasus region between the Black and Caspian seas. Their efforts began in 1816 when a cousin of Denis Davydov, General Alexei Ermolov, made the first incursion. He achieved little lasting success, but the Russians did not give up on their plans for conquest. The conflict resumed in earnest in 1829 and continued for thirty long years of irregular warfare, finally culminating in the surrender of the Chechen leader Shamil. He was a contemporary of the great Algerian insurgent Abd el-Kader and had actually met him briefly when they were both still young men, before their lives were overtaken by war. Shamil was the classic insurgent type of bandit—as opposed to the "noble robber" and "avenger" types—what Eric Hobsbawm has called "the primitive resistance fighter."[1] His defense against invasion was epic and highly skilled, often running rings around Russian forces—literally—a situation depicted so searingly by a veteran of this fighting, Leo Tolstoy, in his wonderful novella *The Raid*.

In the decades after Shamil's surrender, social bandits, insurgents, and avengers continued to flourish, and the Russians never felt secure about their control of the Caucasus. The Chechens proved, again and again, that they were among the best natural fighters in the world. Their strength was augmented by the Sufi brand of Muslim mysticism that had come to their country several centuries earlier, giving them a profound, powerful faith to accompany their fighting spirit. They struggled against tsarist rule, then, after the Russian Revolution, against Communist control. They were still resisting Russian suzerainty in the late 1930s, even as the great fascist threat loomed.

In the dark days of World War II, when German armies drove deep into the Caucasus, the Chechens tried to come to a friendly accommodation with the invaders. But the Germans had little aptitude for reaching out to unhappy Soviet subjects—yet another cause of their defeat in the East— and when the Nazis were finally driven back, Joseph Stalin had almost all the Chechens deported in retaliation for what he viewed as their treachery. Over a few weeks, beginning in late February 1944, about four hundred thousand Chechens were resettled, many to Kazakhstan, others farther away in Siberia. They were to remain in exile for thirteen years, sustained by their social structures, Sufi practices and dreams of home.

Nikita Khrushchev, a relatively more liberal-minded successor of Stalin, decided to "pardon" the Chechens. During 1956–1957, in a conciliatory move, he allowed them to return to their ancestral lands. In addition to sending them home, Khrushchev sought to reintegrate the Chechens fully into Soviet society. No doubt he was guided in this policy by his belief in the tenet of the Communist faith which held that class, and the equality and fraternity of all workers, would always trump ethnicity. George Kennan, perhaps the greatest American observer of the "Soviet experiment," viewed this belief as a fatal flaw. For, as he noted, "national feelings have shown themselves to be more powerful as a political-emotional force than ones related, as is the Marxist ideology, to class."[2]

Kennan was right, and Khrushchev's policies unwittingly set a time bomb ticking in the Caucasus. In the last three decades of the Cold War, Chechen nationalism did not die but rather waited for its moment, like a tree in winter waiting for spring. That spring came with the dissolution of the Soviet Union in 1991, when independence from Moscow was first declared by separatists in Chechnya. They had cleverly supported the successful democratic opposition to the coup plotters who briefly overthrew Gorbachev in August 1991 in a vain attempt to restore the central power of the Soviet Union. Chechen solidarity with Gorbachev's democratic reforms made it hard for the rising Russian political star, Boris Yeltsin, to crack down on them, at least overtly. So the policy developed in Moscow eschewed brute force, aiming instead at the cultivation of a friendly anti-separatist "front" in Chechnya, one that was intended to keep the republic well within the Russian Federation. If Chechnya ever escaped Moscow's gravitational pull, other non-Russian republics within the federation were sure to follow.

Between the winter of 1992 and the summer of 1994, jockeying for position by both sides was intense, and it was clearly a prelude to armed conflict. Thanks to Khrushchev's reintegration policy toward the Chechens, a number of them had risen to command levels in the Soviet military, most notably air force general Dzhokhar Dudayev and an artillery colonel named Aslan Maskhadov. Dudayev had been elected the first president of the Chechen Republic in September 1991, while Maskhadov was soon to rise and become chief of staff of the fledgling Chechen military.

Given that Dudayev had to deal with all manner of affairs of state, the demands of planning for the republic's defense fell for the most part on his colleague's shoulders. Maskhadov had been born in exile in Kazakhstan in the fall of 1951 and was a young boy when his family was allowed to return to Chechnya. He reached manhood intent upon becoming a professional military officer, his most challenging service coming in the waning days of the Cold War, when he was posted first to Hungary and then later to Lithuania. Maskhadov got his first serious glimpse of separatism in the wake of the Lithuanian declaration of independence in March 1990. After many months of simmering tensions, Soviet forces were called out to curtail the growing unrest in January 1991.

Just days before the American air force unleashed its strategic bombing campaign against Saddam Hussein in the first Gulf War, Maskhadov partici-pated in a military crackdown against Lithuanian freedom demonstrators. Thirteen of them were killed in this attempt to show that the Soviets were still in control of their country—yet another of the world's events that have come to be known as "Bloody Sunday."

Maskhadov did his duty in Lithuania but suffered growing doubts about the rectitude of such actions. Gorbachev had second thoughts too and allowed a referendum on independence to be held the following month. The pro-independence faction won with a whopping 90 percent of the voters affirming the anti-Moscow line. Lithuania was on its way to freedom, and just ten months later the Soviet Union itself would disinte-grate. Maskhadov retired from the army shortly thereafter, returning home to Chechnya and affiliating himself with the independence movement. Events in Lithuania tugged at his conscience, but the prospect of Chechen freedom quickly won his heart.

For an artillery officer, Maskhadov showed considerable aptitude for irregular military operations. In the skirmishing between the pro- and anti-Moscow factions, Maskhadov developed and increasingly oversaw a campaign comprised largely of small-scale, hit-and-run firefights. His forces also mounted many raids on trains carrying munitions—though these may have been sham actions, providing cover for illicit arms deals made with corrupt Russian officials. Whatever the truth of the matter, a profusion of weapons reached the insurgents.

It turned out that the arming up of the Chechens happened just in time, for Moscow, reluctant to be seen as intervening directly, was pass-ing weapons to friendly lowland clans in the north who feared being ruled by Chechen highlanders from the mountainous south. And a stream of Russian "volunteers" was trickling into the pro-Moscow faction's ranks, leavening them with skilled professionals. When they finally moved against the insurgents in November 1994—a direct drive on the capital, Grozny—Maskhadov and Chechen rebel forces were waiting. The genius of their defensive concept of operations lay in the wide dispersion of hundreds of small fire teams, armed with little more than rocket-propelled grenades (RPGs). The pro-Moscow faction was swiftly routed.

The Russians redoubled their efforts and sent in some forty thousand of their own regular forces a month later, at Christmastime. Maskhadov had prepared even more thoroughly for this second assault. His small bands,

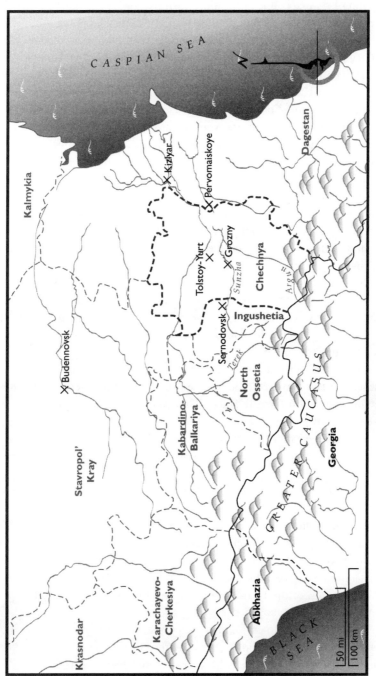

Conflict in the Transcaucasus

amounting by his account to no more than five or six thousand fighters in all,[3] employed a bewildering array of irregular tactics, popping up out of sewers and fighting from various floors of high-rise buildings in the city center. They learned to hit the front and rear vehicles of Russian convoys first, in order to immobilize the convoy, then struck at close range with sawed-off RPGs—shorter barrels made for greater velocity—that had napalm charges attached, starting fires on the inside and often blowing up the invaders' tanks. Chechen *ghazavat* fighters were an early generation of suicide bombers, specifically used to blow up tanks and other armored vehicles. In the words of two journalists who were eyewitnesses to much of this conflict, "the lack of fixed defenses and the mobility of the small groups of fighters were in fact their strength."[4]

Thus an archetypal irregular battle unfolded. An invading army comprised of big, balky formations was beaten by forces just over a tenth their size—and with no air support—because the defenders had broken themselves into small teams of no more than a dozen or so each, fanned out across the city, and swarmed the enemy in a series of simultaneous attacks from all directions. Maskhadov's motto was "less centralization, more co-ordination."[5] It was a defensive version of the swarming style that Garibaldi had employed on the offensive in his fight for the city of Palermo more than a century earlier.

Unlike the royalist forces whose leaders capitulated in the face of Garibaldi's attack, however, the Russians only redoubled their efforts when their first assaults on Grozny failed. Thousands more Russian troops were poured into Chechnya, advancing in areas beyond Grozny even while the fighting still raged there. Dudayev and Maskhadov faced the reality that, after more than a month of hard fighting, Grozny would have to be given over to the enemy.

They now executed a remarkable fighting retreat as the small bands of Chechen fighters headed off in several directions. Most went south to the mountainous region of Chechnya, where they continued to defend, this time in rough country. Other insurgents were deployed well behind the Russian lines to strike at vulnerable posts and logistical nodes as circumstances permitted. Often, like Kitson's pseudo gangs, the Chechens—many of them veterans of the Red Army—dressed up as Russian troops to infiltrate them before opening fire.

Still, sheer weight of numbers kept the Russians moving forward, despite casualties now mounting into the tens of thousands among killed, wounded, and missing. The Chechens suffered even more severely, in relative terms. Comparatively they may have lost only over two thousand fighters killed in action by this time, but this was a large percentage of their total combat forces engaged in the campaign.

At this point a desperate diversionary raid was mounted on the southern Russian town of Budennovsk by one of Maskhadov's colleagues, Shamil Basayev. Where Maskhadov was a professional soldier with a flair for irregular operations, Basayev was at heart a terrorist. Perhaps he was driven to such extreme behavior by the loss of much of his family in a Russian air raid fewer than two months before the attack on Budennovsk. Perhaps he was enraged by the indifference of the international community to Chechen suffering. As he once asked the journalist Anatol Lieven, who was reporting from amid the fighting, "Who cares about our moral position? Who from abroad has helped us, while Russia has brutally ignored every moral rule?"[6]

There would be continual, growing tension between Basayev and Maskhadov in the coming years, but now, in June 1995, there was consensus about the need to do something very dramatic in order to arrest further Russian progress on the ground in Chechnya. That something turned out to be Basayev's infiltration of just over a hundred Chechen fighters, including several female snipers, into the town of Budennovsk, which they completely shot up, killing scores of innocent people.

Engaged by Russian forces, Basayev's men holed up in the city hospital with more than a thousand hostages. After Russian troops failed in their attempts to storm the hospital, Premier Viktor Chernomyrdin entered into direct negotiations with Basayev for the release of the hostages. Basayev's condition was the Russians' suspension of military operations in Chechnya. His raiders were to be guaranteed safe passage home and would take some hostages along on the return route as insurance.

The terms of the deal struck along these lines were honored on both sides—no doubt a surprise to all involved. The resulting respite in the war in Chechnya proper was to give Maskhadov—by now promoted to general—time to plan for an offensive to drive the Russians out of his country. But his was to be no guerrilla hit-and-run campaign, nor was it to rely on terrorism, though terrorist acts were to be committed. Instead Maskhadov would pioneer a concept of operations in which a force of just several thousand fighters, formed up in hundreds of very small units, would mount an offensive directly against a far larger, more heavily armed enemy force that enjoyed complete air superiority.

That Maskhadov prevailed in this campaign provides either evidence of one of history's most exceptional military miracles or a persuasive example of the inherent superiority of a small, swarming irregular force against a traditionally organized opponent. In either case, a true master of the battle-field emerged to carry it off.

*   *   *

Before the fighting resumed, however, an actual chance for peace arose. Maskhadov, the former Russian army officer, negotiated with the enemy an agreement by which Chechens would turn in their arms, or promise to keep them in their homes, as invading troops gradually pulled out. Through the summer of 1995, it seemed that this phased withdrawal might work. Elections were even planned, with the Russians again supporting a pro-Moscow faction that would bring the rebellious republic back under control. But violations of the agreement by both sides grew during the fall. All too many innocent Chechens and hapless Russian recruits were being killed.

By year's end the prospects for peace had seriously dimmed. The Chechens now mounted their second significant terrorist attack outside their own territory. Early in January about two hundred Chechen fighters under the command of Salman Radujev made their way to the town of Kizlyar in the Republic of Dagestan. Their apparent goal was to strike the airfield there, destroying Russian aircraft and possibly seizing some of the cargo supposed to have just arrived. But when they reached the airfield there were few aircraft to destroy and little cargo to speak of. The Russians, who may have known that the attack was coming, responded to the assault and put the raiders on the run.

Radujev and his men made their way southwest to another town, Pervomaiskoye, still in Dagestan but on the border with Chechnya. The Russians had them trapped, however, and the best Radujev could do was to order large numbers of hostages to be taken. As happened in Buden-novsk, the Chechens seized a hospital and, as before, Russian forces massed for an assault. This time there were to be no negotiations; the Russians decided to flatten the town and kill all the terrorists, even if doing so meant the inevitable loss of many innocents.

Before the Russians could act decisively, however, yet another ter-rorist act unfolded on the Black Sea, where pro-Chechen gunmen seized the Russian ferry *Eurasia*. They took some two hundred passengers hostage in the hope of using them to guarantee the safe passage of Radujev's raid-ers out of Pervomaiskoye. Oddly, when the Russians refused to accede to their demands, the gunmen released those they were holding and went into custody themselves. And so the fighting in Pervomaiskoye continued.

After beating off a number of armor-and-infantry assaults, the Chechens made their break for home—joined, it seems, by quite a few of their hostages, who feared that the Russians were about to level the town and kill everyone. To help with the breakout, Maskhadov mustered several attack teams operating from inside Chechnya to strike at the Russians standing between Radujev and home. It was an important diversion, allowing the raiders to make a circuitous escape, heading northeast out of Pervomaiskoye. To create even more confusion, Maskhadov ordered simultaneous small-scale attacks at several locations throughout Chechnya.

While Radujev's raid failed, about two-thirds of his strike force returned safely. It was thought that Radujev had been killed, but he resurfaced several months later. The real consequence of this incident, however, was to confirm the resumption of the war. In the following months the fighting grew in intensity. New Russian offensives were mounted against other built-up areas in Chechnya, most notably at the small city of Sernodovsk in February 1996. Another terrorist incident occurred in March with the hijacking of a Turkish Cypriot airliner—ending, as events did on the Black Sea ferry, with the surrender of the hijackers. Their goal, it seems, was to draw attention to their cause, not to appall the world with wanton violence.

But such nuanced measures had little effect on Moscow, and the fighting escalated. In April the Russians caught a lucky break, killing General Dudayev with a rocket that homed in on his satellite phone while he was talking on it.[7] Now the Chechens had lost their president. But their fighting spirit remained high; soon Maskhadov launched a campaign that looked much like Vo Nguyen Giap's Tet 1968 Tet offensive, in that he ordered attacks throughout the country, from the mountains to the plains, from rural to urban areas. It was a strategic swarm, rocking the large, conventional Russian field army of well over fifty thousand men back on its heels.

The centerpiece of Maskhadov's offensive was his direct assault on Grozny in August 1996. With an attacking force about one-tenth the size of the occupier's garrison of some twelve thousand, Maskhadov split his men yet again into well over a hundred small teams. They advanced from every point of the compass, some crawling through the sewers and others climbing to the roofs of the high-rise buildings located in the city's center. Maskhadov's men attacked both from below and above, creating a truly vertical battlespace that gave the Russians fits. Even their aircraft suffered as the Chechens shot down four helicopters on the first day of the fighting.[8] Shamil Basayev was Maskhadov's key subordinate in these days of brutal dawn-to-dusk struggle.

After more than two weeks of fighting that turned Grozny into a smaller-scale Stalingrad, newly reelected Russian president Boris Yeltsin sent his adviser on security affairs—and chief political rival—former general Alexander Lebed, to negotiate with Maskhadov. Lebed was a veteran of tough counterinsurgent battles against the *mujahideen* in Afghanistan during the 1980s and brought a field soldier's practical views to his discussions with Maskhadov. The two developed a rapport—there is a wonderful photograph of them playing chess during a break in their talks—and arrived at an agreement to withdraw Russian troops from Grozny, and soon after from Chechnya. In return the Chechens would not declare independence, and a final determination of their relationship with Russia would be postponed for five years.

Thus the agreement reached at Khasavyurt brought an end to the fighting that had seen both sides suffer grievously. Soldiers in each army had been killed in the thousands; but it was the Chechen people who had taken the heaviest casualties. Official Chechen figures developed after the war put the number at 87,500.[9]

In the Chechen elections that followed, the two leading presidential candidates were Aslan Maskhadov and Shamil Basayev, the former campaigning on a conciliatory policy toward the Russians, the latter on continued confrontation. Maskhadov won with 59 percent of the vote, a result that Basayev seemed to accept with good grace. The loser was invited into the new president's cabinet, and he accepted. As Carlotta Gall and Thomas de Waal noted of these two men's willingness to continue working together, "there seemed to be little possibility of an 'Afghan option,' as some Russian observers fondly predicted, in which the commanders on the victorious side started fighting each other."[10]

Still, tensions continued between the two men over relations with Russia as time ran out on the five-year truce. Maskhadov hoped for peace; Basayev planned for war. Lebed, the calmest, clearest voice on the Russian side against renewing the war, had been used cynically by Yeltsin and was now being blamed for "losing Chechnya." The hawks were thus on the rise in Moscow, just waiting on a *casus belli*. With his invasion of Dagestan in August 1999, Shamil Basayev gave the Russians all the reasons they could ask for to renew the war against the Chechens.

*   *   *

For most Americans, awareness of the deadly seriousness of rising Muslim militancy came only in the wake of 9/11. For Russians, the alarm was sounded two years earlier, in the summer of 1999, when Shamil Basayev decided on his own to launch an offensive *jihad* (the 1994–1996 fighting in Chechnya is more accurately described as defending against a Russian invasion) in Dagestan. Earlier in 1999 Basayev and his followers succeeded in pressuring Maskhadov into imposing *sharia* Islamic law in Chechnya; now they sought to expand the realm that was to be governed in this way. But Basayev's raiders were countered by a determined Russian defense. In hard fighting, the Chechens were driven back.

In the wake of this repulse, several terrorist bombings occurred in a number of locales around Russia, killing hundreds and wounding thousands. As a leading scholar of this conflict, Mark Kramer, observed of these events, "the circumstances of the attacks were never adequately explained, but the Russian government promptly blamed the Chechens."[11] Thus the hawks in Moscow now had their justification for action, a war on terror. In September, Prime Minister (and soon to be president when Yeltsin resigned at the close of 1999) Vladimir Putin ordered military action against the Chechens. What has followed since has been nothing short of a bloodbath.

Tens of thousands of Russian troops soon poured into Chechnya, supported by massive aerial bombing. By November they were crossing the Terek River on their way to Grozny, which they captured in February 2000. This time they did not simply roll their tanks into town, to be ambushed by small Chechen fire teams. Rather, the Russians themselves had learned how to work in smaller teams. Their special forces (*spetsnaz*) and naval infantry in particular showed considerable aptitude for this kind of fighting. Indeed, their improved performance in this campaign recalled their eventual victory over the Finns in the Winter War of 1939–1940. In that conflict the Finns had also relied on small, mobile fire teams to befuddle the much balkier Russian formations, but after stinging early reverses the Russians had begun to operate in a similarly skillful way.[12]

None of this is to suggest that things went smoothly for the Russians. Maskhadov, Basayev, and their minions put up a stern fight, defending Grozny for months and thereafter mounting countless raids and ambushes throughout the country. Russian casualties were high, in the tens of thousands. Their losses and the elusiveness of the enemy enraged them so greatly that they were spurred to commit terrible atrocities against the Chechen people. A woman described the horror of the Russian advance to the French journalist Anne Nivat: "We hid for four days under a pile of manure. . . . That's how we were able to escape. But almost all our neighbors disappeared. When we came out, there were bodies everywhere."[13] As Mark Kramer has noted, the suffering was such that between 1999 and 2004, the population of Chechnya was reduced from just over one million to about seven hundred thousand. Many tens of thousands were killed, and hundreds of thousands of others have left the country.[14] The population has continued to decline in recent years, though less precipitously.

Maskhadov, forced into a defensive crouch that left him only the ability to mount jabbing raids and ambushes, nonetheless pursued his campaign. He skillfully dodged Russian attempts to kill him with the same kind of homing missiles that had taken out Dudayev, and kept some semblance of order in Chechen insurgent operations. All the while he hoped that his forces' ability to continue fighting would induce the Russians to return to the bargaining table. But two factors were now working against him: improved Russian military performance had induced significant Chechen factions to side with the invaders; and Shamil Basayev, not content with a defensive war of attrition, was agitating for a renewed terrorist campaign in Russia proper.

More effective Russian military action was a thorny problem, but it was one that Maskhadov was trained to cope with. After the fall of Grozny he made sure to husband his resources carefully, avoiding direct combat in favor of a shift to the use of improvised explosive devices, the same tactics used in Iraq and Afghanistan against American forces. Maskhadov also employed a small number of elite snipers to create disruption among the Russians, both at the front and in rear areas. He set traps for helicopters—a principal means of Russian tactical mobility—and knocked out eighteen of them in the first six months of the war.[15] Maskhadov also continued the practice of using his small combat teams to infiltrate Russian positions and set ambushes.

In short, Maskhadov found a way to maintain a protracted resistance to the Russians, even against their improved tactics and growing ability to turn some Chechens to their side. But he could not restrain Basayev from launching his terrorist invasion of Russia, which prompted outrage and redoubled Moscow's resolve to crush the Chechens. The first major move in the new terrorist campaign was the seizure of hundreds of hostages at a Moscow opera house in October 2002 by some fifty Chechen men and women *smertniki* (kamikazes). Putin refused to negotiate with them and employed both anesthetic gas and *spetsnaz* troopers to kill almost all the terrorists. More than a hundred hostages died too, but Russian resolve was demonstrated.

Undaunted, the Chechen terror campaign continued with suicide bombings in Russian subways and elsewhere, often perpetrated by women operatives known as Black Widows, wives of men who had been killed in Chechnya and who now sought revenge. The Widows' most spectacular attacks came in August 2004 when two of them boarded Russian airliners wearing bomb vests and blew themselves up. Both planes went down with all passengers and crew killed.

The airline bombings were followed a month later with a terrorist assault on a North Ossetian middle school by a team of about thirty fighters. They took more than a thousand hostages; Putin once again took a hard line, refusing to negotiate. Instead he mustered a significant military force, including a team of Russia's elite Alpha commandos. Fighting soon erupted, with more than four hundred of the hostages killed along with almost all the terrorists. While this catastrophe caused a firestorm of criticism of Putin's methods, Basayev's goal of weakening Russian resolve was not achieved. The average Russian was angrier with the terrorists than at the usual ham-handedness of the military.

Maskhadov understood this, and continued to try to rein in Basayev and other extremists, but he could not change their minds. So he continued his campaign of ambushes and raids, hoping to wear down the Russians through attrition. To this strategy in the field he added a renewed effort to negotiate peace. But here too he failed. Alexander Lebed, with whom he had crafted a peace agreement a decade earlier, had died in a helicopter crash in April 2002. It seemed that Maskhadov could talk with no one about prospects for peace.

In January 2005 he struck out on his own, declaring a unilateral, conditional cease fire. Chechen fighters would act only in self-defense; they would mount no new attacks. Violence levels began to drop in the wake of Maskhadov's announcement, and it appeared that the Russians put out peace feelers, indicating their willingness to open talks. Encouraged, the Chechen leader made his way to the village of Tolstoy-Yurt in March. But instead of diplomacy he found death.

None of the exact circumstances are yet certain, but it seems that Russian troops and pro-Moscow Chechens had laid an ambush for Maskhadov. He went down in a hail of bullets or a grenade blast, or both. His fellow Chechens said he had died heroically, taking on the ambushers alone, to cover the withdrawal of his bodyguards he had ordered to escape. From Moscow the report was that his incompetent security detail had gunned him down with their own panicky, ill-aimed fire. Whatever the details, or distortions, Maskhadov was dead.

The Chechen insurgency virtually collapsed in the wake of this profound loss. Mark Kramer has observed that the impact of his death "cut deeply into the Chechens' morale and weakened the spirit of resistance."[16] A year later, in July 2006, Basayev was blown up when explosives he had gathered for use on a raid accidentally detonated. More and more Chechens began to reach accommodation with the Russians. Events were finally unfolding as they had in the nineteenth century, when violence gradually waned in Chechnya. Sporadic fighting in the southern mountains continued, and still goes on today, conducted by a few hundred holdouts. In the spring of 2010 Chechen terrorists launched yet another attack on the Russian transit system, though this one paled in comparison to their earlier "spectaculars."

Of all the masters of irregular warfare considered in this book, Aslan Maskhadov seems to have suffered the most ignominious fate, his cause the greatest setback. Perhaps so. Yet what he accomplished in the field is among the most amazing results achieved in all military history. For he was no simple raider or guerrilla. Rather, he built a radically new kind of military force, one comprised of countless small, lightly armed bands doing direct battle with a large, industrial-age army—and winning. His campaigns in the 1994–1996 war will be studied for ages by all military professionals and no doubt by new generations of insurgent leaders as well.

Even Maskhadov's skillfully conducted defensive operations in the second war with the Russians bear close scrutiny. The Russians' renewed effort, launched late in 1999, featured both far greater resources and manpower and vastly improved tactics. That Maskhadov was able to hold Grozny for months in the winter of 1999–2000 and retain his freedom of movement throughout so much of Chechnya for years after the fall of the capital is a remarkable testament to his generalship.

That he was just as great a statesman may be seen in his success in negotiating peace with Alexander Lebed, his skillful balancing between the moderate and radical factions in his own government, and even in his final, unilateral effort to halt the fighting while restarting negotiations for a truce with the Russians. There was a clear nobility about the man whose first name means "lion" in several languages of the region. Like C. S. Lewis's noble lion Aslan, who sacrificed himself to bring an end to a terrible tyranny in one of the Narnia tales, Aslan Maskhadov also gave his life with a similar hopeful vision in mind. Whether his sacrifice will help free the Chechens is uncertain; but the skillful way he fought and his nobility of character and purpose—in short, the ways he lived and died—are sure to inform and inspire countless others for generations to come.

20

MASTER LESSONS . . .
AND A LOOK AHEAD

If there is a common theme that runs through the stories of the masters of irregular warfare, it is their resilience in the face of defeat and other adversity. Where the great captains of the more conventional battlefield often marched through their careers with long strings of impressive victories, guerrillas, insurgents, and raiders frequently struggled through repeated rough patches, regularly losing battles and large tracts of territory. Caesar suffered hardly a single reversal in battle throughout his long career in the field; Napoleon spent well over a decade in high command without so much as a drawn fight. Had either suffered serious losses as often as the greatest irregular warriors, their careers would have been sharply foreshortened. Of the traditional war leaders who rose to eminence, only Frederick the Great of Prussia lost battles very nearly as often as he won them, yet remained in the field long enough to achieve his aims. Among irregulars, however, a war record like Frederick's is more the norm. A leader of guerrillas, insurgents, or raiders with an unbroken string of victories is quite rare.

Nathanael Greene is perhaps the best exemplar of this pattern. During the American Revolutionary War he failed to win even a single battle yet completely wore down the forces of his opponent, Lord Cornwallis, and prepared the way for ultimate victory at Yorktown. And he is hardly alone. Francisco Espoz y Mina saw his Spanish guerrilla forces virtually wiped out on three occasions, yet he rose again and again, finally prevailing over the French occupiers of his country. Giuseppe Garibaldi did win defensive victories in his insurgent campaigns in South America, but he suffered crushing defeats in Europe, especially in his heroic, doomed defense of the Roman republic. Yet he persisted, and in the end his Thousand freed Italy. In more recent times Vo Nguyen Giap's countrywide irregular offensives in Vietnam were repeatedly beaten, first by the French and later by

U.S. forces. But he too held on, defeating the French at Dienbienphu in 1954 and more than twenty years later overseeing the final collapse of the American-supported regime that stood between him and the unification of his country.

Even those irregulars with more imposing battle records suffered in other ways. Abd el-Kader, peerless in an ambush, a raid, or even a pitched battle, had to fight on the run for fifteen years. The situation was virtually the same for Christiaan de Wet and his Boer insurgents, and for the Indian *dacoit* Phoolan Devi, though the active careers of de Wet and Phoolan were much shorter than Abd el-Kader's. Paul von Lettow-Vorbeck won almost all his battles, whether he was the attacker or standing on the defensive, yet he had to relinquish all the territory of German East Africa to Allied forces during World War I. The strategic situation of Aslan Maskhadov in the Russo-Chechen wars was, in this respect, quite similar to von Lettow's.

Sometimes adversity came in the form of social, organizational, or technical constraints. Robert Rogers had to fight hard to get his British masters to take the notion of "ranging" seriously; in the end he was able to convince them to transform all their regular forces in North America into capable bush fighters. Mina was at first snubbed by the Spanish nobles who were trying to lead resistance from a distance, yet eventually they made him a general in charge of the most important area of guerrilla operations. Denis Davydov had to lobby hard to be given permission to form even a small unit of deep-striking raiders to harass Napoleon's forces in Russia—but he succeeded, and contributed mightily to their defeat. Charles Lockwood had to cope with a mix of difficulties as he was putting together his "submarine insurgency" against the Imperial Japanese Navy: his skippers were too stodgy and his torpedoes didn't work. Yet he mastered both challenges and conducted the most effective irregular naval campaign in history.

Aside from their sheer indomitability in the face of defeat and other seemingly intractable problems, the masters of irregular warfare often showed a ruthlessness rarely seen elsewhere, save perhaps in the rise of some tyrants and many crime lords. Mina provided archetypal insight into this aspect of insurgent leadership with his systematic killing of rival guerrilla commanders so as to consolidate his own control. The noble Abd el-Kader took to executing tribal leaders who seemed to have gone over to the French occupiers of his beloved Algeria. George Crook, the great Indian fighter renowned for treating Native Americans with compassion and respect, had early on showed his darker side. During the Civil War he tacitly allowed junior officers under his command to execute captured rebel guerrillas so as to avoid the problem of their being paroled and returning to the fight. Even T. E. Lawrence showed ruthlessness from time to time, personally executing a tribesman during one crisis—to prevent a blood feud from erupting—and on more than one grim occasion allowing his Bedouins to cut down helpless fleeing or surrendering Turkish troops.

Beyond these traits of doggedness in defeat and cold-bloodedness, so commonly found among many of the masters, other insights may be drawn from their careers that still resonate profoundly and carry important lessons for military practitioners in this new era of irregular warfare. Indeed, it is difficult to see the continuing relevance of Frederick the Great's "oblique" order of battle or Napoleon's onrushing columns. Frederick's flanking attacks may have informed notions of modern maneuver warfare, and Bonaparte's frenetic operational tempo may have prefigured *blitzkrieg*, but the landscape of battle today is bereft of traditional foes waiting to be outflanked and overrun. Instead of being massed, they are dispersed and must be found before they can be fought—like the tribal warriors that Rogers contended with and that Crook met a century later, or the insurgents that Frank Kitson made an art of exposing before he engaged them. The wars against al Qaeda and other terrorist networks, and even those conflicts to come against other nations, are more likely to take on an irregular hue.

*   *   *

From the lives and campaigns of the masters of irregular warfare, several insights may be drawn. In particular, five related pairs of concepts have borne deeply upon the phenomenon of irregular warfare—and, in my view, will continue to shape the future of conflict in important ways.

Transformation and integration. These two concepts have to do with the alternate possibilities of reconfiguring an entire force or creating a subordinate irregular component and allowing it to operate in tandem with more traditional formations. Robert Rogers provided the first glimpse of the advantages that could present themselves when a whole army became attuned to irregular operations. His elite rangers may have contained in their ranks the best bush fighters operating in the North American wilderness of the mid-1700s; but their most important contribution was in diffusing their techniques to the remainder of the British forces. The improvement of the British between Braddock's opening defeat at the hands of a small Franco-Indian force and Amherst's capture of Montreal five years later was nothing short of miraculous.

Paul von Lettow-Vorbeck was another bush fighter who turned a total force toward irregular warfare. Throughout the hard-fought World War I campaign in East Africa, von Lettow was always vastly outnumbered and cut off from supplies and reinforcements from home. Yet his remarkable little army more often than not held the initiative, mounting a major offensive into Mozambique even after several years of relentless pursuit by considerably larger British and other Allied forces.

Perhaps the best modern example of a force that became almost completely imbued with irregular fighting skills may be found in the Chechen insurgents who fought under Aslan Maskhadov's command. Not only were they able to conduct hit-and-run raids against a far more numerous Russian force; they also fought them head-on and, in their first war, won outright. Even in the second war, aspects of which still rage on today, Chechen irregulars fought hard and well, at least until Maskhadov himself was killed.

For all the attractiveness of creating an entire force capable of operating in this manner, it is not always possible. Indeed, it seems a somewhat rare phenomenon. More often it is necessary to employ a skillful blending of conventional and irregular troops and operations. In the eighteenth century, Nathanael Greene drew the blueprints for this manner of fighting, then executed such a campaign in the field. His tough Continentals forced the British to concentrate against them; when the Redcoats did so, his irregulars ran wild. When the British dispersed to chase the guerrillas, Greene's regulars advanced in threatening ways. Lord Cornwallis was always caught between at least two fires, which is why Greene won and in the process changed the course of history.

Although T. E. Lawrence was less tightly tied to regular forces during World War I in the Arabian desert, he did rely on British sea power to support his irregulars' advance, and he coordinated his many raids with the advance of Allenby's large regular army. The result was a remarkable victory against very sturdy Turkish opponents who had previously beaten the Allies badly in pitched battles at Gallipoli, and who had held their own in the fighting in Palestine and Mesopotamia.

Without doubt the finest modern example of integrated guerrilla and conventional operations was provided by Vietnam's Vo Nguyen Giap, whose mix of these methods proved powerful enough to defeat the French and then the Americans. While his record includes the great conventional victory in 1954 at Dienbienphu, his forces were beaten badly during 1968's Tet offensive and once again in the 1972 Easter offensive. Absent his ability to pursue a guerrilla war alongside and in between major offensives, Giap could never have won.

Today, a decade on in the terror war begun by the 2001 attacks on the United States, al Qaeda and its affiliates still seem to be emulating Aslan Maskhadov's model of one force that can conduct either fleeting raids or more protracted swarming engagements against regular forces in the field. Thus isolated terrorist attacks around the world have been coupled with more protracted insurgent campaigns in Iraq and Afghanistan.

The American and Allied response to this challenge has been to integrate conventional and irregular forces—witness the opening invasion of Iraq, or the surge there and later in Afghanistan, along with the special operations task forces who were engaging in their own raids. In the long run the Rogers model of complete transformation may offer the promise of better results for the counterterrorist coalition than the Greene framework of integration.

Rogers's achievements in the field, like Maskhadov's, suggest that a force configured for irregular operations may also do well even when facing a traditionally configured foe. Their results buttress the argument in favor of pursuing full transformation instead of integration. Even if such a complete change is infrequently found in history, the great successes that have resulted when militaries have remade themselves in this manner suggest that the model should not be dismissed in favor of the integrative approach.

Narratives and nation building. Another theme that runs through the history of irregular warfare over the past 250 years concerns the "story" that impels individuals to action. Quite often the narrative is tied to the creation or freeing of a homeland, whether real or imagined, like Osama bin Laden's cherished "caliphate." Recognizing the story can be a powerful key to understanding the appeal, persistence, and in some cases the ultimate victory of a range of irregular leaders.

Perhaps the most common narrative is about the need to eject an occupying force and win or restore the nation's freedom. Greene clearly saw the campaign in the south during the American Revolution in these terms. So did Mina and Davydov, operating respectively in Spain and Russia during the Napoleonic Era. Christiaan de Wet also fits this mold of the resister to the occupation of his country. Closer to the present, Josip Broz Tito also followed this path, even though the land for which he fought, Yugoslavia, was the recent creation of international diplomacy.

For other irregular masters, the act of resisting occupation forces proved an essential step in the process of nation building. There was no truly compelling idea among the Arab tribes of a nation called "Algeria" before Abd el-Kader launched his insurgent campaign against the French. And there was no modern "Italy" before Giuseppe Garibaldi, with conceptual help from Mazzini, began his crusade to drive the French and Austrians from his country. Lawrence too found the allure of nationhood a lively basis for recruiting Arab fighters and sustaining tribal support for his operations. "Nation" was a driving concept for Giap and Maskhadov as well, though Giap used the notion far more successfully.

Win or lose, fighting under the banners of self-liberation and nationhood, each of these masters understood that the ability to conduct an irregular campaign depends heavily upon having a compelling narrative. This is much more the case than in conventional wars. Take, for example, the performance in World War II of German soldiers, who fought with great skill and valor for a regime many despised and a cause almost all knew was irretrievably lost. Insurgents could never perform as well if they didn't respect their high commands and believe wholeheartedly in their cause. This makes for a fascinating difference in social dynamics between conventional and irregular wars.

The power of the notion of nationhood is such that, in some cases, leaders of counterinsurgent forces have been able to use the allure of a nation-related narrative to help bring about the surrender or defeat of their foes. The great Indian fighter George Crook was able to accomplish this time and again in his campaigns, treating Native Americans with respect and doing his utmost to make sure they would enjoy some sense of sovereignty on lands reserved for them after the end of the fighting. A century later Frank Kitson did something similar, persuading members of the Mau Mau to switch sides, in part on the basis of a shared vision of a free Kenya.

A modern echo of this narrative theme has been heard in the more recent counterinsurgent campaigning in Iraq. The fierce resistance of Sunni tribes to the U.S. occupation was tamped down in 2007–2008 partly by the assurance that, by their joining the Americans in the fight against al Qaeda operatives, their country would be freed, peace would come, and U.S. forces would withdraw. Thus the Sons of Iraq arose to fight alongside their former enemies. The counterinsurgent effort in Afghanistan has been less successful in using these themes to turn hard-core opponents into allies.

Deep strikes and infrastructure attacks. It is commonly thought that an edge in tactical mobility is crucial to the success of long-ranging special operations, and that terrain exercises a profound shaping influence on irregular warfare in general. But the masters of this mode of conflict suggest the need for nuance when thinking along these lines. For example, mobility should be thought of in relative rather than absolute terms; the critical point is the need to move and act faster *than the opposing force.* A similar point holds with terrain, which is a constraint for both sides. The problem is not so much with rough country, dense jungle, or high mountains; it is much more a question of whether a force is willing to change its ways to adapt to the demands of such settings.

Robert Rogers built a force that could move faster in the North American wilderness than even the Indians. This enabled him and his striking force to cover hundreds of miles over exceptionally rough terrain, most of the time on foot, and then to launch shattering blows, like his raid on St. Francis during the French and Indian War. Denis Davydov took advantage of General Kutuzov's strategy of trading space for time in the campaign against Napoleon in 1812, creating a force of cavalry raiders that regularly struck far behind the French lines.

By his actions, largely mounted against the invaders' supply convoys, Davydov began to marry the deep strike to the notion of crippling the enemy's infrastructure. Abd el-Kader adopted a similar method also against the French in North Africa in the 1830s and 1840s. But his and Davydov's attacks were confined to supply wagons. With the coming of rail transport and telegraphic communications in the mid-nineteenth century, a whole new world of opportunity opened up for irregular raiders to cripple the advance of modern field armies. The clear master of this sort of campaign was the Confederacy's Nathan Bedford Forrest who, with quite small forces, threw a very large monkey wrench into Union plans in the western theater of operations during the Civil War. Given that rail and telegraph lines then ran mostly in tandem, Forrest's task was made a bit easier: both target sets were in the same place. This pattern still held at the time of the Boer War, some thirty years later, when Christiaan de Wet was able to act much as Forrest had before him. During World War I, Lawrence's riff on this theme was to do enough damage to cripple, but not so much as to force enemy withdrawal from advanced outposts that were costly to hold.

After Lawrence, deep commando raids coupled with attacks on transport and communications infrastructures persisted as a mode of irregular warfare but seemed to have less strategic impact. During World War II all major combatants fielded such raiding forces, yet no leaders of the stature of Rogers, Davydov, Forrest, De Wet, or Lawrence emerged. Despite a great many commando coups mounted during this war, their strategic impact, as many studies have shown, seemed to diminish. The one great exception was in the war at sea, where Charles Lockwood proved that a deep-striking irregular campaign could be waged with a small number of submarines, and that it could have a profound effect on the supply system of a modern maritime nation.

In more recent times the Chechens attempted to revitalize the classic notion of the deep raid; but in their case these attacks were designed to weaken Russian resolve. The Chechens enjoyed mild early success with this technique—for which Aslan Maskhadov had little appetite—but such actions soon brought down the most powerful blowback on the Chechens themselves. The return of the deep raid as a means of striking at infrastructure may require some fundamental rethinking of the concept.

Networks and swarming. In an organizational sense (as opposed to its electronic or social connotations), a network is characterized by the dominance of lateral linkages among many small nodes, cells, or units. It features great autonomy on the part of field forces, with the central command—such as it is—remaining concentrated on the big picture rather than the tactical details. Swarming is the way networks fight—their many small formations tend to attack enemy troops and other targets simultaneously from several directions.

While some masters of swarm tactics did not operate in network fashion—Nathan Bedford Forrest being the prime example, but see Garibaldi's operations in Palermo, too—the most successful practitioners married this doctrine to a highly networked organizational structure. During World War II, for example, Tito's great success in Yugoslavia came in large part from his ability to see the need for a countrywide swarm. His widely dispersed forces were ordered to mount attacks throughout the areas occupied by German and Italian troops and their other allies and collaborators. Tito did this even as Axis regulars were mounting major offensives against him, driving ever southward, and *Jagdkommando* units were relentlessly hunting down his soldiers.

Tito was able to counter the Axis initiative in this manner partly because the swarming tactics his soldiers employed caused such great consternation, hammering home the point that this was not a linear campaign that could be concluded with the usual sort of straightforward advances. But Tito could not have won without his willingness to trust in his local commanders, many of whom were of differing ethnicity and might even turn against him. Yet for all these risks, Tito realized that the gains to be made by delegating authority out to the edges of the insurgent network far outweighed the potential problems.

The other great swarm network of World War II was the one built and sent into battle by Charles Lockwood. His relatively small numbers of submarines were dispersed throughout the extensive Japanese maritime empire, attacking it simultaneously at several points on any given day. Aside from the technological demands of such a campaign—submarines with long-range cruising capability, and stealthy enough to operate in waters otherwise controlled by enemy forces—Lockwood understood the need to empower his skippers with almost complete tactical discretion. Once he found the right officers, those most comfortable with taking the initiative when commands from above were few, the campaign caught fire and did more damage to the enemy than any other American military activity of the Pacific War.

By way of contrast, it is interesting to note that in the Battle of the Atlantic Lockwood's German counterpart, Admiral Karl Doenitz, ran his U-boat campaign in far more controlled fashion. While the Germans were able to add a tactical swarm to their operations, in the form of wolf-pack attacks on convoys, Doenitz's insistence on maintaining close control over these forces via radio ran the fatal risk that the Allies might break his codes and either find his subs or reroute their convoys out of harm's way. In the event, his codes *were* broken, many of his U-boats were found and sunk, and the courses of many Allied convoys were diverted away from contact with his forces. A "full Lockwood" approach was probably not possible for Doenitz; but something less centrally controlled might have given his U-boats a much better chance of winning.

In the postwar era, Giap made use of a Tito-like, countrywide swarm, first against the French then later against the Americans. Like Tito, he also assigned a great deal of local authority to cadres dispersed throughout Vietnam. Both the French and U.S. forces, in their respective periods of involvement, dealt reasonably effectively with the swarms they confronted. The French response was a combination of garrison-type forces and small raiding units; the Americans, at least early on, emphasized the use of small "combined action platoons," of just a few dozen soldiers each, who lived and fought side by side with local anti-Communist fighters. Only when the French reverted to a major conventional offensive and the Americans switched to their "big unit war" did they both go awry. Had one or the other stuck with the notion of forming their own networks to defend against Giap's swarms, Hanoi likely would not have won out in the end.

Of all the masters I have surveyed in this book, Aslan Maskhadov showed the greatest capacity for empowering networks and building a concept of operations around the notion of swarming. His 1996 offensive, which drove the Russians from his country, will stand as one of history's great campaigns. For it was a very tough test: against vastly superior Russian numbers and firepower, Maskhadov relied on small teams of twelve to twenty men each, and gave all of them great discretion as to how and when to engage the enemy. His networked swarm succeeded brilliantly. But, in an ironic turn, it was Maskhadov's inability to rein in his network that led to the ill-advised invasion of Dagestan and the eventual return of a far more effective Russian force. In this respect Maskhadov's tale is a profoundly cautionary one for those who embrace notions of networking: what you create you may not be able to control.

Cooptation and infiltration. One of the most important developments in irregular warfare emerged during the decades-long nineteenth-century struggle against the Native American tribes of the West. While it is easy to say that the brave fight of these essentially Stone Age peoples was doomed from the outset, the truth is that they often enjoyed better armaments (thanks to gunrunners) and greater mobility than the U.S. military units arrayed against them. The Apaches in particular seemed to hold a persistent edge against their adversaries. That is, until George Crook hit upon the idea of convincing some of his former foes to join the fight on his side. He did this largely with subtle, skillful psychological appeals and genuine compassion for the plight of these doomed peoples.

Thus Crook was able to subdue the Apaches with a very small force in a reasonably short span of time, where those who had come before him had failed with large numbers of troops and years of field operations. Crook was on to something: it is often possible in irregular warfare to reach out to enemy fighters with every chance of persuading them to switch sides. Still, there are few examples of this practice among the other masters. Tito recruited antifascist Italian soldiers who wished to join his partisans, but they fought like any other guerrillas, simply augmenting his existing force rather than arming it with infiltrators. It seems that only Frank Kitson truly captured the spirit of Crook, and even did him one better.

In Kenya, Kitson's innovative pseudo gangs not only relied on the recruitment of former Mau Mau fighters, they also operated in a highly deceptive fashion. That is, they wandered about the battle zones looking and acting like insurgents while in actuality they were secret scouts for the British—and sometimes even conducted the raids and ambushes that did so much to cripple the Mau Mau. In this respect Kitson married a brilliant new concept of infiltration to the practice of cooptation.

Among modern echoes of Crook and Kitson, the loudest has been heard in Iraq during 2007–2008 when former insurgents switched sides and began to fight against al Qaeda cadres in their country. These stalwart Sons of Iraq did far more to improve the situation on the ground than the rather modest surge of American reinforcements that arrived around the same time. The extent to which Crook-like cooptation may have extended also to Kitson-like infiltration is yet unclear; but if one day there is an end to terrorist networks, their defeat will almost surely be at the hands of the inheritors of Crook and Kitson.

Infiltration was practiced also in a manner resembling the deep strike, but conducted over a protracted period. When Rogers, Davydov, Forrest, de Wet, and Lawrence mounted deep raids, their forces generally went out and came back to a home base. This was also true of Lockwood's long-ranging submarines. But Orde Wingate gave a whole new meaning to notions of infiltration with his call for a capability to operate far behind enemy lines for indefinite periods. His Chindits, particularly the second expedition, proved that infiltrated forces could, with adequate air support, subsist, persist, and triumph.

Wingate's ideas have sometimes been conflated with notions of heli-borne assault, especially of the kind that characterized the period of American involvement in Vietnam. But this is the wrong lesson to draw, as these latter-day air assault forces resembled short-duration raiders—that is, they went out, hit their targets, and returned. Wingate's infiltrators, while they did have strongholds, were located far from any sort of friendly infrastructure. And they operated in this fashion for months at a time. Seen in this light, Wingate's concepts retain their cutting-edge feel, and thus he still awaits the coming of a modern master able to interpret the twenty-first-century implications of his mode of irregular warfare.

* * *

Having surveyed the past 250 years of irregular warfare, we have these remaining questions: Who will be considered the masters of this era? and What may come next for irregular warfare? Given that the key issues raised by earlier masters—from variants of military reform to nation building, networking, and on to swarming—remain in lively play, these questions are highly relevant.

Will Osama bin Laden one day be ranked among the masters? Certainly the attacks on the United States that he orchestrated and the organization he formed, which held up with such resilience against strong counterblows, suggest that his impact on global security affairs has been profound. But for all bin Laden's emphasis on elaborate networking, he has had great trouble in empowering his minions to maintain a faster operational tempo. While, al Qaeda cadres and affiliates have pulled off a few major attacks over the past decade, and a few more small-scale "wave attacks" here and there, they have never developed a capacity for sustained swarming. This limitation, probably more than any other factor, will prevent bin Laden from ever being seen as one of the masters of irregular warfare.

If al Qaeda is good at networking but doesn't do much swarming, the reverse seems to characterize the U.S. military, which now does a great deal of swarming but is loath to network. Save for the physical network of small outposts in Anbar province in Iraq in 2007–2008, complemented by the social network of ties to former tribal insurgents, American field forces have done little networking over the past decade. Among senior American military leaders, army generals David Petraeus and Stanley McChrystal achieved the best results against the terror networks. Petraeus was responsible for the networked swarm in Anbar that put al Qaeda forces on the run and sharply reduced violence there; McChrystal led the elite task forces of swarming raiders operating in other parts of Iraq. But this approach was curtailed, and the endgame in Iraq still hangs in the balance. In Afghanistan, where Petraeus and McChrystal went next, the shift they called for there looked far more like the big-unit approach in Vietnam than a swarm network. Thus the jury is still out on bin Laden, Petraeus, and McChrystal. Not one of them has been able to combine networked organizational forms with sustained swarm tactics.

In other key areas, bin Laden has striven for full transformation of his cadres while his foes have concentrated less successfully on trying to achieve some degree of integration between conventional and irregular capacities. American nation-building efforts have at best muddled along, and al Qaeda's narrative of a restored caliphate has never really caught on. Neither side has gravely injured the other's infrastructure, al Qaeda's being the physical haven in Waziristan and its virtual haven in cyberspace. All have had their innings at cooptation—the Americans in Anbar, particularly—but none have used infiltration well.

Where the central players in the terror war seem not to measure up to the standards of mastery, another candidate emerges if we consider Hassan Nasrallah of Hezbollah. Over the past few decades he and his organization drove the Israelis from Lebanon, largely by fielding a fully transformed fighting force built around swarm networks, then fended them off again in fighting in the summer of 2006. In terms of nation building and narrative themes, Nasrallah has also proven himself to be quite adept, his organization even rising to form a key part of the Lebanese government. He has also encouraged cooptation campaigns to extend the reach of his core network, but so far he has demonstrated little capacity for deep strikes that might pose serious threats to Israeli or other enemy infrastructure. Even so, as a work in progress Hassan Nasrallah has a shorter way to go to achieve a fully demonstrated mastery of irregular warfare than bin Laden or any of the leading American candidates.

This analysis might of course be overtaken by a future in which irregulars become armed with weapons of mass destruction. A few nuclear or biological weapons in the hands of Osama bin Laden or Hassan Nasrallah would change the game completely. For these men command networks that are virtually impervious to threats of retaliation in kind. How could a terror network be nuked in return if it struck first by, say, destroying a major American city? Or if terrorists infected with deadly diseases, in their communicable incubation phases, simply wandered about airport terminals in the United States? The darkest possible future for irregular warfare is the one in which terror networks seize such capabilities.

Indeed, it is this possible future that should convince us that taking a "long war" view of the struggle against terror is completely wrong-headed. Instead the spirits of Crook and Kitson need to be rekindled in some modern master attuned to the skillful use of their respective methods of cooptation and infiltration. Both won out quickly against difficult opponents who had successfully resisted the brute-force efforts of their adversaries for many years. Their techniques offer us the best way ahead, perhaps the only way to defeat the networks before they arm themselves with the deadliest weapons.

Leaving aside the specter of mass destruction, in the near term the greater likelihood is that "mass disruption" will be pursued by the next aspiring master (or masters) of irregular warfare. In the physical world this would consist of a capacity for mounting many small-scale attacks; but the concept may also be applied in the virtual world. Modern society and security depend heavily upon cyberspace-based systems whose disruption would inflict enormous costs upon all. We know that these systems, despite the proliferation of stout firewalls and other security measures, are highly vulnerable.

The only saving grace of the moment is that hackers who possess the technical skills to mount highly disruptive attacks are not sufficiently radicalized to want to do so. And those terrorists with the desire to commit acts of mass disruption don't yet have the skills to accomplish them. But at some point this gap between motivation and capability will close, opening up the prospect of a virtual covert war of all against all, of the kind described by Frederik Pohl in his dystopian classic *The Cool War*. This cool-war world does not demand that the malefactors be disaffected terrorists. Indeed, in Pohl's tale the leading nations themselves are drawn to the apparent promise of secret wars of mass disruption.

Whoever starts the next war, whether nation or network, we can be almost fully assured that the conflict will unfold largely along irregular lines, in either the physical or virtual world, or both. This prospect should provide us with all the reason we might need, right now, to scrutinize the many methods of the earlier masters. For victory in future conflicts will increasingly incline toward the side that demonstrates a deeper understanding of how to employ such concepts. In this respect the long debate between the leading conventional and irregular military theorists and practitioners that has flared continually since the 1750s seems finally to be over. The irregulars have won—a sure and troubling portent of the darkness that lies ahead.

NOTES

1. WAR "OUT OF THE DARK"

1. *Guerrilla* is the Spanish word for "small war."

2. The term *commando*, which enjoys widespread modern use, initially referred simply to a unit of mounted infantry of some 100 to 150 guerrilla fighters.

3. Caleb Carr, *The Lessons of Terror* (New York: Random House, 2001), 12.

4. "Guerrilla warfare," "insurgency," and "partisan operations" should all be thought of as synonyms.

5. See Loretta Napoleoni, *Insurgent Iraq: Al Zarqawi and the New Generation* (New York: Seven Stories Press, 2005).

6. Joint Staff, *Irregular Warfare Joint Operating Concept* (Washington, D.C.: U.S. Department of Defense, 2007), 5.

7. James Kiras, "Irregular Warfare," in *Understanding Modern Warfare* (New York: Cambridge University Press, 2008), 234.

8. The seminal article is by William Lind, K. Nightengale, J. Schmitt, J. Sutton, and G. Wilson, "The Changing Face of War: Into the Fourth Generation," *Marine Corps Gazette,* October 1989, 22–26.

9. See T. V. Paul, *Asymmetric Conflicts: War Initiation by Weaker Powers* (New York: Cambridge University Press, 1994).

10. For this expansion upon Paul's initial concept, see Roger W. Barnett, *Asymmetrical Warfare: Today's Challenge to U.S. Military Power* (Washington, D.C.: Brassey's, 2003).

11. Friedrich August Freiherr von der Heydte, *Modern Irregular Warfare in Defense Policy and as a Military Phenomenon*, trans. George Gregory (New York: New Benjamin Franklin House, 1986), 3.

12. Admiral McRaven introduced and analyzed the notion of "relative superiority" in his *SPEC OPS: Case Studies in Special Operations Warfare* (Novato, Calif.: Presidio, 1995).

2. FRONTIERSMAN: ROBERT ROGERS

1. Winston Churchill, *A History of the English-Speaking Peoples*, vol. 3, *The Age of Revolution* (New York: Cassell, 1957), 148.

2. At the time of this war there were some eighty thousand French colonists in North America but more than 1.5 million British settlers.

3. Cited in Richard Holmes, *Redcoat: The British Soldier in the Age of Horse and Musket* (London: HarperCollins, 2001), 41.

4. Fred Anderson, *Crucible of War: The Seven Years' War and the Fate of Empire in British North America, 1754–1766* (New York: Knopf, 2000), 411.

5. Under the mercantilist policies of the time, trade goods were to be shipped first to Britain, marked up in price, then sent back out to the American colonies.

6. Francis Parkman, *Montcalm and Wolfe: The Decline and Fall of the French Empire in North America* (New York: Collier Books, 1962), 301.

7. For a complete listing of these rules, see Robert Rogers, *Journals of Robert Rogers of the Rangers* (London: Leonaur, 2005), 58–65. A somewhat bowdlerized version of the plan of discipline also appears in Kenneth Roberts's novel *Northwest Passage*.

8. Francis Russell, *The French and Indian Wars* (New York: American Heritage, 1962), 46.

9. Anderson, *Crucible of War*, 241.

10. Cited in Parkman, *Montcalm and Wolfe*, 300.

11. Anderson, *Crucible of War*, 410.

12. Cited in John R. Cuneo, *Robert Rogers of the Rangers* (New York: Oxford University Press, 1959), 53.

13. Another reason why the French alliances with the Native American tribes had begun to falter was that the hundreds of hostages taken by the Indians at the time of the Fort William Henry massacre brought smallpox into the villages of their captors, decimating many settlements and curtailing the general appetite for plunder.

14. See Rogers, *Journals*, 125–26, for a remarkably dispassionate account of what had to have been a searing experience.

15. On both these points, see Anderson, *Crucible of War*, 542–43.

16. From a letter written by Washington to the president of Congress, June 27, 1776.

17. See John F. Ross, *War on the Run: The Epic Story of Robert Rogers and the Conquest of America's First Frontier* (New York: Bantam, 2009), 436–41.

18. The great account of irregular warfare in the northern theater of operations is Howard Swiggett's *War Out of Niagara: Walter Butler and the Tory Rangers* (New York: Columbia University Press, 1933).

19. R. E. Dupuy and T. N. Dupuy, *The Compact History of the Revolutionary War* (New York: Hawthorn, 1963), 463.

3. FIGHTING QUAKER: NATHANAEL GREENE

1. Russell Weigley, "American Strategy from Its Beginnings through the First World War," in *Makers of Modern Strategy*, ed. Peter Paret (Princeton, N.J.: Princeton University Press, 1986), 410.

2. Mark Mayo Boatner III, *Encyclopedia of the American Revolution* (New York: D. McKay, 1966), 981.

3. Alfred Thayer Mahan, *The Influence of Sea Power Upon History, 1660–1783*, 7th ed. (Boston: Little, Brown, 1894), 376.

4. See Hank Messick, *King's Mountain: The Epic of the Blue Ridge "Mountain Men" in the American Revolution* (Boston: Little, Brown, 1976).

5. Cited in Terry Golway, *Washington's General: Nathanael Greene and the Triumph of the American Revolution* (New York: Holt, 2005), 232.

6. Theodore Ropp, *War in the Modern World* (London: Macmillan, 1962), 91.

7. Theodore Thayer, "Nathanael Greene: Revolutionary War Strategist," in *George Washington's Generals*, ed. G. Billias (New York: Morrow, 1962), 131. Emphasis added.

8. Derek Leebaert, *To Dare and to Conquer: Special Operations and the Destiny of Nations, from Achilles to Al Qaeda* (New York: Little, Brown, 2006), 295.

9. Russell Weigley, *The American Way of War: A History of United States Military Strategy and Policy* (New York: Macmillan, 1973), 27.

10. Not to be confused with Charles Lee, mentioned earlier in the chapter.

11. Cited in Bruce Catton, *The Civil War* (New York: American Heritage, 1961), 177.

12. Cited in Dupuy, *Compact History of the Revolutionary War* (New York: Hawthorn, 1963), 400.

13. Thomas Fleming, *Liberty! The American Revolution* (New York: Viking, 1997), 323.

14. Weigley, *American Way of War*, 36.

15. Charles Francis Adams, *The Works of John Adams* (Boston: Little, Brown, 1852), 7:487.

4. GUERRILLERO: FRANCISCO ESPOZ Y MINA

1. This is certainly the case with the two classic multivolume histories: William Napier's *History of the War in the Peninsula* (London: Folio Society, 1828) and Charles Oman's, *History of the Peninsular War* (London: Greenhill, 1903–1930). Among modern historians, Charles Esdaile argues in his *The Spanish Army in the Peninsular War* (Manchester, England: Manchester University Press, 1988), 141–43, that the guerrillas did more harm than good.

2. David Chandler, *The Campaigns of Napoleon* (New York: Macmillan, 1966), 660. For a survey of the studies that downplay the guerrillas' importance, see J. L. Tone, *The Fatal Knot* (Chapel Hill: University of North Carolina Press, 1994), 186n9.

3. Lynn Montross, *War Through the Ages*, 3rd ed. (New York: Harper, 1960), 527.

4. His memoirs, however they may be overstated, give a stirring account of the day-to-day course of one of the key insurgent campaigns. See Juan Martín Diez, *Military Exploits* (London: Nabu Press, 1823).

5. Details of this action and Javier's subsequent moves are described in Tone, *Fatal Knot*, 77–80.

6. On Mina's struggles with various competitors for command and his ultimate recognition by the regents, see Tone, *Fatal Knot*, 101–2.

7. This action is described by Mina himself in his *Memorias* (Madrid, 1962 edition), 36.

8. Cochrane, who would serve as the model for Frederick Marryat's naval hero in his novel, *Mr. Midshipman Easy*, would go on later in life to help establish navies in some of the Latin American republics that rebelled against the reimposition of Madrid's authority, which had been interrupted during the French occupation of Spain.

9. For an account of the importance of irregular warfare techniques to Napoleon's defeat in Russia, see the next chapter.

10. Elizabeth Longford, *Wellington: The Years of the Sword* (New York: Harper & Row, 1969), 211.

11. This figure comes from Tone, *Fatal Knot*, 131.

12. See Mark Kurlansky, *The Basque History of the World* (New York: Walker, 1999), 143–44.

5. HUSSAR POET: DENIS DAVYDOV

1. Walter Laqueur, *Guerrilla: A Historical and Critical Study* (Boston: Little, Brown, 1976), 110.

2. Georges Lefebvre, *Napoleon: From 18 Brumaire to Tilsit, 1799–1807*, trans. Henry F. Stockhold (New York: Columbia University Press, 1969), 275.

3. The Poles were loyal to Napoleon because he put their country back on Europe's map after Prussia, Austria, and Russia had partitioned it out of existence in 1795.

4. Carl von Clausewitz, *The Campaign of 1812 in Russia* (London: Greenhill Books, 1992), 192.

5. Denis Davydov, *In the Service of the Tsar against Napoleon: The Memoirs of Denis Davydov, 1806–1814*, trans. Gregory Troubetzkoy (London: Greenhill Books, 1999), 115.

6. Hussars were the least encumbered (or protected) of the types of cavalry of the time, their swiftness and stealth commending them to irregular operations. By way of contrast, cuirassiers wore front and back armor and, with weapons, weighed in at about three hundred pounds on the backs of their horses.

7. Davydov, *In the Service of the Tsar*, 69.

8. Armand de Caulaincourt, *With Napoleon in Russia*, ed. and trans. George Libaire (New York: Morrow, 1935), 46. The long-lost original manuscript was found at the Caulaincourt family château in 1935.

9. Clausewitz, *Campaign of 1812 in Russia*, 187.

10. Cossacks, whose name may go back to an ancient word for "bandit," were thus quite well suited to working with the hussars.

11. A good summary of Davydov's outreach to Russian villagers, and his instructions to them, may be found in Laqueur, *Guerrilla*, 45.

12. Caulaincourt, *With Napoleon in Russia*, 148.

13. Davydov, *In the Service of the Tsar*, 134.

14. Napoleon's largest intact forces were roughly thirty thousand troops under his subordinate Macdonald—mainly compliant Prussians—who had been besieging Riga on the Baltic coast. But as Macdonald moved to link up with Napoleon, seventeen thousand of the Prussians deserted. Thus there were few relatively fresh forces remaining.

15. Count Philippe-Paul de Ségur, *Napoleon's Russian Campaign*, trans. J. David Townsend (Boston: Houghton Mifflin, 1958), 143.

16. Davydov, *In the Service of the Tsar*, 155.

17. David Chandler, *The Campaigns of Napoleon: The Mind and Method of History's Greatest Soldier* (New York: Macmillan, 1966), 859–60.

18. Davydov, *In the Service of the Tsar*, 209–10.

19. See Bernard Pares, *A History of Russia* (New York: Knopf, 1948), 316.

6. DESERT MYSTIC: ABD EL-KADER

1. The city would officially be given its modern Turkish name, Istanbul, in 1930.

2. Cited in Edward Behr, *The Algerian Problem* (New York: W. W. Norton, 1961), 17.

3. Sufism is that branch of Islam that emphasizes the direct experience of the divine by various forms of meditation, contemplation, and, sometimes, repetitive physical movement. This last practice is best known to us through the sword dancing of the so-called Whirling Dervishes.

4. Alexis de Tocqueville, "Second Letter on Algeria" (1837), in *Writings on Empire and Slavery*, ed. and trans. Jennifer Pitts (Baltimore: Johns Hopkins University Press, 2001), 17.

5. The proclamation is cited in John W. Kiser, *Commander of the Faithful: The Life and Times of Emir Abd el-Kader* (Rhinebeck, N.Y.: Monkfish, 2008), 51.

6. See Behr, *Algerian Problem*, 19, and Kiser, *Commander of the Faithful*, 63.

7. Kiser, *Commander of the Faithful*, 82.

8. Kiser, *Commander of the Faithful*, 116.

9. Antoine Henri de Jomini, *The Art of War* (London: Greenhill Books, 1992), 29.

10. Douglas Porch, "Bugeaud, Galliéni, Lyautey: The Development of French Colonial Warfare," in *Makers of Modern Strategy: From Machiavelli to the Nuclear Age*, ed. Peter Paret (Princeton, N.J.: Princeton University Press, 1986), 379.

11. C. E. Callwell, *Small Wars: Their Principles and Practice* (London: University of Nebraska Press, 1996), 83.

12. Kiser, *Commander of the Faithful*, 175.

13. Cited in Behr, *Algerian Problem*, 23.

7. NATION BUILDER: GIUSEPPE GARIBALDI

1. V. I. Lenin, *Imperialism: The Highest Stage of Capitalism* (New York: International Publishers, 1939), 76.

2. Mazzini's exhortation to his comrades is cited in Christopher Hibbert, *Garibaldi and his Enemies: The Clash of Arms and Personalities in the Making of Italy* (Boston: Little, Brown, 1965), 14.

3. Cited in Irene Collins, *The Age of Progress: A Survey of European History from 1789–1870* (London: Arnold, 1964), 283.

4. Laqueur, *Guerrilla*, 130.

5. Nina Brown Baker, *Garibaldi* (New York: Vanguard Press, 1944), 21.

6. Giuseppe Garibaldi, *The Memoirs of Garibaldi*, ed. Alexandre Dumas, trans. R. S. Garnett (London: E. Benn, 1932), 92.

7. Hibbert, *Garibaldi and His Enemies*, 21.

8. The conversation is recounted in Baker, *Garibaldi*, 106.

9. George Macaulay Trevelyan, *Garibaldi's Defence of the Roman Republic* (London: Longmans, Green, and Co., 1907), 203.

10. Trevelyan, *Garibaldi's Defence of the Roman Republic*, 215.

11. The Battle of New Orleans in the War of 1812 was the first in which one side—the Americans under Andrew Jackson—were mostly armed with rifles.

12. Baker, *Garibaldi*, 288.

13. For more on this matter, see Howard Marraro, "Lincoln's Offer of a Command to Garibaldi," *Journal of the Illinois State Historical Society*, September 1943.

14. Cited in Hibbert, *Garibaldi and his Enemies*, 361–62.

8. REBEL RAIDER: NATHAN BEDFORD FORREST

1. Derek Leebaert, *To Dare and Conquer: Special Operations and the Destiny of Nations, from Achilles to Al Qaeda* (New York: Little, Brown, 2006), 357.

2. See, for example, Grady McWhiney and Perry D. Jamieson, *Attack and Die: Civil War Military Tactics and the Southern Heritage* (Tuscaloosa: University of Alabama Press, 1982).

3. On the pull of Jominian and Napoleonic thought on both Union and Confederate senior military leaders, see T. Harry Williams, "The Military Leadership of

North and South," in *Why the North Won the Civil War*, ed. David Donald (New York: Collier, 1960). Clausewitz's work, which expressed some similar ideas about battle and "decisive points," was not yet disseminated throughout the American officer corps.

4. This argument is implicitly supported by Martin Dugard, *The Training Ground: Grant, Lee, Sherman, and Davis in the Mexican War, 1846–1848* (Boston: Little, Brown, 2008).

5. The most thorough account of Lincoln's travails may be found in James M. McPherson, *Tried by War: Abraham Lincoln as Commander in Chief* (New York: Penguin, 2009).

6. Cited in Bruce Catton, *The Civil War* (New York: American Heritage, 1961), 177.

7. The phrase is from Williams, "Military Leadership of North and South," 54.

8. Walter Laqueur, *Guerrilla: A Historical and Critical Study* (Boston: Little, Brown, 1976), 81.

9. Ulysses S. Grant, *Personal Memoirs* (New York: Charles L. Webster and Company, 1886), 2:346.

10. On this period in Forrest's life, see Jack Hurst, *Nathan Bedford Forrest: A Biography* (New York: Knopf, 1993), especially 15–17.

11. Laqueur, *Guerrilla*, 81–82.

12. Hurst, *Forrest*, 383.

13. The Rommel connection is made in Walter Sullivan's preface to Andrew Nelson Lytle, *Bedford Forrest and His Critter Company* (Nashville, Tenn.: J. S. Sanders, 1992), xii.

14. Bruce Catton, *This Hallowed Ground* (Garden City, N.Y.: Doubleday, 1956), 200.

15. On this point, see R. E. Beringer, Herman Hattaway, Archer Jones, and W. N. Still, *Why the South Lost the Civil War* (London: University of Georgia Press, 1986), 248.

16. Hurst, *Forrest*, 139.

17. Cited in James M. McPherson, *Battle Cry of Freedom: The Civil War Era* (New York: Oxford University Press, 1988), 676.

18. Quoted in Robert Selph Henry, *"First with the Most" Forrest* (Indianapolis: Bobbs-Merrill, 1944), 193.

19. Albert Castel, *Decision in the West: The Atlanta Campaign of 1864* (Lawrence: University Press of Kansas, 1992), 346.

20. Cited in Hurst, *Forrest*, 207.

21. The officer was Colonel D. C. Kelley. See John Allan Wyeth, *That Devil Forrest: Life of General Nathan Bedford Forrest* (Edison, N.J.: Blue & Gray Press, [1899] 1996), 573.

22. Cited in Lytle, *Bedford Forrest*, 390.

23. The article may be found in Robert S. Henry, *As They Saw Forrest* (Jackson, Tenn.: McCowat-Mercer, 1956), see especially 20–35.

24. An excellent assessment of these views of Forrest may be found in Paul Ashdown and Edward Caudill, *The Myth of Nathan Bedford Forrest* (Lanham, Md.: Rowman & Littlefield, 2005).

9. GRAY FOX: GEORGE CROOK

1. S. L. A. Marshall, *Crimsoned Prairie: The Indian Wars* (New York: Da Capo, 1972).

2. David Roberts, *Once They Moved Like the Wind: Cochise, Geronimo, and the Apache Wars* (New York: Simon & Schuster, 1994), 57.

3. James M. McPherson, *Battle Cry of Freedom: The Civil War Era* (New York: Oxford University Press, 1988), 753.

4. George Crook, *Autobiography* (Norman: University of Oklahoma Press, 1946), 87.

5. Crook, *Autobiography*, 98.

6. Crook, *Autobiography*, 107.

7. Crook, *Autobiography*, 141.

8. John Bourke, *On the Border with Crook* (Lincoln: University of Nebraska Press, 1971) 150.

9. Martin Blumenson and James L. Stokesbury, *Masters of the Art of Command* (Boston: Houghton Mifflin, 1975), 207.

10. Robert M. Utley, *The Lance and the Shield: The Life and Times of Sitting Bull* (New York: Holt, 1993), 141.

11. Russell Weigley, *American Way of War* (New York: Macmillan, 1973), 162.

12. Perhaps the best account of this campaign may be found in Jerome A. Greene, *Yellowstone Command: Colonel Nelson A. Miles and the Great Sioux War of 1876–1877* (Norman: University of Oklahoma Press, 2006).

13. Mark H. Brown, *The Flight of the Nez Perce* (London: Putnam, 1967), 210.

14. The treaty went into effect on July 29, 1882. See Paul Wellman, *Indian Wars of the West* (New York: Indian Head Books, 1992), 419.

15. The definitive account of this episode is related by Crook's subordinate, John Bourke, in his *On the Border with Crook.*

16. Geronimo said that Chato and the scout Mickey Free warned him of the impending arrest. See Britton Davis, *The Truth about Geronimo* (Lincoln: University of Nebraska Press, 1976), 200–201.

10. VELDT RIDER: CHRISTIAAN DE WET

1. It is close to the German word for farmer, *Bauer.*

2. Winston S. Churchill, *A History of the English-Speaking Peoples*, vol. 4, *The Great Democracies* (New York: Dodd, Mead, 1958), 374.

3. Cited in Byron Farwell, *The Great Boer War* (New York: Penguin, 1976), 40.

4. Farwell, *The Great Boer War*, 83.

5. Christiaan Rudolf de Wet, *Three Years' War* (New York: Scribner's, 1903), 32.

6. Arthur Conan Doyle, *The Great Boer War* (New York: McClure, Phillips & Co., 1901), 434.

7. Thomas Pakenham, *The Boer War* (New York: Perennial, 1992), 348.

8. Farwell, *The Great Boer War*, 261.

9. Farwell, *The Great Boer War*, 256.

10. De Wet, *Three Years' War*, 78.

11. Winston S. Churchill, *Frontiers and Wars* (London: Eyre & Spottiswoode, 1962), 592. Churchill had gotten close enough to the action to be captured by the Boers at one point, though he soon escaped. From then on he kept close company with Field Marshal Roberts and other senior British commanders. Churchill left South Africa after the fall of Pretoria and, later in the year, won election to Parliament as the Conservative member from Oldham.

12. Farwell, *Great Boer War*, 307.

13. Actual battle deaths among the Boers were still quite small and would reach only about seven thousand by war's end, compared to more than twenty-two thousand British soldiers killed in the war. These figures are cited in Pakenham, *Boer War*, 607.

14. De Wet, *Three Years' War*, 225.

15. See Ruth Fry, *Emily Hobhouse* (London: J. Cape, 1929).

16. Alfred Thayer Mahan, *The Story of the War in South Africa* (London: William Clowes, 1900), 203.

17. De Wet, *Three Years' War*, 292.

11. BUSH FIGHTER: PAUL VON LETTOW-VORBECK

1. Thomas Pakenham, *The Scramble for Africa, 1876–1912* (New York: Random House, 1991), 613.

2. Cited in Edward Paice, *Tip and Run: The Untold Tragedy of the Great War in Africa* (London: Weidenfeld & Nicolson, 2007), 25.

3. One of the best accounts of this German maritime strategy may be found in Edwin P. Hoyt, *Kreuzerkrieg* (Cleveland: World Pub. Co., 1968).

4. Cited in Byron Farwell, *The Great War in Africa* (New York: Norton, 1986), 105.

5. Paice, *Tip and Run*, 153.

6. Farwell, *Great War in Africa*, 293.

7. Indeed, victory was somewhat prematurely declared in the leading book about the campaign published back then, J. H. V. Crowe's *General Smuts' Campaign in East Africa* (London: J. Murray, 1918).

8. Edwin P. Hoyt, *Guerilla: Colonel von Lettow-Vorbeck and Germany's East African Empire* (New York: Macmillan, 1981), 162.

9. Paul von Lettow-Vorbeck, *My Reminiscences of East Africa* (London: Hurst, 1925), 212.

10. Von Lettow-Vorbeck, *Reminiscences of East Africa*, 229.

11. Paice, *Tip and Run*, 392.

12. Hoyt, *Guerilla*, 34.

13. Farwell, *Great War in Africa*, 357.

12. EMIR DYNAMITE: T. E. LAWRENCE

1. Plutarch, *The Lives of Noble Grecians and Romans*, trans. John Dryden (Chicago: Encyclopaedia Britannica, 1952), 433.

2. One might argue that attack aircraft made the principal difference in this campaign, but the Northern Alliance enjoyed complete air support for a month before the Special Forces joined them—and showed little progress. Once the advisers were in place, Kabul and Kandahar fell in a few weeks. See Doug Stanton, *Horse Soldiers* (New York: Scribner, 2009).

3. T. E. Lawrence, *Seven Pillars of Wisdom* (London: J. Cape, 1935), 192.

4. Robert Payne, *Lawrence of Arabia: A Triumph* (New York: Pyramid Books, 1962), 105.

5. James Barr, *Setting the Desert on Fire: T. E. Lawrence and Britain's Secret War in Arabia, 1916–1918* (London: Bloomsbury, 2008), 83, 162.

6. Cited in Jeremy Wilson, *Lawrence of Arabia: The Authorized Biography of T. E. Lawrence* (New York: Atheneum, 1990), 192.

7. Lawrence, *Seven Pillars of Wisdom*, 350.

8. Lawrence, *Seven Pillars of Wisdom*, 386.

9. Barr, *Setting the Desert on Fire*, 201–6, offers a case against the truth of Lawrence's story about Deraa, based mainly on lack of corroboration and later evidence of his masochistic tendencies. A more sympathetic but clinically incisive perspective may be found in Harvard psychiatrist John E. Mack's biography of Lawrence, *A Prince of Our Disorder* (Boston: Little, Brown, 1976).

10. The impact of this deception on Turkish leaders and their German advisers is nicely described in Jon Latimer, *Deception in War* (Woodstock, N.Y.: Overlook Press, 2001), 92–94.

11. Lawrence, *Seven Pillars of Wisdom*, 344.

12. B. H. Liddell Hart, *Lawrence of Arabia* (New York: Da Capo, 1935), 384.

13. Lowell Thomas, *With Lawrence in Arabia* (New York: Century Co., 1924), 171. The direct share of prisoners accounted for by the Arab irregulars was about one-third. The numbers of Turks that Lawrence's fighters killed as they tried to surrender remains lost to history.

14. Liddell Hart, *Lawrence of Arabia*, 380.

15. Liddell Hart, *Lawrence of Arabia*, 381, for both quotes in this paragraph.

16. See, in the first instance, Richard Aldington, *Lawrence of Arabia: A Biographical Enquiry* (London: Collins, 1955) and, in the second, Suleiman Mousa, *T. E. Lawrence: An Arab View* (New York: Oxford University Press, 1966).

17. Wilson, *Lawrence of Arabia*, 1084.

18. Robert Graves, *T. E. Lawrence to His Biographer, Robert Graves* (New York: Doubleday, 1938), 129.

19. B. H. Liddell Hart, *T. E. Lawrence to His Biographer, Liddell Hart* (New York: Doubleday, 1938), 191.

20. Cited in Barr, *Setting the Desert on Fire*, 317.

13. LONG RANGER: ORDE WINGATE

1. Walter Laqueur, *Guerrilla: A Historical and Critical Study* (Boston: Little, Brown, 1976), 169.

2. Wingate would come to criticize Lawrence's method of buying the support of Arab tribesmen, and studiously refrained from doing so when recruiting tribal levies in Abyssinia a decade later.

3. Leonard Mosley, *Gideon Goes to War* (New York: Scribner, 1955), 44.

4. Mosley, *Gideon Goes to War*, 62–63.

5. Christopher Sykes, *Orde Wingate* (London: Collins, 1959), 149.

6. Mosley, *Gideon Goes to War*, 58.

7. Lewis Gann, *Guerrillas in History* (Stanford, Calif.: Hoover Institution Press, 1971), 58–59.

8. Mosley, *Gideon Goes to War*, 126–27.

9. Mosley, *Gideon Goes to War*, 138.

10. Thesiger would later in life become famous for his classic studies *Arabian Sands* and *The Marsh Arabs*.

11. Sykes, *Orde Wingate*, 317.

12. Sykes, *Orde Wingate*, 331–32.

13. This critical view was certainly held by General (later field marshal and chief of the imperial staff) William Slim, one of the senior British commanders in India, though he only articulated it in full more than a decade later in his memoir, *Defeat into Victory* (London: Cassell, 1956).

14. Mosley, *Gideon Goes to War*, 194.

15. Winston Churchill, *The Second World War: Closing the Ring* (Boston: Houghton Mifflin, 1951), 67.

16. Wingate's supporters tended to come from those who served under him. See, for example, Derek Tulloch, *Wingate in Peace and War* (London: Macdonald, 1972). More recently, an excellent assessment that sustains the more positive view of the Chindits may be found in J. Bierman and C. Smith, *Fire in the Night: Wingate of Burma, Ethiopia, and Zion* (New York: Random House, 1999). Wingate detractors, including and beyond William Slim, were often drawn from the ranks of more conventional general officers. One of the most thoughtful critiques is Shelford Bidwell's *The Chindit War* (London: Hodder & Stoughton, 1979).

17. *Japanese Monograph No. 134: Burma Operations in Imphal Area and Withdrawal to Northern Burma* (Washington, D.C.: Distributed by the Office of the Chief of Military History, Dept. of the Army, 1957). Cited in Bierman and Smith, *Fire in the Night*, 386.

18. From Mosley, *Gideon Goes to War*, 63–64. Emphasis in the original.

14. UNDERSEA WOLF: CHARLES LOCKWOOD

1. Ronald Spector, *Eagle Against the Sun: The American War with Japan* (New York: The Free Press, 1985), 178.

2. Robert Frank, *Guadalcanal* (New York: Random House, 1990), 601, reflects a final tally of twenty-five American surface ships lost, including two aircraft carriers, and eighteen Japanese ships, including one small carrier.

3. A. T. Mahan, *Influence of Sea Power upon History* (Boston: Little, Brown, 1894), 132.

4. Cited in Carlton Savage, *Policy of the United States toward Maritime Commerce on War* (Washington, D.C.: U.S. Government Printing Office, 1934), 1:389.

5. Article I, Section 8 grants the legislative branch authority over "letters of marque," the principal means by which private individuals could wage war with the patina of respectability afforded by this form of governmental authorization.

6. An outstanding survey of Confederate naval operations may be found in William M. Fowler, Jr., *Rebels Under Sail* (New York: Scribner, 1976).

7. Spector, *Eagle Against the Sun*, 130.

8. The travails of the Mark-14 torpedo are best documented in Clay Blair, *Silent Victory: The U.S. Submarine War Against Japan* (Philadelphia: Lippincott, 1975), 249–54.

9. See Thomas C. Hart, *Narrative of Events, Asiatic Fleet, Leading up to War and from 3 December 1941 to 15 February 1942* (Washington, D.C.: Government Printing Office, 1946), 68.

10. Samuel Eliot Morison, *The Two-Ocean War: A Short History of the United States Navy in the Second World War* (Boston: Little, Brown, 1963), 493–94. See also Spector, *Eagle Against the Sun*, 487.

11. Winston S. Churchill, *The Second World War*, vol. 4, *The Hinge of Fate* (Boston: Houghton Mifflin, 1950), 125.

12. Lockwood describes the use of "pack tactics" in his *Hellcats of the Sea* (New York: Greenburg, 1955). A more recent analysis of Operation Barney may be found in Steven Smith, *Wolf Pack* (Hoboken, N.J.: Wiley, 2003).

13. On the impact of code-breaking, see David Kahn, *Seizing the Enigma: The Race to Break the German U-Boat Codes* (Boston: Houghton Mifflin, 1991). A remarkably detailed account of the direction finding and other technologies—as well as tactics and doctrines—that beat the U-boats may be found in Michael Gannon, *Black May* (New York: HarperCollins, 1998).

14. On this issue, see John Prados, *Combined Fleet Decoded: The Secret History of American Intelligence and the Japanese Navy in World War II* (New York: Random House, 1995).

15. Morison, *Two-Ocean War*, 505.

16. Lockwood's account of this remarkable—yet not atypical—action may be found in his *Sink 'Em All: Submarine Warfare in the Pacific* (New York: Dutton, 1951), 231–36. O'Kane's memoir of these events is in his *Clear the Bridge! The War Patrols of the U.S.S. Tang* (Chicago: Rand McNally, 1977).

17. Spector, *Eagle Against the Sun*, 487.

18. Morison, *Two-Ocean War*, 511.

19. Cited in William D. Leahy, *I Was There* (New York: Whittlesey House, 1950), 441.

20. Lockwood, *Sink 'Em All*, 383.

21. I exclude the spectacular Indian aircraft carrier raid on Karachi in 1971, as that Indo-Pakistani conflict was exceptionally one-sided at sea.

22. John Keegan, *The Price of Admiralty* (New York: Viking, 1989), 274.

15. PARTISAN: JOSIP BROZ, "TITO"

1. See E. H. Cookridge, *Set Europe Ablaze* (New York: Crowell, 1967).

2. John Keegan, *The Second World War* (New York: Viking, 1989), 483–84. A more recent but similar assessment, and one that offers a sharp critique of Churchill's strategy of sabotage and subversion, may be found in Max Hastings, *Finest Years: Churchill as Warlord* (New York: HarperCollins, 2009).

3. Winston S. Churchill, *Closing the Ring: The Second World War* (Boston: Houghton Mifflin 1951), 461.

4. The number grows to over 350,000 when Serb, Bulgar, and Croat fighters are included. See Fitzroy Maclean, *Disputed Barricade* (London: J. Cape, 1957), 248.

5. Walter Laqueur, *Guerrilla: A Historical and Critical Study* (Boston: Little, Brown, 1976), 217.

6. Robert Kennedy, *German Antiguerrilla Operations in the Balkans, 1941–1944* (Washington, D.C.: Center of Military History, U.S. Army, 1954), United States Army Pamphlet, 29–243.

7. These methods are assessed in detail in Otto Heilbrunn, *Partisan Warfare* (New York: Praeger, 1962), 108–10.

8. Heilbrunn, *Partisan Warefare*, 167.

9. Walter Roberts, *Tito, Mihailovic, and the Allies, 1941–1945* (New Brunswick, N.J.: Rutgers University Press, 1973), 228. Laqueur, *Guerrilla*, 217, puts partisan losses in this action at more than six thousand.

10. Maclean, *Disputed Barricade*, 255.

11. Laqueur, *Guerrilla*, 219.

12. Reported in Vladimir Dedijer, *Tito Speaks: His Self-Portrait and Struggle with Stalin* (London: Weidenfeld and Nicolson, 1953), xiii–xv, and Richard West, *Tito* (New York: Carroll & Graf, 1994), 239.

13. This is not to suggest that Tito abstained from extramarital affairs thereafter. But his marriage to Jovanka was the most stable relationship of his life.

14. West, *Tito*, 258.

15. Cited in Jasper Ridley, *Tito* (London: Constable, 1994), 323.

16. Misha Glenny, *The Fall of Yugoslavia* (London: Penguin, 1992), 31.

16. COUNTERINSURGENT: FRANK KITSON

1. Robert Taber, *The War of the Flea* (New York: L. Stuart, 1970).

2. See Brian Lapping, *End of Empire* (New York: St. Martin's Press, 1985), xv.

3. The insurgents' own name for themselves was the Land and Freedom Army. The term Mau Mau used to describe them likely came from the shortening and repetition of *muma wa uiguano*, the oath of unity that all took.

4. Anthony Clayton, *Counter-Insurgency in Kenya* (Nairobi: Transafrica Publishers, 1976), 7.

5. John Newsinger, *British Counterinsurgency* (New York: Palgrave, 2002), 70.

6. Sir Michael Blundell, *So Rough a Wind* (London: Weidenfeld and Nicolson 1960), 170–71.

7. Frank Kitson, *Low Intensity Operations* (London: Faber, 1971), 65.

8. On the British cover-up, see Caroline Elkins, *Imperial Reckoning: The Untold Story of Britain's Gulag in Kenya* (New York: Holt, 2005). For the anecdote about the Churchill letter, see p. 53.

9. These initiatives are described in detail in Otto Skorzeny's memoir, *Skorzeny's Special Missions* (London: R. Hale, 1957), 120–25, 167–74.

10. Frank Kitson, *Gangs and Counter-Gangs* (London: Barrie and Rockliff, 1960), 74.

11. Newsinger, *British Counterinsurgency*, 74.

12. Robert B. Asprey, *War in the Shadows: The Guerrilla in History* (New York: W. Morrow, 1994), 640.

13. On this point, see J. M. Woodhouse, "Some Personal Observations on the Employment of Special Forces in Malaya," *Army Quarterly*, April 1955.

14. See Lawrence M. Greenberg, *The Hukbalahap Insurrection* (Washington, D.C.: U.S. Army Center of Military History, 1995), especially 118–19; and Lawrence E. Cline, *Pseudo Operations and Counterinsurgency* (Carlisle, Pa.: Strategic Studies Institute, U.S. Army War College, 2005), 1–2.

15. A good military overview of this conflict may be found in Stephen Cheney, *The Insurgency in Oman, 1962–1976* (Quantico, Va.: Marine Corps Command and Staff College, 1984).

16. J. Bowyer Bell, *The Irish Troubles* (New York: St. Martin's Press, 1993), 112.

17. Newsinger, *British Counterinsurgency*, 167.

18. Newsinger, *British Counterinsurgency*, 169.

19. See Robin Evelegh, *Peace Keeping in a Democratic Society* (London: C. Hurst, 1978), 29–31; and Newsinger, *British Counterinsurgency*, 169.

20. Charles Townshend, *Britain's Civil Wars* (London: Faber and Faber, 1986), especially the discussion on pp. 32–33.

21. On this point, see Martin Dillon, *The Enemy Within* (London: Doubleday, 1971), 120.

22. Kitson, *Low Intensity Operations*, 29.

23. Lucian W. Pye, *Guerrilla Communism and Malaya* (Princeton, N.J.: Princeton University Press, 1956), 95.

17. PEOPLE'S WARRIOR: VO NGUYEN GIAP

1. Cecil B. Currey, *Victory at Any Cost: The Genius of Vietnam's General Vo Nguyen Giap* (Washington, D.C.: Potomac Books, 2005), 21.

2. The French claimed that she committed suicide, but American intelligence reports support the conclusion that she was beaten to death. See Philip Davidson, *Vietnam at War: The History, 1946–1975* (Novato, Calif.: Presidio, 1988), 7. Their daughter, Vo Hang Anh, survived and was later reunited with Giap.

3. This name was, as Giap put it, an "easier to remember" abbreviation of *Vietnam Doc Lop Dong Minh Hoi* (Vietnam Independence League). See Vo Nguyen Giap, *The Military Art of People's War* (New York: Monthly Review Press, 1970), 50.

4. See the discussion of how Giap drew insights from Napoleon as much as Mao in Currey, *Victory at Any Cost*, 53.

5. Joseph Buttinger, *Vietnam: A Dragon Embattled* (New York: Praeger, 1967), 2:739.

6. Currey, *Victory at Any Cost*, 175.

7. Bernard Fall, *Street Without Joy*, 4th ed. (New York: Schocken, 1967), 44.

8. Michael Maclear, *The Ten Thousand Day War: Vietnam, 1945–1975* (New York: St. Martin's Press, 1981), 47.

9. Vo Nguyen Giap, *Dienbienphu*, trans. Lady Borton (Hanoi: The Gioi Publishers, 2004), 124.

10. Another Democratic senator who had joined Johnson in opposing intervention in Indochina was Mike Mansfield of Montana. His opposition remained steadfast over the years, but he later failed to talk Johnson out of going to war there. See Robert Mann, *A Grand Delusion: America's Descent into Vietnam* (New York: Basic Books, 2001), 156.

11. Lacouture's comment is cited in Maclear, *Ten Thousand Day War*, 49.

12. Bernard Fall's *Hell in a Very Small Place* (Philadelphia: Lippincott, 1967) remains the finest study of this battle.

13. Cited in Davidson, *Vietnam at War*, 305.

14. Currey, *Victory at Any Cost*, 239.

15. John Prados, *The Hidden History of the Vietnam War* (Chicago: Ivan R. Dee, 1995), 57.

16. Cited in Maclear, *Ten Thousand Day War*, 183.

17. Robert McNamara, *In Retrospect: The Tragedy and Lessons of Vietnam* (New York: Times Books, 1995), 243.

18. One of the most notable of these army officers was Lieutenant Colonel Anthony Herbert, whose memoir, *Soldier* (New York: Holt, Rinehart and Winston, 1973), detailed what this kind of war looked like and how he had achieved numerous successes with irregular tactics.

19. Don Oberdorfer, *Tet!* (New York: Doubleday, 1971), 330.

18. BANDIT QUEEN: PHOOLAN DEVI

1. Eric Hobsbawm, *Bandits* (New York: Delacorte Press, 1969), 58.

2. The term is from the Hindustani *dakait*, meaning, roughly, rural secular bandit.

3. John Reed, *Insurgent Mexico* (New York: D. Appleton, 1914), 115.

4. Hobsbawm, *Bandits*, 90.

5. For an overview of the Thugs, see Kim A. Wagner, *Stranglers and Bandits: A Historical Anthology of Thuggee* (New York: Oxford University Press, 2009). The origin of "thug" is the Hindi word *thag*, for deceiver or con man.

6. See Bhangya Bhukya, "Delinquent Subjects: Dacoity and the Creation of a Surveillance Society in Hyderabad State," *Indian Economic and Social History Review* 44, no. 2 (April–June 2007): 179–212.

7. Richard Shears and Isobelle Gidley, *Devi: The Bandit Queen* (London: Allen & Unwin, 1984), 18.

8. There is a lively debate about the facts of Phoolan Devi's life, so I shall stick to consensus views or, in their absence, describe the differing versions of her story.

9. Phoolan Devi, Marie-Thérèse Cuny, and Paul Rambali, *The Bandit Queen of India: An Indian Woman's Amazing Journey from Peasant to International Legend* (Guilford, Conn.: Lyons Press, 2003), 157.

10. Mary Anne Weaver, "India's Bandit Queen," *Atlantic* 278, no. 5 (November 1996): 97.

11. Shears and Gidley, *Devi, the Bandit Queen*, 77.

12. Cited in Irène Frain, *Phoolan* (Paris: Stock, 1993), 252.

13. Hobsbawm, *Bandits*, 26.

14. Weaver, "India's Bandit Queen," 95–96.

15. Devi, Cuny, and Rambali, *The Bandit Queen of India*, viii.

16. Reinhard Bendix, *Nation-Building and Citizenship* (London: Wiley, 1964). Both quotes are on p. 54.

17. Weaver, "India's Bandit Queen," 104.

19. CHECHEN LION: ASLAN MASKHADOV

1. Eric Hobsbawm, *Bandits* (New York: Delacorte Press, 1969), 20.

2. George F. Kennan, *The Cloud of Danger Current Realities of American Foreign Policy* (Boston: Little, Brown, 1977), 185.

3. Stasys Knezys and Romanas Sedlickas, *The War in Chechnya* (College Station: Texas A&M University Press, 1999), 94.

4. Carlotta Gall and Thomas de Waal, *Chechnya: Calamity in the Caucasus* (London: New York University Press, 1998), 191.

5. Cited in Knezys and Sedlickas, *War in Chechnya*, 107.

6. Anatol Lieven, *Chechnya: Tombstone of Russian Power* (New Haven, Conn.: Yale University Press, 1998), 33.

7. For a technically detailed account of how the Russians finally succeeded in killing Dudayev, see Knezys and Sedlickas, *War in Chechnya*, 308–16.

8. Gall and de Waal, *Chechnya*, 331.

9. Cited in Knezys and Sedlickas, *War in Chechnya*, 304.

10. Gall and de Waal, *Chechnya*, 367.

11. Mark Kramer, "The Perils of Counterinsurgency," *International Security* 29, no. 3 (Winter 2004–2005): 7.

12. An excellent account of this conflict may be found in Eloise Engle and Lauri Paananen, *The Winter War* (Mechanicsburg, Pa.: Stackpole Books, 1992).

13. Anne Nivat, *Chienne de Guerre: A Woman Reporter Behind the Lines of the War in Chechnya* (New York: Public Affairs, 2001), 189.

14. Kramer, "Perils of Counterinsurgency," 6.

15. Kramer, "Perils of Counterinsurgency," 34.

16. Mark Kramer, "The Russian-Chechen Conflict and the Putin-Kadyrov Connection," *Russian Analytical Digest*, no. 22 (June 2007): 3.

INDEX

A NOTE ON THE AUTHOR

John Arquilla has been teaching in the special operations program at the U.S. Naval Postgraduate School since 1993. Before that, he was a RAND Corporation analyst. He earned his doctorate at Stanford University and is the author of several books and many articles on a wide range of topics in military and security affairs. His books include *From Troy to Entebbe, Networks and Netwars, Three Circles of War,* and *Worst Enemy: The Reluctant Transformation of the American Military.* His policy work has included advisory roles to senior leaders during Operation Desert Storm and in the Kosovo War. Since 9/11, he has been closely involved in several aspects of the global campaign against al Qaeda and affiliated terrorist networks. In recent years, *Foreign Policy* magazine has listed him as one of the "top 100 global thinkers." He lives with his family on California's central coast.